THE PARISH REPUBLIC:

HLINKA'S

SLOVAK PEOPLE'S PARTY

1939-1945

YESHAYAHU JELINEK

EAST EUROPEAN QUARTERLY, BOULDER
DISTRIBUTED BY COLUMBIA UNIVERSITY PRESS
NEW YORK AND LONDON

1976

EAST EUROPEAN MONOGRAPHS, NO. XIV

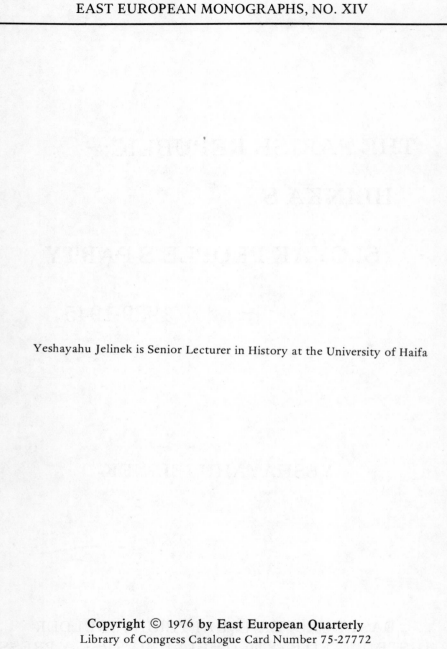

Yeshayahu Jelinek is Senior Lecturer in History at the University of Haifa

PREFACE

When the Hlinka's Slovak People's Party attained supremacy in Slovakia, in March 1939, it was not a new face on the political scene in the Czecho-Slovak Republic. The Party's triumphs paralleled Hitler's success in abolishing the rump Czecho-Slovakia, and it is clear to all that these two events were complementary. On March 14, 1939, Slovakia obtained independence, but in fact became the first satellite of Nazi Germany. The success of the Nazis strengthened the rulers of Slovakia; the defeat of the Reich meant the end of the Slovak state.

Was the cooperation of the Hlinka Party with the Nazis a logical termination of a long development? Would the essence of the policies of Father Andrew Hlinka and his followers suggest the inevitable trend toward cooperation with Hitler? One is easily tempted to think so, particularly if the intransigent nationalistic course of the Hlinka Party between wars and its pro-German line in the late 1930's and the 1940's are taken into account. however, it cannot be denied that a struggle for the territorial autonomy of Slovakia within the Czechoslovak Republic was the most characteristic single trait of the Hlinka Party before 1938. Various groups and individuals, while sharing the fate of the Hlinka Slovak People's Party (HSL'S), went further and demanded complete separation from the Czechs. Still, there is nothing illegitimate in a nationalistic program of a political party, so long as it is acting within the framework of the law, as was the Hlinka Party most of the time. Moreover, it was the duty of the Party to represent its members faithfully and guide its constituency. Though many Czechoslovak politicians objected to the Hlinka slogans and strategy, disagreement could not automatically serve as an indictment of pro-Nazi leanings. The guilt of the leadership of the Hlinka Party lies in the indiscriminate tactics it chose or tolerated in the late 1930's. At that time, extremist elements within the Party took a lead which was irresponsible at best, and treasonable and treacherous by any judicial standards.

The international situation and internal conditions of Czechoslovakia on the eve of the Second World War set the stage for Slovakia's autonomy and later independence. Slovak nationalists claimed that they seized upon the opportunity when it came. Modern history stayed in the shadow of the "sacred" right of national self-determination, and Slovakia was no exception. Slovak development was singular and unique to those people,

PREFACE

and it would not be just to use the same measures for other ethnic groups. One cannot dismiss the defense of Slovak nationalists that, despite Hitler's record, they could not pass up the opportunity to become their own masters. Nevertheless, the morality of the Hlinka Party joining the bandwagon of the Third Reich and its acceptance of many Nazi examples and prescriptions must be evaluated. What is being examined in these pages is the morality of the course taken by or forced upon the Slovak people, using standards of the preservation of a certain degree of well-being for the *whole* of mankind, and of pity and compassion for *all* people.

The wartime leaders of Slovakia, and their advocates after the war, frequently repeated the statement that they wanted to rescue the national existence of their people; that six years of independent living gave higher essence to the Slovak nation. The Slavonic Slovaks chose close friendship with the Third Reich, justifying their step as "national survival"; Hlinka Party spokesmen talked about a policy of necessity and the lesser evil. Yet it would seem that the Party undertook many of its actions out of *free will* rather than from being under pressure of a greater force. It followed a normal course of development rather than reacting to unpredicted intrusions from outside.

During the war, Slovak leaders learned the severe lesson, so well defined in the proverb "He who eats with the devil needs a long spoon." Many of their dreams faded under the impact of the gray reality. Extermination of the local Jewry, harassment of other minorities, and Slovakia's active participation in the battles of the war are sufficient testimony to the waywardness of Slovak leaders.

A student of Slovak history also cannot overlook the deeply religious (i.e., Catholic) outlook of the Hlinka Party. The facts of the Nazi attitude toward religion and the persecution of fellow Catholics in the Reich did not escape the Party leadership. Indeed, Slovak Catholic priests condemned Nazi "neo-paganism." This raises several questions: How did it come about that the Hlinka Party cooperated with the Reich? Were any elements in its *Weltanschauung* held in common by the partners? What kind of regime was established in Slovakia during World War II? What were the Party's actual goals, and to what extent was it able to realize them? What were the conditions for the success or failure in the realization of the Party's goals?

In pursuing these questions, I had to be conscious of the limited scope of my work; I had no intention of fully describing the internal policy of the Slovak state, or the political, social, or economic history of Slovakia during the Second World War. I have concerned myself solely with the Hlinka Party, thereby, I believe, adding insight into the activities of rightist movements and authoritarian regimes. I feel that this work will be useful

PREFACE

both to historians of East-Central Europe and to students of comparative politics.

The sources of my study are listed in the bibliography. For subjective and objective reasons, I could rely only on documentations and libraries in the West. All chapters except the two introductory chapters, for which there exists extensive literature, are based on primary sources as much as possible.

I would like to express my appreciation to Indiana University, which, through a generous scholarship during my graduate studies, made it possible to prepare this work. In particular, I am indebted to the advice and support of Professors Charles Jelavich, the late Vaclav L. Benes, Fritz L. Epstein, and Robert W. Campbell.

Many institutions and individuals contributed information and sources; I list them with gratitude: Indiana University Libraries, Bloomington; the National Archives, Washington, D.C., and Alexandria, Virginia; the Library of Congress, Washington, D.C.; the Slovak Institute, Cleveland, Ohio; the Political Archives of the Foreign Office, Bonn, Federal German Republic; the Central Slovak State Archives, Bratislava, Czechoslovakia; the Hoover Institute, Stanford, California; the Yad Washem Archives, Jerusalem, Israel; the Moreshet Archives, Givaat Chavivah, Israel; and the University of Minnesota Libraries, Minneapolis. The Institute for Contemporary Jewry of the Hebrew University in Jerusalem awakened my interest in this topic and enabled me to collect much important testimony. At all the institutions and libraries I met much good will and help. Also I would like to extend my personal thanks to the individuals involved: Dr. Joseph M. Kirschbaum, the late Professor Ferdinand Ďurčanský, Professor Charles Murin, Dr. Joseph M. Mikuš, Dr. K. O. Rabl, the late Dr. Jozef Lettrich, the late Dr. Matej P. Josko, and Mr. Stephen Revay. Professor George Barany of the University of Denver and Professor William E. Wright of the University of Minnesota read and commented on the manuscript. However, the full responsibility for this work, its defects and shortcomings, lies only with me.

I have appreciated the advice and assistance of many, and all should share my thanks. But above all, my parents and my brother made many sacrifices on my behalf, and they should share any achievement with me.

TABLE OF CONTENTS

TABLE OF CONTENTS

CHAPTER I
A PARTY AND A STATE—1918-1938

Slovakia, a small Slavic nation in Central Europe, seems to fit well Friedrich Engels' description of a people without a history. After living independently within the framework of the Great Moravian Empire for a brief period, the forefathers of the Slovaks disappeared for nearly a thousand years. From the beginning of the eleventh century when it became a part of the lands of the crown of St. Stephen, Slovakia shared the changing fate of the Hungarian monarchy. The ideological influence of the Enlightenment, the French Revolution, and political romanticism—as transmitted by the Germans, Hungarians, and Czechs, which reached its apex in the "Spring of Nations" awakened the self-consciousness of the upper stratum of the Slovak nation. However, a full national revival was yet to come. Bach's absolutism and especially the *Ausgleich* broke and almost killed the Slovak revival. The intensive, and very successful policy of Magyarization which followed the *Ausgleich* removed or oppressed the national consciousness of many members of the Slovak intelligentsia and urban class. Indeed, only the rural village safeguarded the Slovak language and, as a result, rescued Slovak self-identification.

Slovaks of the end of the nineteenth and the beginning of the twentieth centuries were a rather poor country folk. For mountain shepherds and woodcutters, for the valley peasants, religion gave reason and sense to life. A great majority of the population were devout Catholics, although groups of members of the Orthodox and Uniate churches lived in the east and great numbers of Protestants were scattered throughout the country.[1]

It was these Protestants who gave the Slovaks their first national leadership. Because of continued contact with foreign countries where their ministers studied, and strong bonds with Czechs and local German co-believers, the Protestants were saved from the provincialism of their Catholic brethren. A married Protestant minister was able to secure continuity of property, knowledge, and tradition through his children who studied secular subjects, went into politics, and entered into commercial occupations, thus creating the foundation for a middle class.

The case of the Catholics was somewhat different from that of the Protestants. The village priest was not only a spiritual guide, but also often the only educated person in the community, and was very close to his peasant flock. A peasant's fondest wish was that his son would become a clergyman; the dream of his talented son was to be a priest. For the seminary promised an escape from peasant life and also provided the only way for a member of the lowest class to rise in status. Moreover, the prospective priest won the admiration of his fellow citizens not only for himself, but also for his family. The Church accepted and reared these children, and provided them with food and shelter. Once ordained into the priesthood, they would return to the villages of Slovakia to work for the glory of God and the greatness of Hungary.

The Catholic Church ranked among the top institutions promoting Magyarization. While studying in small provincial towns, where the seminaries were located, young theologians underwent a thorough Magyar nationalistic indoctrination. Their congregations followed the political bent of the clergy. When the pastor was able to guard his Slovak consciousness, he spread it among his congregation. If he was indifferent or Magyarized, the national cause found little echo.

The outlook of Catholic priests tended to be rather provincial and conservative. Their knowledge of the world did not extend very much beyond the bishopric in which they served. They fulfilled their vocation by executing their religious obligations and preserving the priestine conditions of life. Most clergy looked with suspicion on new thought, which was indeed dangerous to the accepted older customs. Such a situation occurred in 1895 when the Hungarian government introduced a series of laws aimed at separating Church from State and modernizing the country.

A Catholic layman, Count Nándor Zichy, alarmed by these separationist trends, founded the Christian People's Party in order to fight the liberal government. Several Slovak priests joined the new party, among them Andrej Hlinka, a young cleric from northern Slovakia destined to attain national stature in his struggle on behalf of the Slovak people. In the elections of 1898, Hlinka tried unsuccessfully to become the representative of the People's Party in the Budapest parliament. Three years later he left Zichy—as did many other Slovaks—when he discovered the Magyar-bias of the party. The dissenters joined first the Slovak National Party, a relatively insignificant political movement staffed mainly by Protestants, and later in 1905 made the first formal attempt to create a Slovak People's Party.

A PARTY AND A STATE

Hlinka's nationalistic activities attracted the attention of the authorities, and in 1906 he faced persecution at the hands of his Magyar bishop and the central government. Accused of subversion, Hlinka was found guilty by the court and sentenced to two years of imprisonment. But before he was taken to jail, a major tragedy occurred in Hlinka's village of Černová, where twelve citizens were shot to death and another ninety injured by Magyar gendarmes. The villagers had wanted their native son to consecrate a new church, and the bishop had tried to force another priest on them.

The shooting on October 27, 1907, made Hlinka internationally known over night. He drew the attention of Europe to the plight of Slovaks in the Hungarian kingdom. Constituting an ethnic minority, lacking an aristocracy, an intelligentsia, and imaginative leadership, the Slovaks could hardly ward off the political and cultural pressures of the Magyars. Budapest systematically tried to erase the remnants of Slovak national consciousness, their indigenous culture, even the native Slavonic language. But the obscure priest from Černová became a symbol of the Slovak struggle for survival, and commanded wide support in the country.

Hlinka and the clergy, however, were not the only Slovak patriots. Institutions of higher learning, particularly in Prague, were training a new secular leadership for Slovakia. Many young Slovaks desiring education preferred attending Czech schools to Magyarizing Hungarian universities. In Prague many of them were exposed to direct influence of the philosopher and sociologist Thomas G. Masaryk, himself a Moravian Slovak by descent. The group around Masaryk published a journal called *Hlas* ("The Voice"), and its members were known as *Hlasisti*. They were to have a considerable impact on modern Slovak history.

On the eve of World War I, the Slovak nation was in poor condition. Thousands of Slovaks, unable to find work at home, had emigrated abroad. Thus the country, economically underdeveloped and suffering from many social maladies, was barely able to resist the strong denationalization efforts of the Magyar rulers. Significantly, these conditions were also more or less prevalent among the ethnic Germans, the Ukrainians in east Slovakia, and the Jews. Hatred toward Jews, already diffused by ultramontane priests, fed and grew on both social maladies and an awakening nationalism.[2]

The Slovak urban population welcomed the outbreak of World War I with patriotic celebrations. The nationalistic opposition either kept silent or supported the government. Although Slovakia's desire for independence slept (as did that of Bohemia and Moravia), some Czech exiles began a campaign to break up the old monarchy. Masaryk began to work among the Allies on behalf of his people. He and his collaborators in Russia and the West quickly recognized the advantages of Slovak support. Both Bohemia-Moravia[3] and Slovakia had a long tradition of somewhat sentimental, idealistically-minded cooperation; nevertheless, mutual knowledge and real understanding between them was rather limited.

Masaryk's group found useful allies in a small number of young Protestants originally from western Slovakia, who proclaimed before the world the Slovak desire to join the Czechs in a common state. Several former students of Masaryk flocked quickly around their teacher; but there is some doubt whether these young Slovaks could be regarded as genuine speakers for the majority of their people.

Other "representatives" of Slovakia were American colonies of emigrants from what was known as Upper Hungary. These various self-appointed representatives of Slovakia cooperated with Czechs. Together they signed a number of agreements and resolutions demanding the creation of a Czech-Slovak state. The most often mentioned resolution was the agreement of Pittsburgh, Pennsylvania, of May 30, 1918, which promissed much to the Slovaks. Two of the most important and controversial paragraphs provided for a Slovak diet and stipulated the tasks of duly accredited representatives in the liberated homeland in elaboration of the agreement's details. This document was only partially fulfilled; in the heated disputes of the later days, each side quoted only those sections which best fit its own partisan needs. Similar to the Slovaks, representatives of American societies of emigrants from the Carpathian Ukraine demonstrated the desire to have their ancient fatherland made a part of Czechoslovakia. This demand was sanctioned and approved in the peace treaties of 1919.

Meanwhile, at the end of the war, Slovakia was in a state of social and nationalistic ferment, although the nationalists at home were not fully informed of the action of the emigres abroad. On October 30, 1918, two days after the Czechoslovak Republic had been proclaimed in Prague by a faction of the Czech national leadership, a randomly assembled number of Slovaks (some regions of the country, in particular the east, were not represented) met in the city of Turčiansky Sv. Martin. The 106 men convened, including many of the most prominent citizens of Slovakia, belonged mostly to the National and Social Democratic parties. Not knowing that the Republic had already been proclaimed in Prague, the assembly accepted a resolution professing the desire to join the Czechs in a common Czechoslovak state.

They were not aware that Austria-Hungary had accepted United States President Woodrow Wilson's demand for the right of self-determination for the peopleof the Monarchy. Count Andrassy, the foreign minister of the Viennese government, had done this in his October 27 reply to Wilson's letter of October 18, 1918.[4] Dr. Milan Hodža, a respresentative to the Budapest parliament of the Slovaks living in southern Hungary, reached the city of Turčianský Sv. Martin on a later date. Since he was already acquainted with Andrassy's letter, he altered in part the previously accepted document. By updating the Declaration of Martin, Hodža made it appear that the new Republic was accepted.[5]

Thus it cannot be accurately stated that in the proclamation of the common republic, Czechs and Slovaks met all legal needs required for such a step. Hungary often repeated the demand for a plebescite in Slovakia, convinced that the majority of the population would profess its faith in the tradition of the Crown of St. Stephen. Also, the fathers of the new state were not sure whether they could rely on the better judgment of the Slovak people, and objected strenuously to the requests of Budapest. However, given the situation of Slovakia at that time, the new state was the best possible solution.

The Slovak people had no reason to continue an association with the defeated Magyars, notorious for their oppression of minorities. A huge and formidable mountain barrier cut them off from Poland, so connections with this nation were few, besides which, Poland had too many problems of her own to be in a position to help. Still, Slovakia was not prepared for a separate existence. Thus the new union obviously made sense. The long contact between the cultural elite of both nations, the close relationship of their languages, and the mutual benefits to be drawn by each side added justification for the connection.

Unfortunately, many great differences between the two peoples were underestimated or not taken into account in the wave of emotional optimism: differences in economic activities, social life, degree of devotion to religion, mentality, tradition, and history. Although these factors were not of sufficient strength to invalidate the justice of the union, they became a cause of considerable trouble later, when the elation of the first days subsided.

The initial collision happened as soon as the first large groups of Czech people arrived in Slovakia in 1919 to help organize local administration and life. True, some of them though of themselves as "colonizers," bringing enlightenment to a backward country. But even the most honest of the Czechs soon discovered that ideals and reality were two different things. The industrious, free-thinking, social-minded, somewhat jovial Czech found himself in a deeply religious, rather old-fashioned, conservative country with a high appreciation for the ethos of the aristocracy. Under-developed and backward, Slovakia was short of enterprising individuals. The German and Magyar groups, previously the dominant people, did not adjust to the change quickly. The Lutheran and Jewish minorities were first to adapt themselves to the new mood of life. In mentality, the Slovak Lutherans were much closer to the Czechs than the Slovak Catholic major-ity was and they were also regarded as more trustworthy. Thus the Pro-testants were well represented among the leaders of the new Slovakia.

Zealous to secure the region, to break the Magyar influence, and to take revenge on the old government, the newly established bosses began to purge the country of Magyarones (i.e., Magyarized Slovaks). Employes who previously displayed Hungarian patriotism, some for economic rea-sons only, were replaced by incoming Czechs. Slovak Catholics constituted a large part of these dismissed "Magyarones," and their bitterness was un-derstandable. The central government did not trust the Catholics who, as a result, felt ostracized from public jobs, from investments, and from a share of power. The priests, whether Magyarized or not, became suspi-cious of the new government in Prague.

The Slovak priesthood had had high expectations of the new Republic. It had hoped to increase the influence of the church in the country, to im-prove its own economic conditions, and to fulfill personal ambitions. Thus the Catholic priests were frustrated as their hopes failed or were slow to be realized. The government of Prague, remembering the close ties of the Vatican to the Hapsburgs, was inimical to Catholicism. Czech statesmen planned separation of state and church, thus hurting the feelings of con-servative Slovaks. Instead of abolishing the liberal Hungarian legislation of 1895, Prague intended to reinforce secularization of life in Slovakia. It nationalized primary and secondary education, until then for the most part under religious supervision. Government agrarian reform threatened the future of the church's estates. Patriotic priests, who had suffered in the past from their Magyarizing superiors, and were looking for rewards and better parishes, saw them slow to come. Father Hlinka and other clerics hoped to become bishops in place of the expelled Magyars, but found these hopes soon thwarted, as the influence of the Hungarian hierarchy on the Vatican, and the disinterested attitude of Czechoslovak officials tem-porarily froze any changes.

The frustrations of the Catholic leadership increased when radical new ideas began to spread throughout the country: people talked of socialism, equality, emancipation of women, freedom of conscience. Finding more problems in the new state than in the previous one, the clergy feared that traditional Slovakia as they knew and loved her was on the verge of disappearing. Yet Hlinka labored much on behalf of the new state: he addressed dozens of public meetings, published appeals to the clergy to support Czecho-Slovakia, and above all, organized the national-minded co-religionists. Slowly, under the pressure of the unsympathetic present, Hlinka's circle began to look for a means of securing the gains while preserving tradition as they understood it. Autonomy seemed to provide the solution. Thus as early as November 19, 1918, this group of clergymen and laymen created a new organization and named it the Christian Slovak People's Party.[6]

The new party had a great appeal for the clergy. Priests joined en masse, and the flocks followed their shepherds. Besides the Slovak-minded churchmen, many Magyarones also joined. While the central government was anxiously rooting out anyone suspected of Magyar ties or sympathies, Hlinka understood the need for leniency and forgiveness. He was ready to accept anyone who would from then on prove himself a Slovak patriot, which, to Father Hlinka, was someone who wanted autonomy for Slovakia. This opposed the old notion that a patriot was one participating in the struggle for Slovak survival and against Magyarization. Many Magyarones were undergoing a difficult psychological transformation: the First World War and the creation of the Republic had transformed many values. Hatred of Czechoslovakia was still evident; reality had to be acknowledged and a means of adjustment found, so these people changed from "Magyarones" into ardent Slovak nationalists. Thus, patriotism in many cases consisted of little more than passionate hatred of the Czechs. Given their unfortunate past, very few Slovaks could demonstrate untarnished nationalistic purity. Former Magyarones-turned-patriots were well represented in the leadership of the Hlinka Party.[7]

Priests remained the central pillar of the Hlinka Party throughout its existence, converted Magyarones contributed the extra touch of an intense anti-Czechism. Dr. Josef Tiso, a young priest of the *Bánovce nad Bebravou* parish, provides a good example of the Hlinka Party brand of patriotism: as early as 1922, Tiso was found guilty of anti-Czech instigations and was imprisoned.[8] His Ordinarius, the archbishop of Nitra, Dr. Karol Kmetko, described Tiso as a "silent Slovak" before the war, i.e., conscious of his nationality but not publicly active.[9] However, there were signs that Tiso was at least a "silent Magyarone." A history professor at the University of Bratislava, Daniel Rapant, made a reasonably clear statement to this effect in a Slovak newspaper in 1944.[10] Professor Vojtech (Béla) Tuka, who had long played an unfortunate role in Slovak politics, was another Magyarone accepted by Hlinka on the above-mentioned basis.

Hence, the Party's demands for autonomy were often attacked as a hidden claim of pro-Hungarian irredenta (i.e., a return to the old boundaries of the crown of St. Stephen). No doubt these feelings existed in the minds of some members of the Party; nevertheless, the great majority of autonomists, the above Magyarones included, were serious in their demands for the creation of an autonomous Slovakia within the framework of the existing Czechoslovak Republic. At first these claims for autonomy had rather clerical and parochial intentions. Unsatisfied ambitions of some leaders contributed to the desire for autonomy. Later, social, economic, and political reasons prevailed: the clerical and parochial ferment underwent a metamorphosis and crystallized into one of the purest expressions of Slovak nationalism.

During the initial period of the new Republic, the Slovak clergy cooperated with their co-believers in Bohemia and Moravia. It was Hlinka who produced the first storm at the very time of the honeymoon of the new state. He was not only very ambitious and temperamental, but also easily influenced, a trait exploited by one of the most talented and dangerous Magyarones, Father František Jehlička, who persuaded Hlinka to go to Paris to submit a petition for home rule in Slovakia. The mission failed, and upon his return, Hlinka was jailed for several months. He was later released without any formal charges filed against him. So when elected in 1920 to the parliament of Prague, Hlinka entered political life with seeds of bitterness sown deep in his mind.

In 1919, following the advancement of forces from the Hungarian Soviet Republic into Slovakia, a Soviet Republic was proclaimed in eastern Slovakia. It was, however, a short-lived creation, and the Slovak Soviet Republic collapsed with the retreat of the Magyar forces. Nevertheless, the influence of socialist ideas on the population was not to be underestimated, as the coming elections proved.

In 1920, the first elections of the Republic took place. Unexpectedly, the Social-Democratic Party polled 46.2 percent of the votes, while the Hlinka Party had to settle for only 17.6 percent.[11] These results dealt a heavy blow to Hlinka, and he regarded them as a grave warning for the future. The priest-politician vowed an untiring effort until "the red Slovakia would turn into a white one."[12] While social questions were the main topic of the 1920 campaign, afterward they were combined with national and religious issues. Shortly after the first elections, the "Ludaks," as party members were commonly nicknamed ceased to cooperate with the Czech Catholics in a dispute over secondary education. In their heated chauvinism the Ludaks found it hard to compromise even with their Czech counterparts.

A PARTY AND A STATE

The Party worked untiringly, and invaded and influenced—with varying success—new areas such as economic institutions, cultural organizations, Christian-social trade unions, and the newly formed Association of Catholic Students, which was to supply the Party with its future leadership. Dr. Tuka became editor-in-chief of the Party's organ, *Slovák*. Hlinka felt that the movement lacked a sufficient number of intellectuals in its ranks and, with the hiring of Tuka, he hoped at least for a partial remedy. Indeed, under Tuka's leadership, *Slovák* rose to the stature of the most censored newspaper in Slovakia. Tuka influenced some young extremists on his editorial board such as Karol Sidor, Karol Murgaš, and Milo Urban (all of whom were to play prominent roles in Slovakia). Following examples of other extremist movements then popular in Europe, Tuka created Slovakia's first storm troops, the *Rodobrana*, in 1923. The government disbanded it the same year; nevertheless, veterans of the *Rodobrana* continued under various disguises until 1938 when it gave way to the ill-famed Hlinka Guard. Tuka also contributed much to the improved organization of the Party, to its propagandistic activities both in the country and abroad, and to its parliamentary work.

Slovakia was not spared hardships in the first years of peace. The postwar economic depression hit strongly, followed by the internal political crisis of Czechoslovakia which occurred after the split in the Social-Democratic Party in September 1920. Slovakia reflected all these changes, and the Ludaks exploited the situation. The Party could count on the support of the clergy and many young people who lent a helping hand in its work. Yet Hlinka's work definitely benefited from his lackluster adversaries. These people, members of the pre-war National Party, then concentrated chiefly in the Republican (Agrarian) Party, enjoyed the benefits and advantages of a position of leadership. Instead of facing the Hlinka Party in open battles, they hung on firmly to their government seats which they considered as rewards for past activities. Given these conditions the future achievements of the Ludaks, such as the results of the 1925 elections, were understandable. Hlinka and his people polled more than one-third (34 percent) of Slovakia's votes, a success never again repeated.[13] The Party became the strongest political movement in Slovakia, doubling the number of her deputies in the parliament, and leaving the runner-up Agrarians far behind.

Between 1925 and 1927, however, the Ludaks underwent a serious crisis, caused by a disappointed constituency and a struggle in the leadership. In spite of the success on the ballot, the Party could offer little to the expectant voter. Hlinka tried to effect a compromise, inducing the other parties to accept changes in the administration of Slovakia. But although the region acquired an extended degree of self-government, for any major decisions it still depended on Prague. The coalition also conceded to the Ludaks in the realm of state-church relations, and in questions of personnel. After negotiations lasting almost two years, the Hlinka Party joined the coalition government in 1927, holding two portfolios. Dr. Tiso was one of the Ludak ministers. The period of understanding proved to be brief.

The party continued to lose ground among the electorate. Dr. Tuka, then a member of the Party's executive, obviously did not favor participation in government either. On New Year's Day 1928, when the state was anticipating the celebration of the Ten-Year Anniversary, Tuka published an article attacking the legal basis for Czech-Slovak common life. In the next year, 1929, Tuka was accused of high treason on behalf of Hungary and subsequently tried. Though the state prosecutor had a difficult time convincing world opinion of Tuka's guilt, not to mention that of many fellow Ludaks, the defendant was nevertheless convicted and sentenced to fifteen years of imprisonment. Only after the war, while searching in the Hungarian archives, were Czechoslovak historians able to produce unimpeachable evidence against Tuka.[14] In spite of the accusation of plotting for Hungary, Hlinka accepted responsibility for Tuka's deeds. In the next elections, the Ludaks polled only 28.2 percent of the votes, followed by the Agrarians with 19.5 percent—a setback for but not the end of Slovakia's mightiest political movement.[15]

The Great Depression revived the fortunes of the Ludaks, in that it deepened and sharpened the social maladies of underdeveloped Slovakia; the Ludaks cleverly channeled the bitterness to their advantage. They presented political autonomy as a miracle drug which would heal all sores of their country.

The Party's nationalistic and religious approach appealed to the imagination of the masses, and Hlinka was able to attract huge crowds. In 1933, Slovakia commemorated the 1,100th anniversary of the building of the first Christian church in its territory, in the ancient city of Nitra. This event was celebrated as the jubilee of the adoption of Christianity in Slovakia. The Ludaks seized control over the government-organized celebration, which took place in the city of Nitra, and demonstrated to all the wide support they possessed. In part, as a result, in 1935 the Party recovered many votes which it had lost in the previous elections. But its success was only partial, and the Hlinka Party joined with the Slovak National Party and two other minor groups, creating a so-called "Autonomistic Bloc." In spite of cooperation with the predominantly Lutheran National Party, a faded relic of the Slovak oldest political organization, the Ludaks polled only 30.1 percent of the votes in the 1935 election, the Agrarians, 17.6 percent. Prague politicians also had few reasons to rejoice, with the Communist Party polling 13 percent of the vote, the Hungarian Bloc 14.2 percent, the Carpathian-Sudeten German Party 1.7 percent, and the Fascists 2 percent, which meant they also believed in autonomy in one way or another.[16] It also meant that a majority of Slovakia's population had no confidence in the central government.

Yet Prague and its Slovak allies refused to see the handwriting on the wall. The situation called clearly for drastic steps, but they were slow to come. The attempt of the designated prime minister, Dr. Milan Hodža, a member of the Agrarian Party, to recruit Ludak support for his government failed. A Slovak, the new premier hoped to solve the problems of his people, but hesitancy, the international situation, and a wave of radicalism inside the country shattered his plans, a failure which, ultimately, can be judged in retrospect to be one of the causes for the tragedy of 1938. Then, in the mid-1930's, the moderates of the Hlinka Party still held the upper hand in their organization, and they repeatedly stated their faith in the Czechoslovak Republic.[17] After the resignation of the first president, Professor Masaryk, on December 18, 1935, the Czechoslovak Parliament elected Dr. Edward Beneš to the highest office of the Republic. The Ludak deputies cast their votes for the new president, though they regarded him as an arch enemy of the autonomist program. No doubt this was a promising gesture of good will, which should not have been ignored. Nevertheless, the parties procrastinated in the negotiations for more than a year, and by 1937 these had come to naught.

During the negotiations, the Hlinka Party underwent changes: it reflected the mounting pressure of right-wing radicalism in Europe and was affected by it. The convention of 1936, held at the spa of Piešťany, proved that a group of fascist-minded extremists was driving the movement. Frustration, disappointment, and expectation pushed the moderates to the background. The Ludaks closed ranks with other parties of parliamentary opposition such as the Sudeten German Party, the Slovak National Party, the Czech Fascists of General Rudolf Gajda, and other minority groups on the extreme right. At the same time contacts were made with foreign Fascist movements, including those of Germany and Italy.

The Ludaks, as well as other discontented segments of Slovakia's population of the right wing, intensified their agitation in the following year of 1937, thus undermining the stability of Czechoslovakia. The Party's younger elements conducted a hate campaign against Czechs, which was crowned by a wave of demonstrations in the fall of that year. The Soviet-Czechoslovak Treaty of Mutual Assistance, signed on May 16, 1935, was a favorite target for attacks. The adversaries charged the central government with "bolshevization of the Republic."[18] Anti-communism, combined with anti-Semitism, turned into the most preferred ammunition of the

Ludak arsenal. The atmosphere became more tense.

Ludaks greeted the new year (1938) with two slogans: "Adieu, Prague," and "Forward! On with the attack in the New Year!" The Party approved and supported the demands of the Sudeten German Party. It objected to the partial mobilization of the Czechoslovak armed forces on May 20, 1938, which was aimed at a possible German threat. When Czechoslovakia entered the gravest crisis in her existence, and fought for survival, the Ludaks provided her with little comfort.

At the twentieth anniversary of the Pittsburgh Agreement a delegation of Americans of Slovak origin brought the original document to Czechoslovakia. The delegation wanted to persuade the central government that acceptance of all provisions of the agreement would save the welfare of the Republic. Close cooperation with the Hlinka Party deprived the American Slovaks of the glamour of impartiality, and hardened the other side. The Ludaks exploited the guests for large-scale propaganda, which climaxed in a huge Ludak demonstration in Bratislava on May 5, 1938.

On May 6, Hodža's Agrarian Party organized a counter-demonstration. An American journalist described it in the following way:

... While the crowd which attended the Hlinka Party's celebration was estimated at approximately 50,000, yesterday's parade through the streets of Bratislava, which were decorated with national flags was attended by about 100,000 persons from all ranks of Slovak life without regard to political affiliation. The gathering turned into a spontaneous demonstration of Czechoslovak unity, a homage to President Beneš and the Slovak element's allegiance and confidence in its leader, Prime Minister Hodža.[19]

Thus, in spite of its popular appeal, the Hlinka Party was far from capturing the hearts of the majority of the Slovak people.

Since 1936 the Ludaks, and in particular the extremists among them, had been developing relations with the Third Reich and its agents in Czechoslovakia. In 1938, while Hitler was conducting his major campaign against the Republic, Ludak officials frequently visited the Reich. The Party's leadership coordinated its policies with those of the parliamentary representation of the ethnic Germans and Magyars; it also followed closely the desires of Nazi agencies in Berlin and Vienna. The Fuehrer was acquainted with the program of the Radicals in the Hlinka Party, as his proclamation on September 26, 1938, evidences: "The Slovaks did not want to have anything to do with the Czechs."[20] After the Munich dictate, the Ludaks felt it opportune to forward the unconditional demand of autonomy without delay. Prague, pressured heavily from every side, her spirit broken and stamina exhausted, had no choice but surrender. The Hlinka Party, still a minority in the country's political structure—though the strongest, most vocal, and most purely Slovak

A PARTY AND A STATE

group at that time—wrestled the power from the central government and usurped the right to represent from its domestic competitors. It proclaimed itself the sole spokesman of the Slovak people.

It is legitimate to assume that in spite of the violent agitation and propaganda. the Ludaks never succeeded in capturing the majority of the Slovak people, and that they probably would not have been able to accomplish this without external development and foreign support. As it was, the flow of events carried them to the fore—perhaps to their own surprise.

The Ludaks staked their existence both on the objective situation then prevailing in Slovakia and on their own grievances as they were made public in the Party's proclamations. Quite obviously, Slovak nationalistic criticisms of the central government had much substance. Powerful Czech industries treated Slovakia as a colony.[21] The laissez-faire economic system worked to the disadvantage of the underdeveloped native Slovak business. Czech economic supremacy in the country was almost absolute, and Slovakia served mainly as supplier of agricultural products, raw materials, and labor.

The Great Depression hit Slovakia hard. The young intelligentsia, often jobless after graduation, were sensitive to the plight of its people. At that time, hundreds of the Czech officials employed in Slovak institutions did not bother to learn the local language. Nationalists denounced the ideology of the "Czechoslovak nation" and "Czechoslovak language" as a Czech attempt to denationalize and assimilate the Slovak people.[22] The administrative centralization of the country as conducted by Prague was another argument of the nationalists. Centralization could indeed by questioned in view of the very substantial differences between Bohemia and Moravia on one hand, and Slovakia on the other. However, the nationalists overlooked the major cultural and social progress Slovakia had made since World War I. The Slovak tongue, which before the war was rarely heard even in the country's elementary schools, became a language of high school and university, of arts and science. The Slovak printed word, Slovak music, and Slovak art took a place of equality with cultural products of other European nations. Illnesses, which for centuries plagued the Slovak folk, disappeared under the treatment of the modern Czechoslovak medicine. The democratic system of the Republic enabled an unprecedented development of social and political associations. A network of public libraries, cultural institutions, and organizations for sport and physical fitness spread over the region. The cultural and social standards of the Slovak people were raised as never before. Yet, in spite of these achievements, many young Slovak intellectuals had only resentful words for the Republic. These embittered young people found a home in either the Communist Party or Hlinka's Slovak People's Party (HSL'S).

During the twenty years of the First Czechoslovak Republic, the Hlinka Party underwent a lengthy development: from domination by several provincial priests and laymen, through a democratic period of a movement sharing a regular parliamentary system, and landing in the midst of authoritarian forces, common in Europe during the late 1930's. In this course, Hlinka and his followers were a living example for the tragedy of nations lacking a democratic and parliamentary tradition. In gentry-minded Hungary, the poor, plebeian, and narrow-minded Slovaks were excluded from power and responsibility. As an underprivileged ethnic minority, the Slovaks were not called upon to participate in parliamentary or governmental work. The dominant Magyars forced their deputies and officials on all national minorities of the Hungarian kingdom. Therefore, when the Republic came into existence a good many Slovaks were ignorant of the rules of the game.[23] The founders of the Hlinka Party intended to defend the interests of the Catholic Church and the traditional way of life in their country. In approaching the new government, they regarded its abilities limitless and made impossible requests.[24]

Lacking precise knowledge of what, how, and where to demand, the Ludaks missed many opportunities in the early days. They took foolish steps, issued irrresponsible proclamations and, when it was already late for any achievement, voiced indignation and anger. The Magyarones, who entered the Party in the very early days, added to its bitterness and radicalization. Then there were requests which collided head-on with a vision of a modern state, and Prague rejected them as well. Thinking in terms of old Hungary, the Ludaks considered Prague's actions as a slight to Slovak national rights. Furthermore, being close to the people, Hlinka's friends sensed the social maladies of the country, and were driven to desperation by the slow pace of the central government in dealing with these problems.[25] It was a combination of these things that resulted in the particular brand of Slovak nationalism represented by the Hlinka's Slovak People's Party.

As time passed, life in the Republic became more formalized and the issues clearer. The Hlinka Party followed the trend: it became institutionalized and gained more legitimacy in its political struggle. The young Slovaks who sought out the Party in increasing numbers demonstrated an aggressive nationalism. Alleged and real discrimination—as well as the drives of a young nation to enjoy all advantages and sentiments of independent living—nourished demands for self-determination on the part of the Party's younger elements.

While the almost unbelievable amount of demagoguery in the Party's publications and speeches would flabbergast a contemporary observer, it would be hard to deny the justice of many of the slogans. The central government, including its Slovak members, left much to be desired in understanding the eastern part of the Republic. Occasionally, the state's leaders were even liable to accusations of arrogance and Czech chauvinism; they were too slow to admit the peculiarities of Slovakia. Their centralized administration, their lack of compassion for the plight of the Slovak economy, and their blind adherence to the doctrine of one and undeniable "Czechoslovak" nation were mistakes hard to forgive.

The Hlinka Party became a rallying point for the unsatisfied Slovaks of various factions. While the religious argument continued to hold a considerable place in the Party's propaganda, the national cause gained in importance. The Party advocated territorial autonomy of the country. In this demand it met the wishes of local business and industry, which hoped to be liberated from the oppressive weight of Czech firms. The Ludaks tried to speak to the workers in the name of the unity of Slovak people and social peace. Social and anti-administration slogans pleased the peasants. In the social field, Christian solidarism and anti-Semitism were the universal answers. The Party considered autonomy as a final remedy for any illnesses. The apparent reluctance to compromise, which marked many of the Czech personalities, drove some Slovaks to desperation and provided a fertile ground for the undemocratic elements. The inherent maladies of Czechoslovakia served Nazi imperialism as a lever against the neighboring republic. And at this stage, the Ludak nationalists failed to see the dangers, failed to appreciate the advantages of a liberal democracy, and turned into voluntary assistants of Hitler. In order to follow the prerequisites of the time, the Hlinka Party also shed its old procedures in favor of authoritarian methods.

On the eve of Munich, the Party (HSL'S) was divided into Moderate and Radical wings. A group of clerically minded personages and laymen, as well as leaders of trade unions affiliated with the Party, made up the Moderates, following the Party's general line in their demands. They were basically faithful to the Czechoslovak Republic and to its democratic system, even though they requested several far-reaching reforms. Dr. Josef Tiso, the Party's ideologist, was the outstanding member of this wing. The Radical group included veterans of Tuka's *Rodobrana* and young intellectuals. An important part of the *Rodobranci* consisted of semi-educated and uneducated men, some of whom embodied a strong social consciousness— Alexander (Šaňo) Mach was its leading figure. The young intellectuals (Nástupists) rallied around the periodical *Nástup* and Dr. Ferdinand Ďurčanský, its editor-in-chief.

Historians often describe the Radicals as "separatists" because of their alleged desire to separate Slovakia from Bohemia-Moravia. Indeed, this wing did want a very broad autonomy for Slovakia, and since the mid-1930's had toyed with the idea of complete separation. The Radicals rejected the parliamentary democracy and democratic system, and cherished fascist totalitarian methods. While the *Rodobranci* had active relations with the Croatian *Ustasha,* the Nastupists observed with interest the Rumanian Iron Guard. In the mid-1930's, both groups began to seek help from Nazi Germany. Hlinka stood between the Radical and the Moderate wings serving as supreme arbiter.

Karol Sidor served as leader of the Polonophile group. The Polonophiles backed Slovakia's close cooperation, and eventual federation, with Poland. While Sidor's personal inclinations were with the Radicals, some of his followers stood near the Moderates. Upon Hlinka's death, which was on August 16, 1938, Sidor hoped to inherit this mentor's position. Sidor's most faithful followers were concentrated in the northwest, in the town of Ružomberok and its vicinity.

Dr. Josef Tiso drew strong support in west-central Slovakia, in the valley of the river Nitra, where his parish was located. The western part of the country, particularly the district near Bratislava known as Záhorie, was the stronghold of the Radicals. The Party's support in eastern Slovakia was not great, nor was the Party supported in the concentration of industrial labor in the upper Hron valley. In the rest of the country, the Ludaks had drawn their usual share of votes and their customary following.

The Hlinka Party had done much better in the small cities and townships of the countryside than in larger urban centers. It could also count on more friendliness from the small peasantry and village proletariate than from farmers with larger holdings. In urban centers, the Ludaks had to compete with bourgeois and socialist parties; the well-to-do peasants preferred the Agrarians. Yet, certain segments of the working class were inclined to accept Ludak leadership. The railroad employes who encountered much competition on the part of their Czech colleagues exemplify such a pro-Ludak group. Finally, the young Catholic intelligentsia, and youth in general, were of much assistance to Hlinka—to the man more than to the Party. They were favorably impressed with the youthful claim of the old tribune, and responded enthusiastically to his nationalistic slogans.

Thus, on the eve of the Second World War, Slovakia was slowly reaching the rank of the developed countries of Europe, with notable achievements in its culture, social, and political life. Yet the country was still backward in economic development and administrative efficiency, and it also lacked a sense of its own worth. The Hlinka's Slovak People's Party was aware of Slovakia's problems, and aspired to provide national leadership. To achieve this goal, the Hlinka Party did not discriminate in the means it used. As we shall see in the next chapter, by exploiting the favorable international conditions after Munich, the Party was able to usurp the power in Slovakia.

The confused and dark days after Munich presented the Hlinka Party with an unexpected opportunity to achieve autonomy for Slovakia. Political circles in Prague were well aware that certain segments in the country's body politic, in particular the Ludaks, constituted a major threat for the Republic. When the government of Dr. Hodža fell on September 22, 1938, following the Munich dictate, President Beneš formed a new government under General Ján Syrový. In this government, the Slovaks achieved wide representaton, with the Hlinka Party being represented by a young Radical, Matúš Černák. Though Černák was not formally a member of the Party at that time, he enjoyed the confidence of its leadership, and in particular of the extremist segment. Scarcely was the new cabinet created when Černák surprised it with an ultimatum on October 3 demanding either immediate autonomy for Slovakia or acceptance of his resignation by the end of the next twenty-four hours. This step was a bold example of the reckless and aggressive policy of the Ludaks, who clearly took advantage of the severely pressed Czechs. Prague, exposed to unilateral demands from the four Munich powers, and threatened by Polish and Hungarian claims for border rectifications, could hardly sustain the rebellious Ludaks.

The ultimatum did not meet with any formal approval by the majority of the Slovak politicians.[1] Had it been accepted, the Hlinka Party would have been sole beneficiary. Pointing out the legal procedure needed for an act like the granting of autonomy, the central government asked for more time. In a move calculated beforehand, Černák resigned his post and left the capital. The government followed suit, leaving the president with the task of formulating a new cabinet. Beneš attempted last-minute negotiations with Dr. Tiso. The president promised far-reaching consequences, which he summarized in a letter to the Slovak statesman on October 4, 1938.[2] The letter never reach the addressee, as Dr. Beneš himself resigned the presidency on October 5, 1938, and left Czechoslovakia shortly thereafter.

In the meantime, the Hlinka Party convened its executive committee on October 6 in the city of Žilina, with representatives of other Slovak parties gathered as well. Though officially labeled a regular meeting, the session aimed at fateful decisions. On the preceding day the Party's leadership had discussed the strategy of the coming meeting. At noon on October 6 the Hlinka Party invited the other parties' representatives to join the meeting which had been in session during the morning. When the guests entered the convention hall of the *Katolický Dom* ("Catholic Haus"), they were presented with a fait accompli: a document unanimously accepted. This "Manifesto of the Hlinka's Slovak People's Party" emphasized the right to self-determination of the Slovak people and Slovakia's territorial integrity. It vowed to "contribute to a Christian disposition of affairs in Central Europe," to fight "against Jewish Marxism" and asked for a "friendly solution to all controversial problems in the spirit of the Munich Agreement."[3] The Slovak bourgeois parties accepted under duress the Ludak "Manifesto." The politicians present then prepared a common proclamation in favor of autonomy for Slovakia.[4]

The frustrations of the last weeks and days had weakened the resolve of those loyal to the Republic. The non-Ludak delegates were afraid of losing completely any share of power in the country. Therefore the veteran Slovak politicians assessed the salvation of the salvageable minimum as their correct course of action. The Žilina agreement could hardly be considered a voluntary and independent action on the part of all parties involved.[5] Acceptance of the "Manifesto" and the common proclamation could be regarded as a surrender to the Ludak demands—would the other parties have accepted the various documents and requests of the Hlinka Party in different circumstances?

Prime Minister Syrový, who also acted as president until the presidential elections, accepted the "Žilina Agreement" and appointed Dr. Josef Tiso to head the Slovak government. Tiso's nomination made public the changes in the Hlinka Party leadership.

The deceased Hlinka had not appointed an official heir, nor had he left a political testament that could be found. Many of Hlinka's followers believed that Karol Sidor would assume Party leadership and Sidor himself was confident of his succession. Yet at the very moment that Sidor felt himself at the pinnacle of his career, he suffered a maor setback. The blow came from the hand of another contender, who, in contrast to Sidor, was strong-willed and had sufficient acumen to defeat his adversary. Dr. Josef Tiso, a priest from a small-town parish, proved here, as he would repeatedly, his abilities as a fighter in the political arena. After becoming the active chairman of the Party's executive committee, he also managed to become the prime minister of an autonomous government. Tiso's success was a victory for the clerical group which wished to prevent a layman from assuming Party leadership, Sidor's devout Catholicism notwithstanding.

Also, Sidor's radical inclinations somewhat frightened many of his fellow Ludaks. The prime minister-designate, on the other hand, knew

THE POSEURS AND THE PRETENDERS

how to make himself acceptable to different factions. He chose one of the leaders of the Party extremists, Dr. Ferdinand Ďurčanský, to head the Ministry of Justice, Social Welfare, and Health. The Ministry of Education went to another ardent Radical, Matúš Černák. Pavol Teplanský (Agriculture, Trade, Public Works and Finance) and Ján Lichner (Transport and Posts) belonged to the Agrarian Party.[6] Tiso kept Interior for himself. The office of Chief of the Office of Propaganda, an innovation in Slovakia's life, also went to the Hlinka Party. Alexander Mach, who assumed this position, was initially the sixth member of the government; thus the Ludaks assigned to themselves four of the six key offices in the country. The cabinet underwent basic reorganization after the bill granting autonomy to Slovakia was accepted in Prague's parliament on November 17.

The new constitutional law divided rights and duties between the central government and the government of the *Slovenská krajina* ("Slovak Land"), the official title of the region. Prague kept control over foreign affairs, defense, state loans, customs, foreign trade, and taxation for common purposes; the remaining prerogatives went to a cabinet in Bratislava. Although this cabinet was responsible to a local diet, the state's president had the privilege of designating the Slovak prime minister. The central government was in need of support from a majority of Slovak deputies in a common parliament, and Slovak ministers were to take part in Prague's cabinet discussions on topics concerning specific Slovak matters. Czecho-Slovakia was the name of the "Second " Republic.[7]

In the new Slovak government, which guided the country from December 1, 1938, until January 20, 1939, Tiso remained prime minister. He accepted additional responsibility for the posts of Interior, Public Welfare, and Health. Ďurčanský became head of the Ministry of Transportation and Public Works. A former member of the National Party, Dr. Miloš Vančo accepted the top post in the Ministry of Justice, while the Agrarian Lichner left the government, further weakening the Agrarian Party's status.[8]

By the action of the Party's Moderates, Sidor was denied not only the premiership but also any cabinet post. In spite of his bitterness, Sidor embarked on two new projects, thus hoping to strengthen Slovak autonomy, the Radical wing, and his own position. In creating *narodné výbory* ("national committees") Sidor hoped to mobilize public support on behalf of autonomy, and to provide a substitute for anti-Ludak municipal boards where their reliability was doubted. He himself officiated as head of the Central National Committee. Sidor's expectations failed to materialize, and the national committees gradually lost importance.[9]

Sidor was to regret his toil in organizing his second project, the Hlinka Guards (HG), because soon afterward it turned into the most effective tool of his enemies. Assisted by Karol Murgaš and Šaňo Mach,[10] Sidor planned on providing the Party with reliable storm troopers. The para-military HG was substituted for the regular armed forces, then under the command of Prague. The Guard could also be used against opposition to the Party in the country, against enemies of autonomy in general, and to disseminate propaganda among the population. But above all, Sidor intended to employ the Hlinka Guard for a forceful severing of Slovakia's ties with Czech lands, if and when the time ever came.

In its appearance and conduct the Guard resembled the Italian Fascist Militia, with some SA trappings. The Polonophiles and the veterans of *Rodobrana* constituted the nucleus of the Guard. From the outset, the Guard included many dubious characters, adventurers, and city and village *lumpenproletarians.* However, the spiritual advisers, attached to the command and to various units, added a religious aspect to the HG not present in other groups. The canon of Bratislava, Dr. Karol Koerper, one of the most influential members of the Party's clerical circle, served as chief spiritual advisor.

Assuming power, the Hlinka Party embarked on a reorganization of the political life of Slovakia. It quickly outlawed the Communist, Social Democratic, and Jewish parties and the Masons;[11] it also disbanded many other cultural, sporting, and youth organizations, and granted their property to the Hlinka Guard.[12] On the other hand, the Carpathian-German Party, Slovakia's branch of the Sudeten-German Party, which had been suspended on October 5, returned to legality on October 9, under the name *Deutsche Partei* (DP) ("German Party"). Its leader, the local fuehrer Franz Karmasin, assumed an unprecedented position of influence. The Magyar Party continued its existence unhindered. The fate of the remaining bourgeois parties was different. The Ludaks persuaded their previous adversaries to apply for a merger with the Hlinka Party, which they did posthaste on November 8, 1938.[13] Only one group, the veteran *Národná strana* (Slovak National Party) refused "unification." After prolonged bickering, the Party preferred voluntary disbandment, which it accomplished on November 23, 1938.[14]

Instead of a spectrum of organizations representing various views, the country's political voice was forcefully muted into one toneless mediocrity parading the title "Party of Slovak National Unity." Neither the Magyars nor the Czechs ever dared to act as arbitrarily in Slovakia as the Hlinka Party did: under a facade of fraternization and forgiveness, it repressed dissent and monopolized political representation. Various spokesmen rationalized the mental straitjacket imposed on Slovakia by arguing that the multi-partied democratic system was inefficient and undermined national unity. However, such rationalization bore witness to the authori-

21

THE POSEURS AND THE PRETENDERS

tarian and intolerant mind of the Ludak leadership.[15] The Ludak minority achieved its supreme position neither because of the brilliance of its leaders nor through the justice of history. The various concessions it made to the ethnic Germans constituted only token payment for the great service rendered the autonomists by the Nazis. The Munich Agreement, after all, had sapped the moral strength of the Czechoslovak people. Humiliated and beaten, the Czechs were major victims of Munich and subsequent events. George F. Kennan, then second secretary in the U.S. Embassy in Prague, wrote that "it is not facetious to say that in Czechoslovakia everybody now has autonomy except the Czechs."[16]

Can one then be surprised that in such a situation the Ludaks won a quick victory? The extremists had early sought help from the Nazis; seeing Prague crippled, the Slovak nationalists knew that they could count on Berlin for support. The Slovak people quickly assessed the new situation and responded accordingly. Only a short time earlier the enthusiasm for Czechoslovakia was still evident.[17] Now a local observer told the American commercial attaché that he was amazed to notice strong anti-Czech feelings developing in Slovakia.[18]

Soon after the Žilina meeting, an "old-new" politician arrived in Slovakia: Vojtech Tuka. Having been paroled by the central government at Bratislava's request, the almost blind and very sick Tuka hastened to his home country. The Radicals prepared an enthusiastic welcome, and the scholar-politician quickly joined their ranks. The long imprisonment had affected Tuka physically, but it had not dimmed his mental faculties or his ambitions. Following the lead of the other Radicals, and like Sidor, Ďurčanský, and Mach, Tuka found his way to the Third Reich. Instead of accepting a professorial post in Bratislava's university as the Moderates would have liked him to do, he became a *Homo Politicus* of the first rank.[19] Having been elected honorary commander-in-chief of the Hlinka Guard, Tuka attracted some of the veteran *Rodobranci* and other Radicals to serve as tools for the realization of his own plans, and his influence soon made itself felt. The cleavage between the Radicals and Moderates in the Party widened. Slovak-Czech relations went from bad to worse, while the Radicals were inclined to instigate hostility. The pro-Nazi leaning of the Hlinka Party appeared clearer and less confused. Meeting first minor German officials and then Goering, Tuka eventually met with the Fuehrer himself, whom he saw on February 12, 1939. On this occasion, the old Radical appealed to Hitler for support in Slovakia's efforts to terminate her connubium with the Czechs. Perhaps more than anyone else, Tuka was the prophet of Slovakia's independence.[20]

German agencies spread their nets over Slovakia and did not omit any opportunity to foster their influence and plans. In this respect, Tuka was a welcome addition to the already widespread ties with the local leadership. " . . .[Slovakia's and Ruthenia's] leaders have been completely won over by the Germans through flattery, cajolery, and display of force," reported an American observer in December 1938.[21] The Viennese Nazis had done much to induce Radical Slovaks to join the German camp. According to a contemporary writer, the Austrian politicians reflected anti-Hungarian sentiments in their support of Bratislava.[22] Berlin's officials were free of the particular Danubian flavor, and pursued a more sophisticated line of friendship both with the Slovaks and the Magyars. Hitler's special nominee for Slovak affairs, William Keppler, with his aide Dr. Edmund Weesenmayer, ranked high among Berlin diplomats. There were in Slovakia at that time a large number of both fairly important and minor agents attached to the SS and Army Intelligence (Sicherheitsdienst and Abwehr). Offices and branches of the German Party served as well-placed centers of anti-Czechoslovak activities. Finally, the consul general of Germany in Bratislava, Ernest von Druffel, officially represented the interests of his government. His office and diplomatic prestige assisted any Nazi agent in need.

It seems, in retrospect, that while the Nazis used the Ludaks efficiently on the chessboard of international intrigue, Berlin was of two minds regarding Slovakian policies. During September 1938, the German leaders were well aware of Magyar aspirations to annex "Upper Hungary";[23] yet at the same time, they encouraged and groomed a rebellious spirit in Slovakia.[24] After the Žilina meeting, Berlin seemed to acquiesce to the reorganization of the Czechoslovak Republic; however, on October 19, when Tiso visited with von Ribbentrop in Munich, the German minister mentioned the possibility of Slovakia's independence.[25] In the meantime Hitler decided to destroy the rump (Czecho-Slovakia) at once, and on October 21 he ordered the Wehrmacht to be ready to accomplish the deed at any moment.[26]

According to a contemporary historian who researched in detail this period, in December 1938 the Fuehrer picked the month of March as the final date for Czechoslovakia's annihilation. In this undertaking, he assigned an important role to Slovakia.[27] Though Hungary's appetite was as evident as ever, the Reich's strategists were supporting the drive for an independent Slovakia as championed by the Ludak Radicals. Budapest had to satisfy herself with discarded pieces of Slovakia's territory, which Italy and Germany allotted to her in a common decision on November 2, 1938. The so-called "Viennese Award," prepared by the foreign ministers of the two Great Powers, was to settle Hungarian claims for rights of self-determination of the Magyar minority in Slovakia. In the future, Berlin would again give serious consideration to the possibility of Slovakia's partition among Budapest, Warsaw, and herself.[28] But at least until mid-March, the Ludaks could expect Nazi backing and good will.

Facing a Slovak-German front, Prague's outlook was not too bright. The Czecho-Slovak loyalists were not fully conscious of the approaching tragedy; they wanted to believe that Slovakia's problems were definitely solved. Hlinka Party Moderates did not applaud the Radical undertakings, either. Many Moderates preferred, in the last analysis, a Czechoslovakia to any other combination, doubting Slovakia's ability to survive as an independent state. The Moderates feared Germany and made no secret of it. Still other Ludaks wanted a Slovak-Hungarian or Slovak-Polish federation. Hence, the anti-Radical forces lacked unity, in spite of their numerical strength. Weakened by internal strife, the Moderates constituted no match for determined pro-German opponents.

During November, the Radicals could not yet muster their full strength, a fact evidenced by the list of candidates for election to the Slovak Diet, held on December 18, 1938. Only four of the leading Radicals—Sidor, Černák, Ďurčanský, and Mach—could be sure of election. The first sixty-three names from a list of one hundred candidates were to constitute the future diet.[29] Tuka's exclusion from the list demonstrated the slackening of Radical power in the Party—an insult he never forgave. After the elections, the Radicals reached the nadir of their influence. External and internal deficiencies harmed their prospects. The Viennese Award cooled Slovak sympathies for the Nazis, and the Reich's annexation of two Slovak outposts, a suburb of Bratislava and the salient of Mt. Devin, added further humiliation. The taking of Mt. Devin, a place heavily steeped in historic memories, particularly offended the country's population. Furthermore, Poland, the self-declared friend of the Slovak people, hastened to fulfill the Munich Agreement to the last detail, as she helped herself to some wretched villages beyond her southern borders. No one came to aid the victimized Slovaks, while friends of the Radicals were the first to harm. Radical attempts to boost their popularity by blaming the Czechs for the misfortune failed, with the Moderates extracting every possible advantage from the bad luck of their adversaries.

Prevailing conditions in Slovakia could not provide comfort for the followers of Sidor or Ďurčanský either. A stormy rush of various Ludak job seekers marked the days and weeks after the Žilina meeting. While some aspired to positions in the new administration, others went after those appointments held by men of the old regime, particularly Czechs. The Ludak ministers wanted to drive as many Czechs as possible out of the country, and Tiso, Černák, and Ďurčanský could hardly have been more successful. The disorganization of the newly established government developed rapidly. Czech employes, exposed to a biting chauvinism, applied by the thousands for transfers to their native lands. Only anti-Semitism could compete in intensity with the anti-Czechism that surfaced. The Ludaks encouraged Jewish emigration, and in the meantime set out to make the Jews' lives miserable through discriminatiory legislation, arbitrary persecution, and physical violence. George Kennan described the new order in Slovakia as having "a predilection for swastika methods in internal politics."(30)

An immediate result of autonomy was a severe economic crisis. Because of the political and social instability, foreign investors and tourists were reluctant to visit the country. Czech and Jewish capital fled, and Slovakia's own monetary resources were limited. While Bratislava's government busied itself in drawing up extensive economic blueprints, it was short on the means of completing them. Only Germany was willing to consider helping Slovakia, but under conditions favorable to her own political ends. The Reich's economists demonstrated great interest in Slovakia's raw materials and minerals; Nazi assistance aimed primarily at enhancing the prestige of the Radicals, and indirectly at the destruction of Czecho-Slovakia.

In order to prove herself, Bratislava badly needed to demonstrate her ability to cope with the problems of the territory. She could choose one of two courses open to her: either reduce the high pitch of nationalistic emotions and strive for respectability, or continue to exploit the propagandistic benefit of patriotic excitement. The former meant compromises with the central government: the payoff would be financial assistance from Prague. A preference for the benefits of prestige over economic needs might eventually cost the loss of sympathies for autonomy. The Ludaks needed to broaden their popular basis and they could do it by having more people owing the government for their well being.

The first wave of office newcomers was interested in supporting autonomy, if only for its material benefits. They were, however, reluctant to go any further and support the Radicals. The country needed a breathing spell. Thus the months of December and January stressed a certain stabilization in Slovakia and a limited willingness on the part of Bratislava to cooperate with Prague. Nevertheless, in spite of more moderation in methods and language, the U.S. minister in Prague still found that

The present regime in Slovakia is one which is openly anti-Jewish, anti-freemason and pro-German. It has adopted a number of its political methods from German models. To this extent it may be said to be at least strongly under the influence of totalitarian ideologies.(31)

In December 1938, the country got a taste of totalitarian elections. The Hlinka Party prepared a single list of candidates of which approximately

THE POSEURS AND THE PRETENDERS

one-fifth were non-Ludaks. Among them were representatives of German, Magyar, and Ukrainian (Ruthenian) minorities, and members of defunct parties. The list leaned heavily toward the Moderates, with clergy as its backbone. Since the deputies of the diet would eventually become the Slovak Parliament, their anti-Radical and pro-clerical leanings were important for the further development of the country. The voting methods also illustrated the nondemocratic nature of the elections: the voter had to answer "yes" or "no" to whether he wanted "a free, new Slovakia"; an affirmative answer automatically endorsed the Ludak list. Each nationality cast its votes in a different location, with uniformed Hlinka Guardists as poll watchers. Under such conditions, the 97.5 percent vote result for the Hlinka Party was hardly surprising (voter participation was 91 percent). The percentage of positive answers among the Jews was even higher. No Jew—or Czech or socialist candidate, for that matter—could run for office.[32] Thus the government gained a reliable voting machine in the diet, which was then able to legalize any future actions. The German consul general in Bratislava recorded Tiso's satisfaction when the prime minister first saw the machine in action.[33]

A reshuffling of the government followed the elections. Composition of the new government signalled a setback for the Radicals. The Radical Černák had to relinquish his Education Ministry post to the Moderate Josef Sivák. Ďurčanský, who kept his post as head of the Ministry of Transportation and Public Works, was rumored going into diplomatic exile as Czechoslovak envoy to the Vatican.[34] With the creation of a new Ministry of National Economy headed by a Ludak, Dr. Mikuláš Pružinský, the Agrarians lost still more of the little influence they had. The single Agrarian in the government, Pavol Teplanský, retained only the portfolio of Finance. Father Tiso remained the prime minister and head of the Ministry of Interior, while Dr. Vančo stayed on at Justice.

Since mid-November, when the new constituional law was passed by Prague's Parliament, Karol Sidor had represented Slovakia in the central government. At the same time, he steadily lost ground in the home country. The nomination to the central government bolstered Sidor's ego and apparently inflated his hopes of increasing his own importance—but to no avail. The veteran politician was away from Bratislava when decisions were made he lost personal contact with the people and could not influence events. While Sidor was drifting toward the line of the central government, Tiso was able to develop close cooperation with the Radicals.

The Radicals, while facing declining importance in their native land, could count on the renewed interest of the Reich. Rumors about Radical intrigues and conspiracies continued to reach Czech politicians.[35]

With the approval and support of Berlin, the extremist forces prepared for the complete separation of Slovakia from other parts of the Republic. These plans gained ground among the Ludak leadership, though it was reluctant to act as quickly as the Radicals wanted and the Nazis needed.[36]

Yet the Radicals were gaining friends, Josef Tiso being their most important convert. The Moderates continued to believe even in the early months of 1939 that the prime minister was still in their camp, although he had already abandoned it. Dr. Tiso never developed any special affecttion for Tuka, Mach, Murgaš, or the HG bands. It was the Nástup group which captured his attention, which lent him a considerable support when necessary, and to which he later transferred quite a few important and responsible posts in the administration and the Party. In Tiso a personal link between the clerical group and the Radicals was established, his primary sympathies with the latter. In turn, the Radicals cemented Slovak-German bonds, drawing a great deal of assistance and initiative from Tuka on one side of the border and the SS on the other. Tuka quickly assumed the role of chief conspirator, and even reached the Reich chancellor. The Tuka-Hitler meeting on February 12, 1939, was so well concealed that only captured German documents revealed the secret after the Second World War.[37] At home, Tuka relied both on the young intellectuals and on a group of *Rodobrana* veterans. The *Rodobranci*, which maintained a semi-autonomist position within the HG, gained a reputation of having low moral standards and questionable intellectual capacities. The Academic Hlinka Guard (AHG), also a semi-autonomous student troop within the HG, constituted the front organization of the Nástup group.

The center of the AHG lay in the Catholic student dormitory Svoradov, where Dr. Jozef Kirschbaum, its commander, lived. Then barely twenty-six years old, Kirschbaum rose to national stature when the Hlinka Party nominated him secretary-general. Openly exhibiting his preference for the Nástup Radicals, Tiso placed Kirschbaum and other reliable Nástup members in key positions.[38] As commander of the AHG and personal friend of Mach, the new secretary-general in fact served as liaison officer between the two Radical groups and the Party and Hlinka Guard.

The Moderate camp underwent more changes. Sidor still favored Slovakia's separation from the Czech countries. The Polish annexation of Slovak territories left him deeply disappointed; German activities disgusted him. Yet while Sidor was still closing the gap of loyalty toward the Republic, the Moderates suffered further defections. The German consul general in Bratislava testified to the apprehensions of Moderates as to what path to choose. Von Druffel reported to his superiors the fear in Party circles that the Germans, if called upon once, would not leave the country again.[39] The Hlinka Party, as revealed thus far, was anything but united in approaching the Ides of March. Its internal strife thus paved the way for Hitler.

In the last stage of the Czechoslovak tragedy, the Ludaks were the protagonists, playing the role performed six months earlier by the Sudeten-Germans. The Radicals grasped Hitler's intentions and willingly cooperated; Tiso understood and followed suit. Sidor also understood and recoiled at the last moment. The remaining Party statesmen were powerless to influence the action.

The final crisis of Czecho-Slovakia was a result of activities in Berlin, Prague, and Bratislava which each influenced the other. Much evidence testifies to Nazi plans for destroying Czecho-Slovakia in March 1939.[40] Berlin continued diplomatic pressure on Prague, while directing its friends and agents in Slovakia to step up the anti-Czech campaign.

On the Slovak side, the Radicals increased their propaganda to promote an independent state. Vojtech Tuka masterminded the attack on the Republic, and Alexander Mach carried out the campaign. In conspiratorial meetings Tuka was hammering home to participants the need for Slovak independence; they agreed to carry out their coup d'etat by March 19 at the latest.[41] Mach, Chief of the Propaganda Office, was busy preparing the population for the coming events. Since February 5, when he had publicly proclaimed for the first time the need for independence, Mach and others had continued to argue openly for a Slovak state. Tiso, in his address to the diet on February 21, demonstrated how much he was in agreement with Radical demands. While failing altogether to mention the Czecho-Slovak Republic, he referred to autonomy as a preparatory stage for the territory's statehood.[42] A more intensified organization of the Hlinka Guard, as well as requests for Slovak military troops, was also in accord with the separatist plans. Bratislava's government entered into independent economic negotiations with Berlin in an open break with the state's constitution, which left foreign relations unilaterally in the hands of the central government. Between March 4 and 6 a plenary session of the Slovak government, also including members of the Party's and Diet's presidiums, discussed the future of the country. Those in attendance agreed on an evolutionary advance toward independence without, however, setting a final date.[43]

Rumors of the pending coup d'etat, the unconstitutional activities of Bratislava, and the decisions of March 6 disquieted Prague. Czech politicians felt that they at least had the right to be informed about Slovakia's plans. Moreover, they saw in the Radical preparation a case of high treason, and decided to act accordingly. On March 9 after brief and not too successful negotiations with Bratislava, President Emil Hácha suspended

Premier Tiso and nominated Jozef Sivák (then traveling abroad) in his stead. At the same time the Czechoslovak Army and Gendarmerie stationed in Slovakia took over control of the territory. The military imprisoned several hundred Radicals, while the others either went into hiding or escaped to Austria. The March crisis, the final stage of the Czecho-Slovak drama, had begun.

Among those who escaped confinement was Dr. Ďurčanský. He fled to Austria, launching a broadcasting campaign in Vienna, and appealed from there for the destruction of the Republic. He also cooperated closely with the Nazi leaders and agents, assisting them in their onslaught against Czecho-Slovakia. Using various German channels of communication such as the *Sicherheitsdienst,* the Foreign Office, and ethnic Germans, Ďurčanský and his friends kept in constant touch with their counterparts on the other side of the border. Responsive to the Nazis and Ďurčanský in Bratislava were Karol Murgaš, chief of the HG staff, and Dr. Jozef Kirschbaum, commander of the AHG. The German minority in Bratislava and the ethnic German leader Franz Karmasin were also exceptionally active. The Nazi Fifth Column tried to increase disorder in Slovakia, organize demonstrations and strikes, terrorize political opponents, and take over municipal government wherever possible. It staged incidents forcing the police and military to act, and then complained vocally about "Czech oppression."

The central government under Prime Minister Rudolf Beran hoped initiallly to discipline the Slovaks through fiscal measures. Only when this expectation failed to materialize, and after believing it had secured Berlin acquiescence, the government took drastic steps. For two days the central government negotiated with the Moderates and Sidor. Then, it suggested to the president that the Slovak premiership be transferred to Sidor's hands. Sidor made a *volte-face* and agreed to follow Prague's lead. He accepted the new position under certain conditions—the release of political prisoners and the submission of the Czecho-Slovak military in Slovakia to his orders; nevertheless, he did accept the fait accompli of Prague. The compromise with Sidor, however, weakened Prague's stand, and induced hesitancy and insecurity in army commanders throughout Slovakia. The Radicals sensed the new situation and doubled their efforts.

German pressure made itself felt as well. High-ranking Nazi officials visited Slovakia frequently. Three days before the crisis, on March 6, 1939, Austrian Reich *Statthalter* Arthur Seyss-Inquart visited with Tiso and Sidor, inquiring about the possibility of proclaiming Slovak independence.[44] Lower Nazi officials repeatedly appealed to Sidor with the same end in mind. On March 11, Seyss-Inquart was in Bratislava again, this time as escort to Dr. William Keppler, an envoy extraordinary of the Fuehrer. Keppler came to see Sidor in a "fact-finding mission." The *Gauleiter* of

Austria, Joseph Buerckel, and Franz Karmasin and others (some 15 to 25 men altogether) also attended the meeting.[45] Buerckel in particular put hard pressure on Sidor, who refused to comply with Nazi plans, declaring himself "a soldier of the Slovak nation," and stipulating that he would accept orders only from the presidiums of the Hlinka Party and the diet.[46] The German guests, arguing on the basis of "Slovakia's petition for independence" fabricated by Ďurčanský in Vienna, were disappointed and offended. Their plans to explode the neighboring Republic from within suffered a temporary setback. Berlin never forgave Sidor his uncooperative mood.

Although Sidor had adopted a rigid stance, there still existed a possibility of enlisting Tiso's good services. Having been suspended from the prime ministry, Tiso spent several days in Bratislava before returning to his parish in Bánovce. During his stay in the capital, the ex-premier held intensive discussions with local politicians, including the Radicals. Then he left for the countryside, where he was visited on March 12 by messengers of Murgaš, Krischbaum, and Buerckel. They urged Tiso to hurry to Berlin for a meeting with Hitler. On March 13 he consented, and after a brief meeting with his fellow Hlinka Party leaders in Bratislava, Tiso left for Berlin, accompanied by Ďurčanský and a Ludak deputy of little note, Stefan Danihel.

To accomplish his plans, Hitler needed an influential Slovak who would be able to provide Berlin with an excuse for the final move against Prague. Sidor had balked at the last minute, but Tiso took the hint and went to see the Fuehrer. Ambassador Walter Hewel kept the minutes from the German-Slovak meeting.[47] Dr. Ďurčanský published his reminiscences: and Dr. Tiso testified about it in Bratislava, as Keppler did at Nuremberg.[48] Hewel's record reveals the strong pressures to which the Slovak politicians were exposed in the Reichskanzlei. Hitler and von Ribbentrop insisted on an immediate proclamation of Slovakia's independence, the latter even suggesting the local radio station as suitable for this act.

Hitler threatened his guests with Hungarian occupation of Slovakia; it is a matter of dispute as to how serious these threats were. The German military doubted the wisdom of strengthening Hungary; they were even more reluctant to permit Poland to create a long common border with Hungary. The propagandistic advantages of an independent Slovakia could not escape Hitler, nor could he shut his eyes to the strategic and economic gains. Among the several possibilities for dealing with Slovakia, the creation of an "independent" satellite must have seemed the most advantageous. Hungarian Army divisions served Hitler only as a threat beyond the wall.

Were strong pressures really necessary for Ďurčanský or Tiso? Years later Kirschbaum was to recall the March crisis. He stated:

For Ďurčanský and the writer it was clear that the hour of decision in regard to Slovakia's independence had arrived. In our eyes, it was one of the historical opportunities which numerically small, dominated people cannot bypass without paying heavy penalties.[49]

Moreover Ďurčanský, Kirschbaum, and the Radical circle around Tuka did not look at March 14, the Day of Slovakian Independence, as a "historical opportunity" or as an evasion of "heavy penalties." They toiled hard to prepare for and bring about the day, and provided Hitler with a good excuse for completing his plans.

Nor did Tiso need heavy pressure. His memories of the Berlin meeting were rather pleasant, according to General Ferdinand Čatloš, who testified at Tiso's trial in 1947. Tiso's biographer, Konštantín Čulen, spoke in the same vein.[50]

It would seem that Wilhelm Keppler's testimony before the U.S. Military Tribunal at Nuremberg offers at least a partial explanation for the apparent contradiction. In Keppler's opinion, Hewel probably misunderstood the real meaning of the meeting in the *Reichskanzlei*. During the interview with the Fuehrer, the Slovaks were more concerned with economic and technical matters for the future than with independence itself. According to Keppler, ". . . the independence of Slovakia had already been decided before I even made Tiso's acquaintance."[51] As a defendant in court, the Nazi official evidently tried to play down his role in Slovakia's independence. His explanations and descriptions were flawed, but Keppler may have been right as far as the general tenor of the meeting was concerned. For the Radicals, now including Tiso, no pressure was necessary. Hitler's threats were aimed at the Moderates and for the stubborn (as Sidor was believed to be.)[52]

Tiso refused to proclaim Slovakia's independence in Berlin, justifiably regarding such a step as arbitrary and illegal. Instead, he asked to convene the Slovak Diet on the next day, March 14. Again in Bratislava, Tiso addressed the diet and described his interview with Hitler. Tiso recalled the Fuehrer's threats and the dangers posed by Hungary. He explained that independence would eliminate the immediate dangers and would provide the Slovaks with an opportunity for self-determination. The logic of these words could not escape the deputies. Asked by the diet's speaker to vote openly by standing, the deputies were denied even a chance of expressing their true feelings. Thus, in the words of one writer, "The deputies rose from the chairs, some eagerly, others with reluctance . . . . When it came to counting, the voting was unanimous."[53] On March 14, 1939, the Slovak state came into existence. The next day Hitler removed the remnants of the Republic from the map of Europe.

CHAPTER III
THE "FUEHRERS" AND THE FUEHRER—1939-1940

When the Slovak state was proclaimed, the British consul observed that "the reception given to the declaration on Tuesday by the people of Bratislava was lukewarm indeed."[1] The "independence" was quite a surprise to the overwhelming majority of the Slovak people, including most of the deputies of parliament who voted for it. As the previous chapter indicates, independence was in great measure the work of the Radicals; no one had asked the people. The diet, originally elected to run an autonomous territory, turned *via facti* into a parliament.

The First Steps

However, the real power resided not with the deputies, but rather was delegated by Hitler to the caucus of the Hlinka Party. Reichmarshal Goering saved Slovak independence by appealing directly to the Fuehrer when Keppler almost persuaded Hitler to divide the territory among Germany, Poland, and Hungary.[2] As late as March 25, the Fuehrer informed the chief of the high command, Fieldmarshal Keitel, of plans to use Slovakia as an asset in bargaining with Warsaw and Budapest.[3] When von Ribbentrop met Lipski, the Polish minister in Berlin, on March 21, 1939, such a proposal was actually made.[4]

While still discussing Slovakia's fate with Hungary and Poland, the Reich did not lose any time enforcing unequivocal terms of bondage on the Slovak state. Following Tiso's telgraphed plea of March 15, 1939, Hitler extended German protection *(Schutz)* to the new state the next day. On March 19, after three days of Slovak-German negotiations, Dr. Tiso signed the *Schutzvertrag* (a "treaty of protection"). Von Ribbentrop affixed his own signature on March 23, thus formally and officially confirming Slovakia's independence. According to the treaty, German troops could continue to hold a broad strip of the country's western part (the so-called Zone of Defense, or *Schutzzone*), which it had occupied on March 15 and 16. Slovakia agreed to "coordinate" its foreign policy with that of Germany, and made various concessions in military, economic, and financial areas.

Neighboring Hungary did not assent to the proclamation of the new Slovak state, and took the opportunity on, on March 23, to send Magyar troops into Slovak territory. Two weeks later, under pressure from Berlin,

THE "FUEHRERS" AND THE FUEHRER

Bratislava ceded a small part of its territory to Budapest on April 4.[5]

Nevertheless, the new masters of the country were expected to continue with current tasks, and did so. The premiership was given by the presidium to Tiso, who, during the period of autonomy, had emerged as the strongest personality in Slovakia. His deputy, Tuka, enjoyed German support along with Radicals of various kinds, and probably Tiso's backing as well. The premier's rival, Karol Sidor, accepted the position of head of the Ministry of the Interior. Other positions represented the various existing factions. Ministers Jozef Sivák (Education) and Julius Stano (Transport and Public Works) represented the clerical group and the Party's administration. Dr. Gejza Fritz was chosen to head the Ministry of Justice, on behalf of eastern Slovakia. Dr. Gejza Medrický (affiliated with Sidorites), assigned to the Ministry of National Economy, and Dr. Mikuláš Pružinský, in the Treasury, were experts in their fields. Because of his participation in economic negotiations with Germany during the period of autonomy, Pružinský was believed to have created the radical wing of the government, along with the minister for foreign affairs, Ďurčanský. Šaňo Mach, as the chief of propaganda, had the right to participate in cabinet meetings. General Ferdinand Čatloš was chosen to head the Ministry of National Defense not only because of his knowledge of military affairs, but also to represent those of the Protestant faith.

Tiso and Ďurčanský soon emerged as the leading figures in the government, with Tuka and Čatloš, both appearing as Germanophiles, challenging. The Hlinka Guard, commanded since March 15 by Mach, gained some influence. Meanwhile, the Party's rank and file membership was torn by heavy competition for various political and economic appointments.

The state's first major crisis developed around Sidor, who rejected German pressures to conform with their policy, and thus brought down their rage upon himself. Moreover, his friendly relationship with many Warsaw statesmen and his reputation as a Polonophile compounded Berlin's discomfort. Hitler could hardly appreciate such a man serving as a member of his first satellite government. Finally, Sidor's popularity with the Slovak people continued to create an obstacle in Tiso's road to supremacy. German pressure forced Sidor first to take leave and then to resign from the government completely.[6] In the process, he became a magnet which drew together all the forces opposing the Germans and their local collaborators. Not only friends of Czechoslovakia and anti-Nazis rejected the fait accompli of a Slovak state; many members of the clerical group, previously supporters of Tiso, could not sustain his last actions in leading the Radicals in the overthrow of the Republic.

Surrounded by old and new friends, Sidor, the alleged Hlinka heir, was transformed into the position of a dangerous enemy to the new state. His public appearances turned into manifestations against the government and the Germans. Sidor himself was not as enthusiastic as his crowds; indeed, he tried to persuade the German authorities of his friendliness and suitability in order to be allowed to return to his post.[7] However, they continued to suspect him, and the German High Command pressed for his removal.[8]

Tiso and Tuka cooperated in efforts to disarm Sidor for their mutual benefit. They took a clear stand during a session of the Party's presidium on May 15 when an ultimatum was submitted to Sidor to leave the country or be taken under guard. Sidor subsequently accepted appointment as Slovak minister to the Holy See,[9] where his influence was greatly diminished. Although the German consul warned his superiors not to treat Sidor harshly, because there "still exists a possibility that he can be of use to us,"[10] the unequivocal stand taken by most Germans finally made Sidor leave the camp of his Nazi friends.

At the time that the campaign to remove Sidor was about to be concluded, a more serious source of trouble emerged, centering around the Hlinka Guard. A contest among various elements in search of benefit from Germany's confidence and compassion becomes apparent here: who would be the most accomodating and therefore reap the greatest profit from representing German interests in Slovakia? There were many groups vying for the prize, occasionally joining, at other times plotting against one another.

Although the whole Slovak power structure was on the right in the political spectrum, the challengers stood on the left of Tiso's camp. There were Mach and Murgaš, and the *Rodobrana,* including Tuka, within the Hlinka Guard; a group of fanatics called the Slovak National Socialist (or *Aryan*) Party; the Association of Ethnic Slovaks in Austria, organized around a semi-literate businessman, Rudolf Vávra; various Magyarophiles, who had adopted plotting and spying as their vocations, trying to sell their services to the Germans; intellectual idealists; underdogs; intellectual opportunists; and lone wolves of the Čatloš type, who joined the other challengers for personal reasons. This wide variety of figures split and created new groups, often through complicity with German agencies on whose payrolls they were registered at the time. At least three *Sicherheitsdienst* (SD) branches, the SA, Army intelligence, the Embassy, the local German Party and the Reich's Nazi Party tried to spread their nets in Slovakia. Each sought agents with whose assistance they could interfere in Slovak internal affairs.

As long as the Sidor dispute raged, this new trouble source was not clearly visible. Moreover, Tiso, desiring to widen his base, had gladly accepted the Guard's support; during this period, Tuka and Tiso cooperated. When Sidor was deposed, the HG was purged of Sidor's men who, though they retained some posts, lost their influence in the Guard. In the internal strife, the HG commander, Mach, drew closer to the Party and official German agencies; Murgaš, HG chief of staff, and the emerging Otomar Kubala leaned on the SS and the Austrian Nazis. After Sidor's removal, the friction between the Party and the Guards temporarily ceased. The atmosphere cooled further when German anti-Polish preparations entered the final stage. The Guardists were very active during this period. Mach, as chief of propaganda, organized a slander campaign against Poland, and Murgaš was sent to purge the Party's mouthpiece, *Slovák*, of the Sidorites who continued to staff it. As on several previous accasions, Tiso, Tuka, and Ďurčanský were the main forces behind Slovakia's anti-Polish action.[11] The Moderates, led by Party veteran Canon Jozef Buday, clashed with the Radicals over the war with Poland in the meeting of the Party's presidium in September 9.[12] In the following weeks, Tiso quelled the anti-German influence of the Moderates.[13] All Radicals stood behind the premier in the forthcoming Party convention and later supported his election for the presidency.

The Party Congress, meeting on October 1, set as its responsibility the task of electing a new head and officers for the organization.[14] Behind the scenes, fierce battles raged; but the old cast stood firm and defeated the extremists. In this encounter Tiso played a classic game: while leaning on the Radical wing and even launching a covert attack on the Moderates, in his keynote address, he withheld support from the HG candidates. Thus the Hlinka Guard's proposed list of presidium members—Tiso, Tuka, Mach, Ďurčanský, and Čatloš—was rejected by the Party Congress in favor of the list of the executive committee—Tiso, Tuka, Ďurčanský, Buday, and Sokol.[15] Dr. Buday was one of the leading personages of the clerical camp, not known to be an admirer of Nazism. Dr. Martin Sokol, speaker of the parliament, was an important Ludak Moderate, and maintained relations with "Czechoslovak" circles. The failure of Čatloš, the foremost Lutheran in the regime, to receive a presidium post resulted in grave personal disappointment, a certain degree of apprehension among Protestants, and anger among Germans and extremists.[16] Mach's defeat was attributed to the fact that many old leaders did not take him seriously and opposed him for his extremism.

The results placed Tiso as the balancer of the scales between two representatives from each wing. However, Ďurčanský, once a leading pro-German Radical, had changed his colors in the meantime. Remaining faithful to radicalism, he and the Nástup group moved to the right of the

Party's leading core, the clericals. The Nástupists' willingness to compromise over "Slovak values" decreased steadily. The Guardists composed the radical plank on the left. They sought to propagate their ties to the Reich's agencies, and increasingly committed themselves to usage of Nazi terminology. This regrouping proved significant in the coming period.

The election of Tiso as president followed the convention and was a meaningful step toward a sort of Caesaropapism in the Slovak state. The election was smoother than the convention; despite rumors that Tuka and Čatloš were competing with Tiso, the majority of pro-Nazi Radicals still endorsed the priest and did not openly contest the election. Thus ended the first chapter in the state's life.

The Road to Salzburg

The first year of independence found Slovakia suffering from severe economic maladies. The money market was stagnant; industrial prices rolled upward; inflationary pressures bore down on the economy; salaries and prices of agricultural products remained constant. Unemployment was only partially solved by an export of workers to the Reich. The peasantry flooded internal markets with certain products, especially cattle, which sold at low prices; yet there were serious shortages of cooking fat and other foodstuffs. The uncertain future and persecution of the enterprising Jewish and Czech minorities brought investments and building to a halt. The only beneficiaries were German banks, which bought companies and assets far below their actual prices, and local speculators, usually connected with the Party, who tried to compete with Germans for the loot. Old property changed hands but nothing new was created. In a short time a stratum of nouveaux riches sprang up. In contrast to their wealth, misery sprouted in the midst of the workers and lower income group of village populations.

In the wake of poverty, both Communist propaganda and Roehm-like tendencies of the Guard spread through the villages. Violent-tending groups sought help from Germany, and rumors of coups and revolutions in preparation were frequent. The military rioted in several places during the war with Poland; many deserted. Guardists clashed with soldiers, often violated the law, and terrorized the civilian population, especially when citizens were known to be connected with the fallen regime. The administration appeared not only inefficient and corrupt, but also partly unreliable and sometimes inimical to Ludaks and their Nazi masters. Ethnic Germans contributed to the havoc through their boundless ambitions. Members of the German Party felt themselves trustees of the Reich in

Slovakia. Under claims of equality for ethnic groups (*Volksgruppe*), they built a state within a state, requesting additional rights and benefits, and complaining to Germany with every negative response to their demands. A special aggressiveness was employed in the so-called Jewish question. The Germans closed ranks with the Hlinka Guard in attacking Jews, with an eye to their property. Hence, Berlin had many reasons for concern about the situation in Slovakia.

After Tiso became president of the new government, Tuka became premier. Ďurčanský directed both the ministries of Foreign Affairs and Interior. Ambitious and energetic, Ďurčanský held not only his departments but the whole government as well in a strong grip. Soon he became a target for attack by German agencies and local extremists.

George Kennan, while in Slovakia in January 1939, observed that the knowledge of the outside world of the younger elements in the autonomous movement was slight, and " . . . the native leaders are so sadly lacking in experience, in imagination, in breadth of view and in depth of purpose that they cannot hope to maneuver successfully for very long. . ."[17] These sentiments were echoed more than a year later, on April 29, 1940, by a Hungarian deputy.[18] These naive Slovak leaders tried hard to be what they were not. Ďurčanský posed as a minister of a sovereign nation, sending notes to Berlin, protesting misdeeds, complaining, arguing, and demanding. He even developed a doctrine: that Slovakia was the turning-wheel of a continent which could eventually promote understanding in the divided world.[19] Durcansky was interested in creating ties with the Western Powers, and attempted to enter into economic and political relations with them. When German diplomats quickly detected this, it contributed to Ďurčanský's eventual downfall.[20]

The Slovak state had received de facto recognition from Great Britain and France; the United States abstained from any formal recognition. After first protesting the destruction of Czechoslovakia, the Soviet Union proceeded, in the fall of 1939, to recognize Slovakia, and on February 3, 1940, the Soviet minister arrived in Bratislava.[21] He wasted no time in setting up a well-staffed legation, and in creating warm relations with the local government.[22]

At first the Germans were amazed. Originally they felt that since they had created independent Slovakia for their own purposes, Slovakia should have some freedom of action. Later the Nazis grew angry and began collecting evidence against the head of the Ministry of Foreign Affairs. As early as May 23, German Secretary of State Keppler sent an SD report to his colleague, von Weizsaecker, in which Ďurčanský, Kirschbaum, and the Slovak minister to Rome, Zvrškovec, were accused of a minor offense against the Reich.[23] Later the accusations took a more serious turn, such as the message from Minister Bernard that Ďurčanský was blocking the German exploitation of Slovakia.[24]

The list of "sins" grew; Hitler scarcely needed a Ďurčanský, who "obviously attempts to put on airs as if Slovakia were a great power and hardly is in need of German good will."[25] For Germany Slovakia was only a "calling card" to other states of southeast Europe, particularly Slavonic ones; its holdings had to be limited.[26] Either Ďurčanský and his men did not realize this, or they did not really understand the Nazi mind. In any case, Berlin decided to teach them a lesson. What was to end as the most impressive single interference of Germany in Slovak internal policy started as a fairly innocent encounter in the course of the power struggle between the people holding top positions and those seeking to replace them.

After the presidential elections, the Party's left-wing Radicals opened an attack on the ruling circle. Meanwhile, Tiso cemented his ties with right-wing Radicals and enlisted support of the Party's veterans and the country's bourgeois and liberal elements. Dr. Kirschbaum, the Party's secretary-general, staffed the secretariat's already inflated personnel with students and graduates. Key posts in the press were given to young academicians. Young high school and elementary school teachers were hired to run regional Party secretariats. Ďurčanský's friends gained a strong hold in offices under his supervision, in the president's chancellery and parliament's chamber. These people were placed in vital positions since they were not only faithful but professionally trained and willing to work; they provided the Slovak regime with its best qualified and most reliable material.

Indeed, Nastupists were the chief promoters of the authoritarian regime in Slovakia. The secretary-general busied himself studying authoritarianism in its theoretical and practical dimensions, his influence and power were rising.[27] A young theologian, Dr. Štefan Polakovič, earned a position as court philosopher and leading Ludak theoretician by composing a study of what was to be described as "the Slovak ideology."[28] Tiso awarded the 'ideologist" with a teaching position in the university and, later, with a professorship.

Known as the "Young Generation," the juniors were very aggressive in their fight for jobs and vigorously attacked the methods of Party veterans, taking over the very posts the Guardists were interested in. An editorial in *Slovák* on March 30, 1940, entitled "The Duplicity of the Slovak Nationalism," denounced "those, who turned lazy, frozen or even abandoned what they had defended in the past or had fought for."[29] Kirschbaum hailed the efforts of his generation [30], but Sidor angrily complained about these young ones who, he said, were rushing forward to grab with no regard and consideration for anyone, forgetting that Slovak life began long before March 14, 1939.[31] The competition over jobs and functions was sometimes described also as a combat between *Staroĺudaci* and *Mladoĺudaci* ("Veteran Ludaks" and "New Ludaks"). The Veteran Ludaks were members of HSL'S before October 1938, while the others joined the Party only after it came to power. Many of the New Ludaks entered the Hlinka Guard. Aggressive and filled with the zeal of new converts, their attacks added another dimension to the power struggle and political turmoil.

The HG Radicals attempted to attain their goals in the last weeks of 1939 and early 1940 using two tactics: constitutional and subversive approaches. The constitutional campaign attempted to change the structure of the regime and meanwhile deprive its opponents of power. Parliament was the primary target, and was accused of being part of the dead democratic system. Both Radical wings joined the campaign, but the Nastup group retreated from the demand to have the parliament abolished, and insisted only on change in membership.[32] Tiso, who apparently also toyed with the idea of abolishing that body,[33] eventually decided to oppose any alterations at all. The future confirmed his decision when parliament proved to be a valuable asset against the Radicals.

The other method employed by the extremists in attaining their goals was through subversion. Several plans for a coup ("National Socialist Revolution") were initialed and scrapped in turn. The most serious action should have taken place sometime in the second half of February 1940. The preparations were made with help from, or at least with the full knowledge of, SD branches in Bruck-on-the-Leitha and in Vienna, and with some support from the Austrian *Gauleiter* Buerckel.[34] The reasons for its failure are not completely clear; probably the would-be revolutionaries were too busy boasting of their heroism in advance and gave away the secret. The possibility of German lack of interest exists, too.

The real battle began at the convention of the Hlinka Guard on January 6, 1940. There for the first time the hostile voices took a public stand and attacked the leading Slovaks and the situation in the country.[35] Mach, having the ambition but falling short of determination, was propelled forward by other rivals. Murgaš, Kubala and others considered themselves talented enough and destined to personify the new Slovak "fuehrership." The domestic furor caused the Germans to be increasingly concerned about Slovakia, their agents repeatedly warning Berlin that the Reich was headed for trouble.[36] On January 22, 1940, a high official of the German Foreign Office in charge of southeast Europe, Walther Wuester, went to von Ribbentrop.[37] The official summarized his recent trip to Slovakia and suggested that the Reich support Mach.

Meanwhile, members of the Party's caucus kept publishing appeals for unity. An editorial in *Slovák* entitled "The Contemporary Slovak Problem," said "Unity, unity above all. Today the ideological load of a political system is perhaps not as important as unity."[38] However, all unifying efforts failed. The tension between Mach and Ďurčanský grew rapidly, and on March 20, the Guardist took a final step, resigning from the Office of Propaganda. In a letter to the president, Mach attacked Ďurčanský as an enemy of Slovak-German friendship,[39] and in a meeting with him, Mach presented three demands: (1) solution of the Jewish problem, (2) acceptance of his pro-German line by the whole cabinet, and (3) transfer of the Ministry of Interior to a man possessing the confidence of the HG.[40] Mach was not as politically nimble as Tiso, who decided to handle the whole episode as simply a personal problem. The resignation was not accepted, and the Party's leaders started lengthy albeit impotent negotiations. At this time, Mach, as chief of the Office of Propaganda, was scheduled for a visit in the Reich. The aim of this trip was to strengthen Mach's prestige, in accordance with Wuester's recommendation. Both sides decided to freeze the dispute, and when the visit was over, everything was almost forgotten in Bratislava.

A journey by a group of Slovak journalists to the Reich followed. Officials in Berlin tried to make them understand clearly what Germany expected from Slovakia, yet Bratislava was still too slow to grasp the problem. The men behind Mach continued to press, and he renewed his demands for a new job and radicalization of the government's domestic policy.

Ďurčanský did not remain silent, either. When Tuka, Mach, and others sent a flattering greeting to Hitler on his birthday, Ďurčanský pronounced it servile.[41] Mach immediately informed Eduard Frauenfeld, German advisor to the local Office of Propaganda, about that, and asked for advice. He was told to submit an ultimatum, and did, requesting the government to transfer the Ministry of the Interior to his hands by May 15.[42] When the day passed with no action, Frauenfeld was again consulted. The next step was a meeting of all Guardist leaders in the city of Ružomberok on May 19, where a strong resolution condemning Ďurčanský's policy was accepted. It explained that since "certain leading personalities" endangered continuation of the Slovak state, the HG had unanimously decided to act, in order to prevent any harm.[43]

The answer of the Tiso-Ďurčanský clique took the HG Radicals and Germans by surprise. On May 21, 1940, Bernard wrote to the Foreign Office

It is beyond any doubt that Mach is the representative of the pro-German line. Entrusting Mach with the Ministry of the Interior would lead, no doubt, to including many more or less aware, but likable, pro-German Slovak activists into the state apparatus; and it can be, accordingly, the start of a strong German influence on internal Slovak development.[44]

Yet on the same day, Tiso "accepted" Mach's resignation of March 29, and stripped him not only of his position as head of the Office of Propaganda, but also of the command of the Hlinka Guard.[45] The "resignation" was announced on the radio before it was even submitted to Mach, and police occupied the HG headquarters.[46] Berlin took this latter action as an open challenge to Germany,[47] and all German agencies in Slovakia began frenzied activity.[48]

Tuka, until then timid about his actions, found that the last development opened possibilities for enlarging his own power. He therefore submitted his oral resignation to the president.[49]

A published statement of the Party's presidium of May 28, 1940, bearing Tuka's signature, among others, spoke of "political freebooters and egoists, who should be excluded from the political life of the country."[50] Tiso continued in his approach of dealing with the problem of Mach as a personal one, in no way connected to Germany. Thus, he nominated Dr. František Galan, one of the leading members of the Nástup group, as commander-in-chief of the Hlinka Guard. Galan was a reserve officer and his nomination was viewed as stemming from a desire for an increase of military precision in the HG, since Mach himself had no army training. Konštantín Čulen, another man close to the Nástup, took over the Office of Propaganda..

All this, however, was a miscalculation. From the moment Tiso dismissed Mach, the episode ceased to be considered a personal one. Berlin became involved, and there the decision was made. Karmasin persuaded Mach to hide, in order "not to be imprisoned by Ďurčanský." In actuality, the Germans were afraid that some compromise might be made with Mach and the formal pretext for intervention would be lost.[51] They asked Tuka not to submit a written resignation,[52] advised Tiso to avoid taking further steps, and recalled the German minister for consultation.[53]

Slovakia faced a period of eight weeks of uncertainty. Each of those involved tried to influence the decision which was to be made in Berlin for his own benefit, of these, Tuka was the most active.[54] The prime minister retreated from Bratislava to a spa, and there busied himself by writing memoranda, drafting plans for a new government, receiving messengers, and sending couriers to German agencies. Mach, Karmasin, and others spent this time similarly.

Curiously enough, Rudolf Vávra exerted great influence on the formulation of the final decision. Indeed, a memorandum compiled by him and other extremists, calling for curtailment of the rights of the Slovak state and partial abolishment of its sovereignty, influenced Germany's final steps. Several Slovaks were eventually either given jobs or removed from them as a consequence of this memorandum.[55]

At the same time, the men of the Slovak regime worked vigorously, though in vain, to persuade Berlin of their fidelity. On June 5, SA *Obengruppenfuehrer* Manfred von Killinger, who since December 1939 had been inspector of German agencies in southeast Europe, was sent to Slovakia for consultation. He restored Berlin's confidence in Mach, who had almost lost it because of his weak and insecure behavior in the affair. He also had a significant meeting with Tuka. It was then that Tuka learned that Slovakia could expect a political remodeling.[56] After von Killinger left, Tuka invited Karmasin and the journalist Fritz Fiala to meet with him.[57] He tried to convince them that the problem lay not with Ďurčanský but with Tiso because the possibilities for change were limited as long as priests controlled Slovak politics.[58]

Slovakia remained quiet for some time since the Germans had several more important problems to deal with. Then, at the end of July, Bernard returned to Bratislava, and a Slovak delegation including Tiso, Tuka, Mach, and Ďurčanský was invited to visit Hitler at Salzburg.

The talks at Salzburg were in two stages: the more technical meeting with von Ribbentrop alone, and the audience with Hitler of a general character. Von Ribbentrop began unceremoniously, threatening Slovakia with two hundred German military divisions, and requesting immediate personnel changes in the government. After Tiso acquiesced, the group was permitted to meet with the Fuehrer. Hitler did not outline any specific demands; instead, his speech was one of subtle warnings and promises, intended to be a guideline for future Slovakian policy. Again, Tiso could do little except try to blame the usual Slovakian evildoers: the Czechs, Jews, and Magyars.

The Salzburg meeting between Hitler and the Slovak leaders on July 28, 1940, is the most significant event in the historical writing of Ludak emigrants in the West. However, actual influence in Slovakia from the meeting lasted for all practical purposes only seven months. Even during this period, the radical element tried to provoke new Salzburgs, without success. The only real losers were Nástupists, who forgot who the real master of the country was, lost his confidence, and were replaced with more reliable figures. Ďurčanský, Kirschbaum, and a few others were removed from the positions which they had gained fifteen months earlier; yet they continued to enjoy a luxurious life replete with public posts, money, and fame to the end of the war.

In the Foreign Ministry Tuka replaced Ďurčanský, and Mach took over as head of the Interior. František Galan, another Nástupist, was appointed acting secretary-general, the post vacated by Kirschbaum; in Propaganda, Murgaš replaced Čulen. There were a few changes in minor positions, particularly on Ďurčanský's staff. Tuka's power increased, but was not commensurate with his expectations; he was denied not only the presidency, but also the post of Minister of National Defense.[59] For the time being, the Germans tightened their control over the country, sending "advisers" to supervise Slovak offices and enforcing changes in the legislation. Although the Hlinka Guard was more vociferous and influential than before, it remained impotent against Tiso and his camp. The effect of Salzburg was relatively insignificant and short-lived; the shadow of the event itself was the only lasting effect.

Yet what precipitated Salzburg was important: the deterioration of economic and social situations, which undermined the Reich's supremacy; the intentions of the Fifth Column of the ethnic Germans, which occasionally clashed with the intentions of the legal government; the hunger for power and wealth of the HG Radicals, which troubled the ruling establishment; German suspicion of Ďurčanský's foreign policy, and particularly his stand against German economic exploitation; and the demands for a harsher anti-Jewish policy—these may all have been catalytic factors. Two additional issues which would exert their influence later on the situation were those of the Catholic attitude (e.g., plans to realize the preaching of social encyclicals), and Soviet overtures toward Bratislava, which Berlin watched with growing discomfort. This romance developing between kindred Slavonic states was an important motive for Germany's concern and warnings.

Hitler's pan-German mind could not tolerate Pan-Slavism. Apparently, German suspicions were aroused by the widespread communism in Slovakia and local mistrust of the Nazis, caused by the arrogance of the ethnic Germans, the old Polonophilism of Sidor's group, and the friendliness of many Slovaks to the Czechs. Even more obvious were the problems concerning the Soviet Union. It was evident that Russia was sympathetic to the Slovak people, if only because of their common dislike of Germany. Ďurčanský's ideas about the "turning wheel" and memories of the Czechoslovak-USSR treaty added to the misgivings. The Soviet Union seems to have toyed with plans to replace the Reich in Slovakia, if the witness of the Czechoslovak minister to Moscow, Zdeněk Fierlinger, was correct.[60] Constant Hungarian propaganda and denunciations in this direction also nourished German fears.

The Russian question was discussed at the Salzburg meeting; Hitler referred to it while conferring with Tiso and Tuka. A Hungarian diplomat, Ullein-Reviczky, told the American representative in Budapest: "Hitler does not like the trend toward Pan-Slavism, and contemplates a block in Central Europe to thwart Russian expansion and Pan-Slavism."[61]

The first phase of the life of Hlinka's Slovak People's Party in its own state, marred by continuous strife among various Party factions, ended at Salzburg on July 28, 1940. The struggle was not completely internal because of German influence through the effective support of the Hlinka Guard and through suppression of the Sidorites and Nástupists. After the meeting with Hitler, the strife was renewed under somewhat different conditions, leaving only two contentious camps.

Organization of the Party and the State

When the other political forces in Slovakia were absorbed by the Hlinka Party, its name was extended to the "Party of the National Unity." The secretary-general was in charge of making this lyrical name a reality. The president appointed Dr. Jozef Kirschbaum to this difficult job on March 16, 1939.[62] Father Hlinka, who lacked understanding for systematic administration and preferred to keep the party unconditionally in his own hands, had left behind a loosely knit organization. No secretariat of merit existed. Need for an administrative apparatus became evident during the period of autonomy. Moreover, the recently acquired power and new role assumed by the Party demanded its extensive reorganization.[63] The democratic structure inherited from pre-Munich times had to give way to a different one matching the new days. Slovak politicians decided in favor of the authoritarian system, following fashionable examples seen elsewhere. Kirschbaum became the "high priest" of Slovak authoritarianism, and often discussed authoritarianism in addresses, speeches, and in the press.

Tiso could hardly have picked a better man of administrative talents. A skilled lawyer and an experienced politician in spite of his young age, driven by insatiable ambitions, Dr. Kirschbaum set out to reorganize the party entrusted to his hands.

As secretary-general, Kirschbaum endorsed the maxim: nothing outside the Party, everything in the Party, nothing against the Party, everything for the Party.[64] The young lawyer had watched the Italian and German examples closely. Italian Fascism came more to his mind. Indeed, he spoke of Nazism as a millstone. According to Kirschbaum, Nazism and Bolshevism were two such stones, and Slovakia had to find her own way of escaping them, reported *Slovák's* correspondent when the secretary-general addressed students in the dormitory La Franconi.[65] The secretary-general developed his own concepts about how Slovakia should be ruled. The nation should be organized in a single party which was to be built on authoritarian principles.[66] The Party should act as the intermediary between the people and the government. Extensive legislation should clarify, and set down rules for the relations between the Party and the state. The supremacy of the Party must be recognized; it alone should hold political power and regulate the actions of the administration. In other words, the administration was to be static and the Party the dynamic force of the state—and both were to be guided by Ludak ideology. The immediate task was to reeducate the Slovak people in the intentions of this ideology.[67] On April 3, 1939, the secretary-general presented the presidium with a plan of Party reorganization.

Since the Party was the representative of the nation, it needed a sovereign position in the state. The presidium, where Tiso was the leading figure, had to have direct influence on the internal policy, spiritual development, and structure of the state. The initial indication of the change would be reflected in the appointment, rather than the election, of local Party officers after Easter 1939.[68] Kirschbaum worked hard on the project, he studied the problem, compiled theoretical research, and prepared a draft on an authoritarian system in Slovakia. The draft was tailored to increase the stature of the secretary-general in such a degree that he would certainly become the most powerful person in the state. According to the proposal, the Party should be first the regulator and controller of all public life of the entire Slovak nation, and second, it should be the responsible mediator and arbiter between the Slovak people and their government. The Party chairman (leader) would have superiority in the ranks of the state's hierarchy; he would be responsible for maintaining cooperation between Party and state administrations. The secretary-general would be his aide, responsible for the practical work, accountable only to the supreme leader and to the nation; in other words, the Party organs, the cabinet, and the parliament would have no real influence on his deeds. Moreover, the secretary-general would have not only exclusive rights in Party administration, but also considerable prerogatives in state, municipal, and corporate affairs. He would possess the right to send any dangerous person to prison through the Ministry of Interior.

On lower levels, a single man would perform the function of Party secretary and head the civil administration in a district. He must be granted enough power to fulfill his task. The relationship of the district secretary to the secretary-general would be comparable to the former's relationship to the supreme leader.

These, in brief, were the characteristics of this document. It was never legalized, yet its influence was felt in various laws and events while Kirschbaum held office, and even later.

It was simpler to prepare plans than to fulfill them. When the Ludaks acquired power, they were only vaguely prepared to establish an efficient dictatorship. Public support was insufficient; terror tactics were defective and wrongly employed. The HG began to compete with the Party, and there was no SS to destroy it. Some other strong organizations also refused to surrender. Many of the Ludaks were only good-natured *petit bourgeois,* who never dreamed of mastering a country and running a government. The lack of efficiency, demonstrated at the outset, best characterizes the period.

In spite of its shortcomings, Party leadership attempts to enlarge its impact on the population had more than moderate success. The gates of the Party, and of its front organizations, were kept wide open; citizens were encouraged, sometimes forceably, to join. Different front organizations made appeals to the workers, middle class, peasantry, and youth. The Ludaks influenced the clubs of *Actio Catholica.*[69] The Party formed many new branches, giving special attention to the villages. It wanted to reach every settlement, and, through a branch, bring it under control. The Hlinka Guard had the important task of supervising the population.

However, in the Party's attempt to spread its influence, its lack of qualified personnel was a grave shortcoming. The intellectuals, if not strongly nationalistically or clerically minded, despised the ultramontane attitude of Hlinka and his followers. Moreover, Protestants created a large segment of the Slovak intelligentsia, and Catholic chauvinism alienated them. Party veterans in many localities adopted arrogant, self-centered attitudes, hindering intensive recruitment. In order to revive and adapt the Party to the new needs, it appointed young people to local and district organizations—a policy resulting in jealousies and serious problems for Bratislava. Fights between different factions and job competition emerged as by-products of the difficulties of reorganizing the Party. The Party's secretariat worked feverishly to channel these widely straying currents, trying to guide and to put order into displays of vigor and greed.

Yet the Party continued to grow through "intervention," one of the foremost pillars of the Ludak regime; for every governmental job, and many in the private sector, one had to have the recommendation (Party intervention) of the local branch;[70] to accomplish any project in governmental offices, one needed the "intervention" of the Party. When "interventions" flooded the offices, the secretariat published direction for methods of intervention and greatly enlarged its own personnel to handle the enormous task.[71] The importance of "intervention" in the life of the Party and state can be amply illustrated; the corruption following it was remarkable.

The Ludaks used a whole range of methods to force the public into conformity. These methods included control of press, monopoly of organization of public meetings, disbanding or taking over of non-Ludak associations, and oppression of municipal government. Between March 14 and October 31, 1939, the Minister of Interior suspended 541 municipal boards and replaced them with emissaries.[72] The Ludaks permitted only publication of Party papers, and all journals were similarly oriented.[73] The authorities appointed new officers for existing organizations, or at least arranged elections to bring in reliable men.

In spite of its authoritarian procedures, the regime seems to have derived a considerable amount of satisfaction and support from various groups of the population. Disapproval of the narrow-minded policy of the Prague government aided its Ludak heirs. Slovaks quickly filled posts vacated by expelled Czechs. Oppression of Jewish tradesmen helped their gentile adversaries. The fast clericalization of education pleased many.

The law regarding the Party, accepted on September 28, 1939, did not go as far as Kirschbaum had proposed.[74] Nevertheless, it stated that the nation was taking a share in the government only through the Party, which possessed the status of a legal personality. It could use the state's administration to enforce several private actions. The secretary-general was to appoint local officers according to the recommendation of local branches which had the privilege of proposing various public officials. The law did not specify a supreme leader. An elected body or presidium assisted the Party chairman in conducting the Party. The presidium itself included an "executive committee" which would meet more frequently than the whole body. A congress was to be convened every five years which had among its responsibilities election of the chairman and the members of the presidium.

Under the new law, the para-military Hlinka Guard was formally incorporated into the Party body. Paragraph no. 5 (1) proclaimed that the task of the Guard was "to raise patriots, faithful to death to the Slovak nation" and to supervise public life. Further, the Guard was ordered to cooperate with the administration in the state's defense, and in the protection of public peace.

The law of the Party was based on the previously accepted constitution.[75] While the original intention had been to make a strong authoritarian form of government, the results showed a curious mixture of several schools of thought. The authoritarian line prevailed, yet it was based on two different models: one as seen in the countries ruled by the revolutionary right, such as Fascist Italy and Nazi Germany; the other as purportedly contended in encyclicals (particularly those of Popes Leo XIII and Pius XI), and professed in Salazar's Portugal and Schuschnigg's Austria. The Italian *Carta del Lavoro* and the constitutions of Portugal and Austria served as examples for a corporate setup and implemented "Christian solidarism."[76] All these models rejected liberalism and a democratic type of government. The Ludaks wanted to fit the corporate system into the Slovak social structure. While the system was allegedly based on modern Catholic social thought, only right-wing authoritarian states such as Germany, Italy, Spain, and Portugal had created any corporate structures. Yet the constitution kept some traditional liberal elements such as parliament, personal liberties, and a republican form with a president as head of state. The chairman of the committee for the preparation of the constitution, Tuka, himself a professor of law, described these parts as "exercises of words."[77] Nevertheless, they were included in order to please liberal elements, if not the moderates, of the Party and parliament. The country's liberals were particularly influential in economic life, and their cooperation was needed for success in this important field, for creation of an illusion of national unity, and to counterbalance the Radicals. After all, the written paragraphs were not important, their fulfillment was.

The one-party system, and the monopoly of power given to it, conveyed the essence of Ludak authoritarianism. Hlinka's Party became the sole representative of the political will of the whole state. Though the constitution carried a provision for political representation of ethnic minorities, the monopolistic concept remained unchanged, since each group was permitted to have only one party. During some periods, the whole population was entirely deprived of its rights, and many minorities (Jews and Gypsies, and to lesser extent Magyars and Ukrainians) were denied rights for the duration of the Slovak state.

Several paragraphs of the constitution dealt with the leadership. For the time being, no single established "fuehrer" was to be found in the country. Accordingly, an upper "State Council" was created to provide a kind of collective leadership. Besides the president, a prime minister was placed in the foreground of a council of ministers. This separation of functions was intended to increase the status of the president and disassociate his name from unpleasant actions.[78]

The corporate system, designed for lasting social peace and justice, was in reality only a guise for authoritarianism of a different kind, a dictatorship against socially weak segments of the population. The government was given a monopoly in conducting the labor market and the right to fix salaries; workers were deprived of the privilege of organizing themselves and fighting for improved standards of living.

The essential idea behind "Christian solidarism" was shrouded heavily with religious and social demagogy, as the preamble of the constitution demonstrated. The preamble was significant, too, in its denial of the sovereignty of the people, a sacred principle in liberal constitutions. The creation of the Slovak state was attributed to the Lord's will alone, a thinly disguised attempt to make the unholy satellite seem divine.

THE "FUEHRERS" AND THE FUEHRER

The clerical group made untiring attempts to revive the corporate system. At first the Party strove to take over and control associations and organizations which had been uncontrolled until then. This action was described as a unifying process, aimed at increasing the efficiency of the representation of the corporate organizations.[79] The leaders soon added its doctrinaire counterpart: the goal of building Slovakia as a model Catholic state.[80] An SD report reveals that Tiso himself exerted pressure on behalf of the corporate system, with a wish to please the Vatican given as the explanation;[81] there also exists another testimony which admits Tiso's cooperation in this issue with foreign Catholic personalities.[82] The Holy See was never fond of the priest Tiso's presidency. In spite of the warm attention given to Catholic Slovakia, relations with the president remained strained. The Vatican was worried about the political and moral responsibilities which the Slovak clergy was assuming in a secular state, particularly under circumstances of war. Perhaps the hostile influence of Polish and Hungarian Church princes added also to the Vatican's coolness toward the Slovak Catholic hierarchy.[83] Yet the president-priest was very anxious to be well-received by the Church's leadership. That the Catholic hierarchy would be pleased to see the doctrine implemented is not hard to believe. It would furnish the Catholic theoreticians with proof that the corporate system was a real contribution to political science. Tiso meant to accomplish this, but dreaded the danger of failure under Nazi pressure. Thus he temporarily abandoned the plan.[84]

There were other motives for the suspension of the plan, as well. The trade unions, under the formal control of the Party, opposed the intent to abolish their independence. Similarly, various professional organizations related to the Party who had gained monopolies in their fields were reluctant to hand the recently secured power to the corporate organizations. Newspapers published resolutions demanding continuation of the present status or the building of new independent organizations.[85] The opposition of the German minority was very important; it feared the loss of its own institutions and wanted to promote the Nazi system.[86] Quarrels among the Slovak leaders about the future form of the corporate bodies and who would head them increased the number of obstacles.[87] At Salzburg, Hitler gave the *Schuschniggiade* its final blow.[88]

Slovak Protestants were also potential opponents of the corporate plans. The regime's relationship with the Protestants caused continuous friction and added to the disruption of the alleged idyll of the Slovak state. Lutherans had enjoyed a privileged status as a skilled people and as reliable citizens in old Czechoslovakia. Protestants held important positions in the nation's economic and cultural life: many prominent Slovaks including Prime Minister Hodža and Dr. Iván Dérer, leader of the Slovak

Social-Democratic Party, were Protestants. The Protestant success caused strong jealousy among Catholics, particularly the Ludaks. Hlinka and his people made the Lutherans the targets of constant attacks, though religious fanaticism appeared to be mixed with political and economic passions. However, the government needed the skilled Protestants. Economic, military, and cultural necessities proved stronger than animosities.

The government must take the blame for many instances of wrongdoing and discrimination against Protestants. Offenses ranged from petty persecution of the Lutheran press through attacks on the place of the Lutheran Church in the state to open violence against Protestant ministers and laity.[89] Soon after the proclamation of independence, Protestants in the western part of the Republic grew so bitter that they preferred annexation to the "Protectorate of Bohemia and Moravia" to the life in the Slovak state.[90] The Lutheran leadership collected complaints and requests and submitted them to the government, but obtained no results. They were the *Memorandum of the Protestant Clergymen* of November 1939,[91] and the *Gravamina of Slovak Protestants* of May 1940.[92] The *Memorandum* dealt mainly with the Hlinka Guard and the Hlinka Youth, and the Catholic influence in them; the *Gravamina* was concerned more with the acts of government and its agencies. Both expressed the deep anxiety of the Protestants about their fate in the Slovak state.

The prime minister was responsible for one of the major encounters between the Protestant Synod and the government. Tuka tried to break the Synod's leadership and have the Lutheran bishops dismissed, both for "reasons of state," meaning hostility toward the regime, and personal hatred. The encounter failed in the face of the unified stand of Synod members and because of hesitation on the part of the government in opening a major confrontation.[93] Conflicts flared constantly around the new constitution of the Lutheran Church, which was repeatedly rejected by the government.[94]

In summary, the first period of the Slovak state was marked by instability in the political, economic, and social aspects of its life. The Party was torn by internal struggles, opening the door to German interference. The meeting at Salzburg concluded this period.

CHAPTER IV
PARTY FACTIONS

The Ludak Party was not internally cohesive, though its public relations agents were clamoring against the democracy and charging it with splitting the nation.[1] Consequently, one of the Party's leading propagandists, Konstantin Čuleň, stated publicly that, rather than being one unified body, the Hlinka movement consisted of parties and groups. He explained that no ideological differences divided it, but that opinions about the best means of reaching the movement's goals varied.[2] If Čuleň had admitted that competition among those who desired to execute policy also disrupted Party unity, his answer would have been even more truthful.

No formal framework for uniting the party factions suggested itself. Members of factions were identified by a community of goals rather than by formal grouping, although all factions but the Sidorites and scattered "Czechoslovaks" (a nickname for Czechoslovak loyalists) had one type or another of unified command.. The clericals had the College of Bishops, the leadership of *Actio Catholica,* and regular district meetings of priests. The Hlinka Guard was led by its High Command. The Nástup group held informal meetings. The best way to classify the factions is to examine their expressed opinions, intentions, and actions.

Nationalist-Clerical Faction

The most powerful group was the nationalist-clerical camp composed of Catholic laymen and clergy. The proclaimed goal of the clerical group was to establish in the country the so-called "corporate system" based on Christian Solidarism,[3] and an authoritarian government. The doctrines of neo-Thomism were to provide the theoretical background;[4] the names of Othmar Spann, Ignatius Seipel, or Kurt Schuschnigg were often found in the Slovak documents of this period. The Austrian Republic between 1934 and 1938 served as a working example.[5] The fundamental prospect was a kind of theocracy, a state in which the church held supremacy over the secular life. Private property was a sacred *sine qua non.* To enjoy it one should be primarily a Christian, secondarily a Ludak. The Ludaks wanted to have all the advantages of their monopoly of power in business and in society.

One must distinguish between the church as an institution and the actions of its individual members. The institution was represented by its hierarchy, parishes, monasteries, and the like, which were formally linked together. Yet individual members of the church, including dignitaries, members of monastic orders, and the laity occasionally acted independently. Although there is no positive evidence available which would link the Catholic Church as an institution with the Hlinka Party, circumstantial evidence tends to indicate that such activity was considered, perhaps even condoned, at informal meetings. Priests held important positions in the administration of the Party and the state: in 1940, among sixty-one members of parliament, twelve were priests;[6] among eighteen state councillors, three were clergymen;[7] and twenty-seven of fifty-eight county branches and two of six district organizations were led by clerics.[8] The priest-mayor of Bratislava, teacher-priests in the university, priests leading local Party branches or sitting on their committees, on school parent-teacher boards, and many other institutions contributed to an impressive list of clergy in important positions.

Unlike Croatia, another state combining Fascism with clericalism where the movement in power by no means represented the Church,[9] the clergy in Slovakia took a clear stand in identifying itself with the Ludaks.[10] Officially separation between the temporal and spiritual arms was preserved, but there was intensive interference of the clergy in state matters with government sanction. The College of Bishops acknowledged with joy Tiso's election to the presidency, as the Archbishop, Monsignor Karol Kmeťko admitted after the war.[11] It also gave the president and the regime continuous support and advice.[12] The *Actio Catholica,* under the direction of a bishop, was important in coordinating propaganda for the spiritual and temporal arms of the state. Through such affiliated organizations as associations of Catholic youth, women, men, workers, and students, the Catholic Academy of Science, the Catholic Press Agency, and through the press and its mouthpiece, *Katolické Noviny,* the *Actio Catholica* was able to influence wide segments of the population. Finally, there was Tiso's own circle of advisers, which included several influential priests.

Conclusions from these facts alone would give a false impression, however, of Slovak Catholicism's ties with the Party, for the Ludaks never got a total grip on the local believers. Only the stepped-up *Gleichschaltung* since the fall of 1938 helped to create an impression of absolute domination. Even then many individual Catholics were disgusted with the deeds of the "Catholic" government. Disapproval of the government was particularly aroused when it instigated harsh anti-Jewish measures. On the other hand, there were outspoken Nazi-minded clerics in several parishes. Some of them were eventually forced to leave the priesthood.[13]

Tiso himself was the leading clerical personality, but ambitions and pragmatism led him to follow his own way, which was not always that of the clerical group. When, early in his political career, during the period of autonomy, Tiso was elected to the premiership, he already stood near the Nástup group.[14] At that time he also remained the clear choice of the clericals who were alarmed by the prospects of having a Radical and layman (Sidor) as head of the Party.[15]

Tiso manifested great ability in politics; he was what Czechoslovak political usage described as a "realist." Though a strong partisan of "political Catholicism," he was an opportunist and pragmatist rather than a doctrinaire politician. Among those who influenced his thinking and political career were Monsignor Antun Korošec, the celebrated leader of Slovenia whom he met during World War I,[16] Monsignor Ignaz Seipel (later a well-known priest-politician) and the theologian Franz Schindler,[17] who were his teachers at the Austrian seminary Pazmaneum. To these, Tiso's biographer, K. Čuleň, adds the influence of Hungarian Bishop Ottokar Prohazska.[18] Intelligent, militaristically minded, Tiso had clearly made up his mind about which path to follow.[19] Jews described the president as a hypocrite, who was not willing to stretch a helping hand to the persecuted.[20]

Tiso was the leading ideologist of his Party. In the Slovak Republic, the president's aim was to establish "Christian solidarism." In his cooperation with the Germans, Slovakia gained more freedom than might have been expected. Two high-ranking German officials, one during the war, another after it, both described Tiso as "a strong personality."[21] The Reich's cooperation with Tiso was based at least as much on Tiso's own willingness as on their forceful pressure. Von Ribbentrop testified in 1946: "I do know that Tiso had Hitler's confidence."[22] Karmasin put it most precisely: *"Tiso—der grosszuegige Politiker, der innerlich bestimmt nicht allzu deutschfreundlich eingestellt ist, der aber absolut real denkt* (Tiso—the boldly conceived politician, who in his innermost thoughts is certainly not too much of a Germanophile, but who is completely realistic)."[23] After the war, Tiso and his colleagues explained his dedication to the Reich as lip service, paid in order to cheat the Germans.[24]

In spite of his postwar explanation, Tiso in fact admired and trusted Hitler. He said that Hitler made a very deep impression on him as a human being.[25] He understood that his personal fate and the fate of *his* state, was linked with the fate of the Reich.[26] Thus, Tiso remained faithful even after he had been abandoned by friends and after the Nazis had met defeat.

The priest was a shrewd pupil of the Nazi dictator. He kept himself informed on developments in Germany, studied Nazi methods, and applied the knowledge at home. Following the example of the German National Socialist Worker Party (NSDAP), Tiso fought personal and political adversaries, putting into action in Slovakia what he had observed in the Reich.[27] Two such examples are the Party's claims to the right of press censorship aimed at curtailing Hlinka Guard propaganda,[28] and the attempt to attain direct control of the army by demoting its commander to the status of a mere member of the president's chancellery (an action taken when Premier Tuka challenged Tiso).

Milan S. Ďurica, a Slovak emigrant historian, analyzed Tiso's prerogatives in guiding the Slovak state. He argued:

Tiso could intervene in the legislative activity of the Assembly and influence the executive power, reserved to the government, which was responsible to the Assembly and not to the President, only within the limits prescribed by the Constitution of the Slovak Republic.[29]

... at the Salzburg meeting with Germany's intervention in the internal affairs of Slovakia—Dr. Tiso lost a definite part of the effective possibilities to exercise his constitutional rights in regard to persons who were forced by Hitler into the Slovak government, especially with regard to expressed demands of the Germans upon the Slovak government. Such was the problem of expelling or liquidating the Jews. In this period we can hold Tiso responsible, as in the previous period, only in proportion to the effective possiblities of free action which remained open to him after Hitler's intervention at Salzburg.[30]

Ďurica's legalistic approach did not fit this case. No dictatorship has been exclusively legalistic, and the rulers of Slovakia never denied that they intended to have an authoritarian state.[31] This government should be classified as an "autocracy," in contrast to a responsible or constitutional government.[32] Apart from the theoretical objections, the Slovak Republic had a "political system in which the rulers are insufficiently, or not at all, subject to antecedent and enforeceable rules of law. . . "[33] It is possible only to describe how far the dictatorship went, or, using Timasheff's definition of totalitarianism, how many auxiliary functions of the state had to be enforced.[34] Yet, to judge Tiso's responsibility by the number of restrictions placed upon him by the constitution is meaningless for all practical purposes. In the Slovak state, too, "the 'structure of government' has no real significance, because the power of decision is completely concentrated either in a single leader or in a collective body, at least for a limited period."[35] However, while Ďurica argued that Tiso lost "a definite part of the effective possibilities to exercise his constitutional rights," after Salzburg "the power of decision," actually concentrated in his hands, became most absolute in 1942.[36] Between the years 1942 and 1944, only German intervention posed any effective limits on Tiso's power. Dependent upon, and nourished by, the authority of the Vodca,[37] and because of the need for his consent, the Party, the government and the legislature could hardly be considered as independent.

Tiso's rise to power can be attributed to (1) the formal rights given by a consecutive legislation of the parliament; (2) rights he possessed as head of the Party, the body holding the monopoly of power; and (3) growing personal prestige and development of charisma around himself.

The president activated, and frequently used, his constitutional prerogatives, particularly when fighting his political opponents, and was strongly and effectively supported by the speaker of the parliament. Every constitutional change added to the leader's (Vodca) prerogatives and increased his power as dictator.[38] Thanks to the new "Law on the Party,"[39] the "Law on the Slovak Working Community" (Slovenská pracujúca pospolitost')[40] and others, Tiso accelerated his influence in an unprecented way.

Tiso's prestige was partly augmented in artifical ways. The Ludak leadership understood the need for a personality with strong appeal, one that could compete successfully with the Guardist camp and better rule the masses. The cult of Tiso's personality began before he was elected to the presidency; it grew steadily and occasionally took Byzantine measures. Nevertheless, Tiso's personal charm, his image as a man of the people, should not be denied.[41] His psychological understanding of his "flock," the results of his experience as a parish priest, must also be acknowledged. Tiso liked to be regarded as priest-shepherd; many of his speeches sounded like sermons, a technique especially applied while addressing the country folk.

Gradually, Tiso concentrated his powers and developed some of the features of a totalitarian leader.[42] Though he was not another Hitler or Mussolini, one of his ministers described him as the "one who decides and others accept."[43] A strong and temperamental person with broad prerogatives and upheld by local and foreign (German) prestige, Tiso was able to achieve almost as much as any other fascist dictator of his era.

Laity Faction

The laity of the People's Party held important administrative posts, but in policy-making it had to acquiesce to the clergy. In contrast to the priests, this lay group was very heterogeneous. Many were teachers who taught in Catholic parochial schools; others served in remote villages where the priest was their single intellectual companion. Teachers always were very much esteemed in Slovak society and had key responsibility for spreading new ideas. When they became nationalists, the effect they had on their neighborhoods was very similar to that of the nationalistic priests. However, since these people were free of Magyar influence and were partially trained in Czechoslovak institutes, there was less hatred of the Czechs among them. In 1940, eleven of sixty-one parliament members were elementary and high school teachers, the second strongest group in the House, among them some of the most fanatical Ludaks, including "court-historian" Dr. František Hrušovsky, and several principals of Catholic institutions.

The lawyer was also prominent in Slovak life. Law became the most frequently pursued college curriculum for Slovak youth, as this profession promised a good income and raise in social status. Two additional reasons attracted Slovak youth to the law and lawyers to the Ludaks: they represented the young Slovak bourgeoisie, which suffered heavily under pressure of Czech competition; and their anti-Semitism was shared by Hlinka and his followers. The Party, which desperately needed nonclerical intellectuals, warmly accepted lawyers, placing them in prominent positions.

The social upper class was another important segment in the Ludak lay leadership. Included in this group were industrialists as well as men of the financial world and land owners. Their reasons for joing the Party were obvious.[44] Deserving of particular mention are those members of the upper class who were engaged in agriculture and industries connected with agriculture. Playing only a minor role during the Czechoslovak Republic, they were now able to surmount old competitors, members of the Agrarian Party, and rise to supremacy. The Ludak clique of the "big" business, tied closely with the Party's caucus, gained control over Jewish and Czech properties. Soon Slovakia saw the creation of a political-economic oligarchy, which included laymen as well as clergy. Its wealth was almost unprecedented in this poor country. German capital and ethnic Germans, who were as hungry for property as the Slovaks were,[45] constituted obstacles to the oligarchy. Hatred between the Slovak nouveaux riches of the clerical camp and between the Guardists and ethnic Germans led to constant quarrels and was crowned by a *monstre-procès* in the spring of 1941.[46]

Completely opposite from the oligarchy were the officers of the Christian Trade Union. In spite of fanfare extolling Christian love and cooperation between employers and employes for the sake of society, a sharp class war broke the peace. Indeed, the Ludaks held no Christian love for the workers.[47] Since the days of the old Republic when the Slovak labor class strongly favored the Social Democratic and Communist parties, antagonism had been developing which remained evident in the independent state [48] The communist Gustáv Husák commented, "The Christian trade-unionists were known by their democratic, or at least more democratic attitude."[49] They never came to a full understanding with other Party leaders.

PARTY FACTIONS

HG Radicals

"Hlinka Guard" is only a convenient label for a diverse group of men unified only by an extremist *Weltanschauung* and the lust for power. The HG Radicals were the direct foes of the clericals. Most of them were in one way or another supported by German agencies. They lacked a firm coordinating power, such as the church was for the clericals, and the influence of the HG high command varied. It was strongest immediately after the proclamation of independence and for a few months preceding and following the Salzburg meeting. Then a gradual decline began, and in 1943 the HG high command was incorporated into the Party's secretariat, becoming one of its branches. After the Slovak National Uprising in the fall of 1944, the Germans revived the autonomous HG for a short, but very harmful, period.

The social composition of the Hlinka Guard reflected its changing fortune. During the period of autonomy, the Guard was the fastest-growing single organization in Slovakia, and anyone feeling himself important was anxious to be a Guardist. Naturally, under such circumstances, many career-seekers started their social advancement with membership in the storm troopers. At this stage, the Hlinka Guard was drawn from the middle class, augmented considerably by anarchistic elements from the bottom of Slovakia's society.

A few weeks following the proclamation of independence, the HG represented a true sample of the social composition of Slovakia. During this time Hungary's aggression against the new state turned the Guard into the outstanding defender of the country's integrity. As the Slovak army was still in its infancy, many patriots found in the HG an organization for defense against the Magyar troops invading Slovakia in March 1939. Thus, when diplomatic actions stopped the Magyars, the HG lost part of its raison d'être.. The subsequent purge of Sidorites and the upsurge of the extremists depleted the good will and the patriotic aura of the Guard. It was losing respectability and representation while becoming a center of various declassé individuals, of men seeking power and property, and of pro-Nazi fanatics. With the gradual withdrawal of the middle-class elements, the Hlinka Guard reflected more and more the aspirations of the economically weaker segments of Slovakia's population, the urban and rural proletariat.

When socialist parties and trade unions were either outlawed or curtailed, the storm troops provided almost the only official outlet for grievances of the poor. Commanders and officers of the Guard exploited extremist tendencies for their own political ends. The regime profited, however, from these recent alterations in the storm troops, for the HG functioned as an important safety valve, channeling some elements which otherwise would have been even more dangerous. During 1941-42, the Hlinka Guard gradually mellowed. Many Guardists, satified with the looting of Jewish property, lost interest in further activities. Others retreated under the pressure of Tiso's camp. Still others, disappointed from unfulfilled expectations, became apathetic and even anti-Ludak and subversive.

The various factions in the Hlinka Guard were small. Individuals would place their loyalties first with one group and then another, seeking new opportunities. Tiso described the HG, in January 1941, as "generals with no troops."[50] With one exception he was correct: when the regular Guardist sensed that there was loot to be had, as during the anti-Jewish measures, the commanders were never short of men.

The SD files contain memorandums prepared by two of the most significant groups of the Hlinka Guard: the *Rodobrana* and the intellectuals. These memorandums best reveal the aims and goals of these groups. The *Rodobranci* wrote their memorandum in August 1940,[51] repeatedly emphasizing the service of its authors to the state. Seven of its twenty-three paragraphs applied for special rights such as appointments as security officers, the holding of arms, and membership on various committees, the acceptance of which would have meant handing the whole population over to the unrestrained terror of a power-hungry band. Three other paragraphs asked for economic advantages because "[We] have the right for the above-mentioned positions and have earned it." Five additional points dealt with the need for anti-Jewish measures. The remainder of the document dealt with organization of the HG. They requested for *Rodobrana* a status similar to that of the SS in the Reich. The Hlinka Guard was to be given the role of the German SA. Intellectually, this paper was rather unimpressive and should not be regarded as representative of the group's theoretical thinking. It bears witness only to the moral stature of its composers.

The other memorandum, written by the intellectual group, met a much higher standard.[52] At least four of its authors belonged to the so-called *Náš Boj* (Our Struggle) group composed of the elite of the Slovak pro-Nazis. The memorandum dealt with such matters as the definitions of the Slovak nation and its territory, and of civil rights; an advocacy of basing the state on national-socialist principles; the concept of labor as the highest human value everyone had the right and duty to work; the rights and tasks of the capital; a demand for the solution of various acute social problems, support of the family, and attention to public health; and suggestions for ways of achieving the socialization of culture. Then the authors stated: "We adhere to the basis of positive Christianity." A description of the desired status for the army and para-military organizations such as the

Hlinka Guard and Hlinka Youth followed. The memorandum suggested that every member of the nation be required to be educated in the virtues of personal courage and national loyalty in order to be prepared to serve in the army and in the HG. Jews were to be denied any public or social functions, their right to private property, and it was felt that they should be excluded from the national body and put in ghettos until the Jewish question could be solved internationally.

This memorandum reveals certain aspects of the HG Radical mind. It strongly emphasized social problems; so-called "Nazi" views were blended with those of "positive Christianity," in order to blur the distinctions between them; and the tone of the memorandum's nationalism was aggressive, but its racial approach hidden. The memorandum can be considered as representative of Guardist intellectuals and as departing from the official ideology, particularly in its social emphasis and clear devotion to National Socialism.[53]

Much of the power of the HG was concentrated in the hands of a few individuals. Its commander-in-chief, Mach, remained with the HG almost to the very end. He gave public speeches from time to time and aroused some enthusiasm, but, as the importance of the Guard diminished, found he needed additional backing. Finally, after the collapse of Italy, he made peace with Tiso and entered his personal suite. The president did not regard him as significant,[54] so he let Mach vent himself while he continued to conduct state affairs undisturbed.[55] Mach's pact with Tuka was one more of convenience than cooperation.[56] Even though the Germans supported Mach, they were never sure whether Mach was their man. Mach was too much of a fanatic and opportunist to accept the Germans and follow them implicitly;[57] he needed the Reich in order to have an independent Slovakia, and to fulfill his personal ambitions.[58] When the Nazis became disenchanted with him, Mach was ready to abandon his well-wishers.[59]

Among powerful Radicals were Karol Murgaš, Mach's old competitor, who lost his power in 1942 partly because of intrigues against Tiso, and partly because of drunkenness. Later Murgaš confronted his conscience during a visit to the eastern front and became anti-German.[60] Another was Otomar Kubala, who was Mach's most dangerous rival, and eventually replaced him. Kubala was a crude man and a Nazi fanatic, holding allegiance to the Reich to its downfall. He was the most important person in the circle around the monthly *Náš Boj* (Our Struggle), where ardent Slovak pro-Nazis gathered. The German adviser *(Berater)* to the HG, SS *Obersturmbannfuehrer* Viktor Nageler, led this group.[61] In the fall of 1943 they counted only about 150 men, but this number composed the elite of Slovak pro-Nazi extremists. The circle included several teachers of Bratislava University, writers, journalists, physicians, lawyers, high-ranking HG officers, and others. In spite of the group's background, *Náš Boj's* influence upon public life was comparatively insignificant.

The most outstanding member of the radical camp was the prime minister, Professor Vojtech Tuka. In retrospect, he is seen as a tragic figure, an ambitious dreamer ready to pay heavily for fulfilling his dreams, which ended on the gallows. Tuka was a thinker who believed in fate and destiny, a man of reason unable to translate thought into deeds. Misfortune, both personal and national, plagued him from birth. In aristocrat-oriented Hungary, he was a pariah, in Slovakia he was often accused of being a Magyarone or a Magyar. He wanted to reunify Slovakia with Hungary, not for the sake of *Regnum Mariannum* nor out of allegiance to the crown of St. Stephen, but for his own sake. If he could not be a great Magyar by birth, then he would become one by deed. He probably hoped that, with the reunification of Hungary, he would become a national leader—another Mussolini.[62]

Tuka was accused of being Nazi-minded, but his convictions lay in this direction before Hitler came to power. Cooperation with the Reich did not originate from ideological conviction but from his dream: if he could not be a *Nemzetvezető* ("Fuehrer" in Magyar) in a bigger country, he could at least be a *Vodca* ("leader") in a small Slovakia. This was the base for his fight with Tiso. Tuka nourished in vain the hope that Hitler would present him with the local leadership. Tuka's hopes, and those of the Hlinka Guardists, were doomed to failure as surely as the hopes of the Iron Guardists and their leader Horia Sima in Rumania.[63]

Professor Tuka's personality emerges clearly from a study of his works, behavior, and deeds.[64] He was described by one biographer as a student devoted to his studies. At the top of his class, he received two university degrees, in law and in political science. Tuka wanted eventually to become a university professor, and at twenty-six was appointed to teach constitutional law in a lycée in Pecs, Hungary. In 1911 he completed his degree work at the University of Budapest.[65] *A szabadsag.* ("The Liberty") was his first work, already showing his appreciation for revolutions and for rule by elites and strong individuals: "Freedom must be a monopoly of great and brave souls."[66] His second and last scholarly work, written while Tuka was in a Czechoslovakian prison, was *Die Rechtsysteme*. A comprehensive and outspoken sound scholarly presentation, the book is an analysis of various types of societies and governments.

In the book, Tuka defines a parliamentary regime with a coalition government as a *Holokratie* (a "mob state"),[67] and rejects it because such is based on the social contract. No equality exists in this system, according to Tuka, because its founders usurped the power.[68] Its parliament is but a playground for parties.[69]

Tuka wrote that an imperfect state of a *tumultine* ("riotous") type creates a *tumultive* ("riotous") atmosphere. When moments of crisis approach, the state system breaks down, leaving the people in a state of uncertainty.[70] Such a dramatic situation calls for a great *hero*, who, when he appears, is in the center of events. His success or failure depends on fate, a mystical power beyond human understanding.[71] A talented and able hero, a genius, will have an impact for generations.[72] Yet there are true leaders and false leaders, only fate decides which is which.[73]

In a sense there seems to be nothing unusual in this study. Yet, considering Tuka's journey to Munich in 1923 to see Hitler's attempt at a coup d'état,[74] and the creation of storm troops in Slovakia in the same year,[75] his ideas begin to take on more significance. In the fall of 1939, while introducing his cabinet, the new premier described Hitler in these words " . . . his abundant genius appears too in the vision of what has to be done, what the forces of history prepared and even predestined, what should come and is coming in spite of the obstacles, with no possibility of prevention."[76] In *Die Rechtsysteme*, Tuka used the Latin proverb *"Quod in operando utilissimum, in scientia verissimum"* (What we use in operation, we verify in science). Tuka seems to have understood the lesson of the postwar period and tried to proceed accordingly.

Although Tuka did not fit his concept of "the hero," he had good reason to believe in himself. When the Czechoslovak government closed the Magyar University in Bratislava in 1918, all the teachers except Tuka left for Hungary. He remained jobless, and in 1921, when he was about to accept an inglorious governmental appointment, Hlinka offered him the editorship of *Slovák*. Thus, instead of becoming a bureaucrat, overnight Tuka became editor-in-chief of one of the country's leading dailies and found himself in the center of the political ferment. A similar situation occurred in 1938 when he met Hitler a few weeks after he left prison; shortly thereafter Tuka was nominated deputy prime minister. Tuka continued to climb, becoming premier, until fate finally turned against him.

Vojtech Tuka's belief in himself naturally included a great deal of self-admiration. He repeatedly paraded his martyrdom on behalf of the Slovak people.[77] While addressing the parliament in the fall of 1939 as prime minister, he declared: "Few of you see today these clouds appearing on the Slovak sky. Probably I see better. And I stay here, holding the full moral and historical responsibility . . ."[78] Returning from Salzburg, he said: "I suffered because I wanted more bread and justice for you in the free fatherland. Now I expect faithfulness and constancy [and ask] you to

serve willingly the nation and meanwhile prepare a better future for your-
selves."[79] In spite of Tuka's efforts, the people did not share his esti-
mate of himself. Tuka's malicious character, selfishness, and lack of
flexibility prevented him from being warmly accepted by the people.[80]

Tuka also failed as an administrator. His dry, legalistic manner lacked
the elasticity needed for his post. When he attemptd to broaden his power
and authority, and created new offices, his feud with Tiso intervened, and
Tiso declined to confirm the men nominated by Tuka, eventually abolishing Tuka-sponsored offices altogether.

Premier Tuka conducted his relations with the Germans in a servile
manner and did not miss any occasion to please them. While visiting von
Ribbentrop in October 1940, Tuka's hosts were astonished to hear him declare that he "would like to ask permission to look around a little in the
rooms where world policy was being made."[81] The talks between Tuka
and von Ribbentrop were conducted in the manner of pupil speaking to
teacher.[82] German missions in Slovakia repeatedly expressed their gratitude to Tuka, because they could get almost anything from him.

In order to gain popularity in the country, Tuka actively participated in
irredenta of the Slovak state against Hungary, in spite of having been on
the payroll of the Hungarian foreign minister for years.[83] In addition,
Tuka approached the Reich several times asking for spoils from the territories of Moravia and Carpathian Ukraine.

These and other exploits were in vain, for Tuka did not succeed either
with the Germans or the Slovaks. His position further declined because
there were many dubious characters in his personal circle.

For a long time, General Ferdinand Čatloš stood near the HG Radicals.
A Protestant by faith and a soldier in the Czechoslovak legions in Russia
during World War I, Čatloš' career encompassed loyalty to Czechoslovakia,
the state he had fought for, then to the extremist pro-German group in the
Slovak Republic, and finally back to Czechoslovakia. Thus, in 1944, the
general contacted the illegal Communist Party and tried to join the Slovak
National Uprising.[84]

Čatloš deserted the Czechoslovak flag, as did many other separatists, in
search of a quick career. The Ludaks were pleased because they needed
Protestant and, particularly, military support. Yet, Čatloš was not accepted into their inner circle, nor was he fully accepted by the Germans, suspicious of him because he had been a Czechoslovak legionnaire in World
War I.

Although Berlin pressed constantly for the discharge of legionnaire
veterans from the army, they were its backbone and could not be release-
ed.[85] Caught in this conflict and growing bitter toward the clericals,
Čatloš closed ranks with the Guard. He sought not only to persuade the

Germans of his faithfulness, but also to oppose the Party's mainstream. The mouthpiece of the HG, the daily *Gardista*, and many leading Guardists, themselves Catholics, supported Lutherans against clericals in spite of Lutheran coolness toward the state. Their reason for this may be expressed in the saying that the enemy of my enemy is my friend. Therefore, Čatloš found friends who also opposed the clerical camp. However, he soon became overworked; the creation of a new army and politics proved to be beyond his stamina. At least three times he tried to resign his post. Competition between the Guard and army caused tension in the officer corps; the constant turmoil in the country resulting from the Guard's activity disquieted the military. The need for political calm and order while getting organized eventually made Čatloš move to Tiso's camp. He was tired of the fighting among the factions. After Stalingrad, he also tired of the Germans.

Nástup

Besides the HG, the other important non-clerical faction was the Nástup group. This group was the only genuinely Slovak contribution to the world of the modern extreme right. During the first period of the independent state, it was a leading power.

Nastup was not a mass movement and had no pretensions as such. Rather, its members considered themselves an elite group of nationalistic Slovak students and college graduates. When the Hlinka Guard was created, Nástupists organized an autonomous *Akademická Hlinková Garda* (the "Academic Hlinka Guard", AHG).[86] The students possessed an esprit de corps of "intellectuals" (*inteligenti*) and scorn for others. After Salzburg, the new minister of interior, Mach, dispersed the AHG along with other Nástup remnants. Mach explained his step, "It was a mistake to organize an exclusive group of students; one must not make a distinction between a worker and somebody who does not work."[87] Nástupists recognized their affinity with another student-led extremist movement, the Iron Guard of Rumania.[88] Indeed, they had some common characteristics.

The world outlook of a Nastupist was based upon nationalism, the Catholic faith, and a disregard for parliamentary democracy.[89] It was the nationalism which caused them to clash with Germany.

Nothing can better describe this kind of nationalism than Countess Waldeck's comment on the Iron Guard: "Unbridled nationalist egoism being the very essence of totalitarianism, it was inevitable that every country which went Fascist, no matter how spontaneously, had one aim: the preservation or restoration of its national independence and integrity, which was why it would bound to turn against German domination."[90]

Ďurčanský and his friends only continued the battle which began in the old Republic. The most succinct popular definition of Slovak nationalism was coined by a young Radical, Matúš Černak: "Ours is this piece of land under the Tatra mountains, and to us belongs its whole output."[91] The Germans raged with anger when Kirschbaum, while addressing a Party meeting, declared: "To be just does not mean to retreat. We have to realize that whosoever relinquishes a position which can be defended for Slovaks, steals and squeezes the nation's property."[92] This statement does not mean that Kirschbaum or his followers were anti-German, however. Wrote the Countess Waldeck:

> This sharp nationalist egoism, which was the raison d'être of the Guardist revolution, was bound to conflict with German interests. It was what all Fascist revolution was about, which was why the Nazis will be in trouble wherever in Europe they achieve Fascist revolution.[93]

> The Guardists were not disloyal to Germany, but their first loyalty belonged to Rumania, and the second loyalty too, and their third and fourth. Then there comes nothing for a long space and the next loyalty after this belonged to Germany.[94]

This description fits the Nastupists well. Unfortunately for the Nastupists, they as well as the Iron Guardists, forgot what they owed to Germany and thought only of what they would get from her. The Hlinka Guard, which replaced the Nástup group, was an extremist group, but lacked the originality and self-confidence of Nástup. Hlinka Guardists were only a reflection of Germany's power, mere stooges. Therefore, the Nástupists were liquidated and the Guardists seated in their chairs.

The nationalism of Nástup was not limited to questions of property. Nastupists were expansionists and chauvinists. Kirschbaum stated in an interview with a journalist of *Slovák*: ". . . our task . . . is to widen the borders of the Slovak state as far as to include the last village of the territory given us by God."[95] Yet, Slovak scholars found that the last village is as far east as Užhorod, as far west as to include a third of Moravia, and almost as far south as Budapest.[96] With regard to anti-Magyarism and anti-Czechism, there were few who could compete with the journal *Nástup* and its readers. The Nastupist attitude toward the Jews was no better.

Religion was another sacred principle of Nastupists. Although they proclaimed themselves in favor of the Christian faith, Catholicism was predominant. Nastupists staffed the leadership of the Association of Catholic Students and other youth organizations. Kirschbaum represented Slovakia in the international Catholic organization, *Pax Romana,* and in similar bodies.[97] Nevertheless, *Nastup,* its editors, and its followers did not get the benediction of the Party's clericals in the period before the War. This curious phenomenon occurred for at least two reasons. One reason had roots in the fact that the Nastupists were a secular element: they were basically anti-clerical. The students disliked the leadership of the clergy; although being firm followers of Hlinka the man, they preferred lay supremacy. Probably they had themselves in mind. On the other hand, the clergy, many of the prewar school and loyal to the old Republic, disliked the young Radicals who were their adversaries. For the extremists the Catholic religion was, however, not a faith but a national mark of distinction and identification. Disregarding the idea of faith, they turned religion into a national demonstrative value, a battle cry. While discussing the spiritual world of the Slovak youth, Kirschbaum said: "What is constant in our national character cannot be changed for one must not let the young people lose the ground under their feet. And this is Christianity, and our nationalism with its Christian flavor, conserved in our national tradition."[98] In advancing this concept of Slovak nationalism, the Nastupists were the most genuine representatives of the official ideology of the Slovak state.

Sidorites

Removal of the Sidorites from the state may have served the Nazis as a precedent for their request to dismiss the Nastupists. Sidor's Polonophile group suffered two heavy blows from which it never fully recovered. Sidor's removal from the Party's leadership and his diplomatic exile meant the loss of the most important and most influential member of the group. Nevertheless, other members still continued to play major roles. They held positions in the Party's administration; they ran the press, particularly the daily *Slovák*; and they were active on the local level. After Sidor's fall from favor, his faithful lost ground in the Hlinka Guard, while the extremists profited. Yet in other spheres Sidorites managed to hold their positions, partly because of the wide support Sidor enjoyed as an alleged anti-Nazi.

When the attack on Poland drew near, the Germans could not afford to tolerate the Sidorites any longer. Sidorites were suspected of pro-Polish espionage and sabotage activities.[99] The board of editors of *Slovák* were the first victims. Murgaš took over the paper and expelled the Sidorites. Poland's defeat brought about their complete ruin. Slovakia grabbed spoils from her unfortunate neighbor, and a wave of anti-Polish jingo-enthusiasm swept over the Polonophiles.[100] In the Party's congress at the end of October 1939 the Sidorites formally lost the strong posts which they had previously held. In subsequent months, these "Veteran Ludaks" (*Starol'udaci*) suffered because of intense competition from the "Young Generation."

After Salzburg, however, came a reconciliation, for the Party needed the help of the experienced Sidorites against the HG Radicals. The blows the Sidorites suffered led a few of them to actively denounce Germany. They participated in meetings where the acts of the Czechoslovak government in exile were discussed. Some Sidorites were also active in the anti-Nazi underground. In postwar Czechoslovakia members of this group took a bigger share in public life than the remnants of any other Ludak faction.

It is somewhat irrelevant to discuss the aims of the Sidorites. Yet, although they were not in the mainstream of Ludak clericalism, they could, nevertheless, easily find a common language with the clergy. Indeed, Pavol Čarnogurský, one of Sidor's followers, was very active in the *Actio Catholica* during and after World War II. While in the Vatican, Sidor became the voice of Slovak Catholicism, apart from the state's official line. Sidorites generally followed the clerical fascism represented by Tiso and the Party's clerical group.

"Czechoslovaks"

The most scattered faction within the Hlinka Party was that of the so-called "Czechoslovaks."[101] Actually, their relative loyalty toward Czechoslovakia was their single shared attitude.

The Ludaks never constituted a compact entity with the Slovak people and so had to force themselves upon the nation. During the period of autonomy, they consumed other bourgeois parties and hoped to either indoctrinate the population or terrorize it. The ruling HSL'S claimed to be the same after as before the unification, with the exception that it now included the entire nation.[102] The HSL'S, being a minority, had a difficult task, particularly since it lacked experience and specialists. Thus it was forced to open the doors, if not of the Party, at least of the administration, to a wide variety of opponents. These included economic specialists, anti-Ludak Catholics, Lutherans, democratically minded army officers, and even Czechs.[103] Nine men (including five Protestants) who were non-Ludaks held seats in the parliament in 1940 (there were sixty-one members).

The "Czechoslovaks" who held admistrative posts were more important than those in political life.[104] Dr. Imrich Karvaš and Dr. Martin Mičura were typical of these administrators. Dr. Karvaš, a Catholic and governor of the Slovak National Bank, was educated in the democratic spirit of Czechoslovakia, and remained loyal to it. A brilliant economist who, because of his position, belonged to the elite of Slovakian society, he was also a black sheep in the regime, and actively aided persecuted Jews and Czechs and the underground movement. Dr. Mičura was the president of the Supreme Court of Slovakia. Prior to the independence, he had been one of the chief officials in the Czechoslovak judiciary. His judicial career in addition had a political flavor; he also headed an anti-Ludak Catholic party.

These men seems to have accepted jobs from the Ludaks for a number of reasons. Obviously they needed the income and the jobs were the kind their social background and training had prepared them for. Another reason is that for many of these "Czechoslovaks," some of whom were careerists, the new regime offered opportunities not available to them in the former government. Yet another reason arose from their appreciation of the expediencies of the political situation in 1939 and 1940. Independent Slovakia was woefully short of qualified personnel at the administrative level some of these "Czechoslovaks" felt that it was the lesser evil for them to adjust to, and make the best of, the given situation rather than to let the ethnic Germans or fanatical Ludaks capitalize on the shortage by filling the vacant posts themselves.

These people were appointed primarily because of the critical shortage of reliable brainpower. The Ludaks hoped to persuade the old adversaries to join them. Furthermore, Slovakia was a small nation where many people were mutually acquainted, and the leaders found it hard to be cruel in such a familiar environment. Tiso once wrote: "There are people who are accustomed to sweet strings, but we need these also; therefore, let them have the strings."[105] Tiso was right. Many Slovaks, previously loyal to Czechoslovakia, discovered a new Eldorado, a chance to make a fortune. they too occupied Czech posts and aryanized Jewish property. Finally, Tiso needed the "Czechoslovaks" as a corrective to the Radicals. Whether he had illusions about their loyalty, one can only wonder. Nevertheless, they served him and for a long time served him well.

Slovak Army

The army was the Achilles heel of the regime. In the officer corps there were more anti-fascists than in any other single institution. In spite of continuous purges, many democratically minded officers remained.[106] There were many reasons for this. Ludaks were always weak in the armed forces. The proportion of Protestants in the officer corps was high. Socially, the officers were very close to the intelligentsia, another soft spot in the regime. When the army was short of skilled men to fill out the corps, teachers were recruited, even drafted.[107]—and many teachers were anti-fascists at heart. Further, the war and participation at the Russian front, where the soldiers were eye witnesses to German atrocities, brought about a change of mind in many more.[108]

THE PARISH REPUBLIC

The Slovak underground had seen many officers as its leaders and commanders of the anti-Nazi and anti-Ludak Uprising in 1944. Quite a few, including generals, paid with their lives for loyalty toward Czechoslovakia.[109] The aims of the heterogeneous assortment of "Czechoslovaks" can be simply defined: the renewal of Czechoslovakia, though with various reservations.

The Party was able to coordinate the action of the majority of its factions. Nevertheless, the Party's structure was extremely fragile, and when more difficult times arrived, it broke down.

The Salzburg meeting of the Slovak leaders with Hitler closed the first period of the Slovak state. From the summer of 1940 on there raged an open struggle between Tiso and Tuka, the encounter ending by the spring of 1942 with Tiso's victory. Tiso took a strong stand in the governmental reshuffle which followed the meeting with Hitler. German documents reveal stormy and dramatic discussions in the Party's caucus. The president rejected Tuka's requests for the appointment of certain friends to public positions, and refused to dismiss certain others scheduled by the HG for dismissal. Mach refused to take the oath of office for his new post and threatened to resign if his demands to be allowed to choose his own aides in the Ministry of Interior were not met.[1]

The German military attaché wrote "it still seems that certain leading figures did not understand the importance (*schwerwiegende Aussprache*) of the Salzburg talks in their whole sincerity."[2] The new German minister, Manfred von Killinger, was a Nazi fanatic. He told Tuka and Mach to erase the words "resignation" and "capitulation" from their vocabulary.[3] Nevertheless, personnel changes were relatively minor, and involved few (but influential) posts. Only some members of Nástup were dismissed, and Mach, Murgaš, and Kubala were placed in important places.

Why did not the Germans punish Tiso for his firmness against Tuka? The lack of qualified leaders among the Radicals required preservation of those of the clerical camp. Mrs. Waldeck says that the Germans regretted that the Rumanian Iron Guard "had only Horst Wessels, and not a single Wohltat, Funk, Schacht, Goering, or Hitler himself."[4] The Slovak Hlinka Guard, however, had not even Horst Wessels. Those close to the Consul Rudolf Vávra were very disappointed for not being placed into any position in Slovakia. Killinger sent them a message arguing that they were *"willkommene Reserve."*[5] The Germans were well aware of the mediocrity of the HG Radicals.[6] Berlin doubted the ability of Tuka and Mach but needed them as a corrective to the opposite camp. The long-term effect of Salzburg, then, was to create a regime combining the skill and popularity of Tiso's men with the checks and balances of the Hlinka Guard. Berlin knew that Tiso, as a conservative Catholic priest, could not become an ardent Nazi. However, they still had full confidence in him, although they had doubts about his people. Thus the Tiso-Tuka-Mach triumverate was the most convenient solution for the Nazis. Suspicious personnages had to be gradually eliminated from power, and Tuka had to have German endorsement at every step of the Nazification of Slovakia.[7] This policy of Berlin became apparent in the following few months.

Meanwhile, Berlin sent a group of "advisers" to Slovakia, including one assigned to the Party and another to the Hlinka Guard; they were to guide and supervise Slovakia's activities. On October 1, 1940, the adviser for the Guard, SS *Obersturmbannfuehrer* Viktor Nageler, asked instructions from *Reichsicherheithauptamt* (RSHA, the Supreme Office for Security of the Reich).[8] His letter, in which he wondered whether creation of a strong and efficient organization in the Party and Guard "which could be eventually used against the Reich itself" was a wise and right act, revealed Germany's suspicion of Slovakia. He proposed only to build a kind of structure which would remain firmly in the hands of the adviser, and be ready for his use.[9] Himmler's files show that the HG was expected to smooth indirectly the Germanization of the Slovak people.[10]

The New Battle for Power

However, Tuka thought that his hour to become fuehrer had arrived. From August 1940 to February 1941 the long battle for power continued, interwoven with ideological and personal aspects. In this struggle Tuka represented what the Germans described as "the so-called 'national-socialist' direction,"[11] and Tiso, defending his Presidency, fought for confirmation of Catholic supremacy.

In order to build and strengthen the resistance, Tiso's camp concentrated on organizing the Party, its arms, and ideological propaganda. As early as August 6, 1940, the presidium gave a vote of confidence to Tiso, and proclaimed that from now on he would be the final deciding power of the Party.[12] In an additional action three weeks later, the presidium asked the parliament to change the constitution to make it consistent with the spirit of the leadership principle.[13] Emphasis was put on strengthening the Party's apparatus at all levels. The secretariat began publishing its own organ, *Organizačné Zvesti* (Organization News), and a campaign of indoctrination spread over the nation with the formalizing of the ideology of *L'udové Slovensko* (People's Slovakia). This ideology had to match the coin of "Nazi Germany" or "Fascist Italy."[14] The clerical camp had taken concrete steps toward establishment of the corporate system.

Tuka and his people were not idle during this time. The premier tried to strengthen his camp, to attract more of the Slovak elite,[15] and to purge the Party.[16] The main attack had two objectives: personal and constitutional. With von Killinger's backing Tuka asked Tiso to remove four ministers and substitute his men.[17] The demand was rejected, yet Tuka and Mach pressed for further concessions. For a week in November they paid

WHO IS THE MASTER IN THE HOUSE?

daily visits to the president's residence. Finally, Tiso lost his temper and proclaimed that he would rather go to Hitler and ask him to abolish Slovakia's independence than to appoint Tuka's protégés. The fate of another plan to have Radicals nominated to head the Central State Security Office (Ústredie Štátnej Bezpečnosti, UŠB) and the police, was similar.

The constitutional attack was aimed at the whole framework of the state, particularly the parliament. The prime minister sought to abolish it and replace it with a representative body modeled on the German *Reichstag,* than packing the assembly with his men.[18] The prerogatives of the parliament would then be transferred to the government.[19] The local administration would be fused with that of the Party.[20] Eventually the regime would become a full-fledged fuehrer-type organization with Tuka holding de facto power. Tiso transferred the project to the speaker, Dr. Sokol, who then prepared another plan, strictly according to authoritarian lines, with the president at the top. The premier realized his weakness and withdrew.[21]

While the maneuvers recounted above were occurring, other intrigues were taking place elsewhere. One involved Murgaš, who, ambitious and envious of Mach's success, wanted to head the Ministry of the Interior. To achieve that end, he planned to transfer the presidency to Tuka and the premiership to Sidor![22] His plans failed when Tiso discovered and quelled this plot in November 1940.

Another intrigue developed within the army. The German Military Mission was unhappy about the low standard of the Slovak Army, and so reorganized the general staff. Colonel Štefan Jurech, a talented but extremely ambitious and quarrelsome officer, was appointed quartermaster general (equivalent to chief of staff).[23] A Catholic, Jurech was a longtime enemy of Čatloš and a secret sympathizer with the Hlinka Party. When in power, he clashed with the general and had to be removed. The furious Jurech denounced Čatloš as unreliable in a letter to the president. He gave the names of two other high-ranking officers as evidence, and Tiso invited them to discuss the matter. Čatloš was not informed about the incident, and the general felt insulted and resigned. This resignation coincided with the major plot of this period: the attempt to overthrow Tiso. The HG designed this coup d'etat with von Killinger.

The German minister von Killinger had great expectations for, and a high opinion of, his own ability to deal with affairs in Slovakia. Upon arriving in Slovakia, where he was sent to put the country "in shape," he discovered how simple and unsophisticated the Slovak people were. "How easy it is, ' he wrote to his superiors on August 19, 1940, after being in Slovakia for twenty days, "to bring the Slovak people with one's finger-tip feeling *(Fingerspitzengefuehl)* to the requested line . . ."[24] Von Killinger supported and encouraged Tuka and the HG to storm the government, for he wanted to see quick results in the national socialization of Slovakia. He first resorted to material and moral aid for the Radicals, personally guiding and advising Tiso's foes. Then, becoming desperate and feeling that the *Fingerspitzengefuehl* was betraying him, he attempted a coup.[25] Together with Tuka, at a Christmas party in 1940 they tried to interest Čatloš in their plans,[26] Nageler, Kubala, Mach, and others decided to set up an HG meeting in the spa of Trenčianské Teplice, arm its participants, give them a courageous commander, and march them on Bratislava.[27] However, at that time, Berlin recalled von Killinger, which left the con-conspirators with no guide. The commander was not courageous either. He went to Čatloš (then acting Minister of Interior) and told him everything.[28]

There are many uncertainties regarding the planned coup d'etat and von Killinger's role in it.

He stood behind the HG Radicals by organizing their press campaign and supplying money,[29] pushing Slovakia toward a "presidential crisis."[30] Yet the chaos he seems to have in part fomented seems to have been against the wishes of the German Foreign Office and the OKW. In the words of the military attaché, "it is the desire of the Reich's government, that at this time no great internal political problems of Slovakia be solved," and that, "the leading Reich agencies want to keep Slovakia quiet."[31] It was at this point that Berlin recalled von Killinger. The new minister, SA *Obergruppenfuehrer* Hans Elard Ludin, approached the fuehrer of the ethnic Germans, Franz Karmasin, and warned him that it was Hitler's intention to keep Slovakia in her contemporary state.[32]

Thus, the Guardist camp suffered a reversed "Salzburg." The shock was not as abrupt but the results were deeper and of longer duration. The Germans compelled both sides to make peace on the basis of the status quo.[33] Tiso understood the possibilities of the reversed situation. On January 31, 1941, the first secretary of the German Embassy in Bratislava, Dr. Anton Endroes, wired Martin Luther, head of the Germany section of Berlin's Foreign Office: "Tiso understood Ludin's last mediation as confirmation that from now on he alone would bear the confidence of Hitler."[34] In the same wire, Endroes told about the various steps taken by Tiso to strengthen his supremacy, and about the terrible mood of Tuka and Mach. He was correct in concluding that "if Tiso succeeds in his efforts, he will turn into an uncontested Fuehrer of Slovakia" (". . .selbst-herrlicher Fuehrer der Slowakei werde").[35]

A thorough report of the Supreme Office for Education of the NDSAP presented the background for the Germans' step to preserve the status quo.[36] The change of German ministers seemed to the author the primary reason for the last developments, because the Guardist camp lost its experienced adviser. Developments on the international scene raised the question of whether Tuka and Mach were able to function efficiently in the face of the opposition from Tiso's camp. Experts on Slovakia thought not. Therefore, it became necessary to make a settlement between Tiso and his adversaries. When the Germans asked why the HG Radicals quarreled with the president, they responded that the dispute was mainly with those of his men who caused trouble. As a result of this reply, the Nazis urged their friends to make peace with the priest and to try to remove and replace his men. "Yet," concluded the report, "today Tiso is not afraid of German interference any more." Tuka and Mach made peace reluctantly and became passive. "The clerical clique," according to the report, "now dominates the field, and the question is with whom should we cooperate after the War."(37)

The tenor of Ludin's reports was similar. He expressed doubts about the ultimate loyalty of both Tiso and Tuka, but saw no reasons for change in Slovakia. Any German interference on behalf of Tuka would alienate the Slovak people. Ludin had faith that Tiso was wholly sincere in desiring to cooperate with the Reich. The minister admitted that only Tiso would be able to fulfill the role designed for Slovakia: to supply Germany with various commodities, and to serve as a showcase of the happy Nazi satellite. If this meant submission on the part of Tuka and the Hlinka Guard, then so be it. Ludin realized perfectly well the personal ambitions behind the Slovak leadership duel.

Berlin could hardly expect an efficient government if the Hlinka Guard were in power. In the face of clerical and popular opposition, the chaos in the country would increase, and, ultimately, German interference would be necessary. But Slovakia was supposed to be *die Visitenkarte Deutschlands*(38) and any direct intervention was out of the question. As the Nazis rejected the Nástup group, so they declined to build on the Hlinka Guard. During the war, the choice was inevitable: to hand the power to the clericals.(39) Hitler found it easier to have a modus vivendi with a conservative power which was less nationalistic and more experienced in running the government. As documents disclose, the Germans were not too seriously concerned about the Slovak Catholic Church, in spite of its expected hostility toward Nazism. They believed, apparently correctly, that the clergy knew where Slovak independence came from and, therefore, would support the regime.(40) At least during the war, Germany expected Slovakia to be a faithful ally and to fulfill her obligations. This could be better provided by a traditional—in the case of Bratislava, clerical—regime than by a revolutionary one. The HG Radicals would not be completely abandoned, but would be kept in reserve in case their services were needed.

January 1941 was the last time when the Hlinka Guard and Tuka conducted a full-scale offensive. In most of the future battles, they were on the defensive. Subsequent conflicts were based on personalities, either when Tiso tried to get rid of Tuka completely, or when Mach attempted to strengthen his shaky position. Hence, the year 1941 saw a constant expansion of the Tiso camp. In 1941 the activities of the Hlinka Party were at a low ebb. This climate proved favorable to the clericals who preferred to work unobtrusively, cementing their internal position and leading the country to new adventures.

German SS agents were unhappy with the situation. They accepted the present government as a necessary evil, but worked busily in the HG, gathering reliable men whose physical characteristics were compatible with SS standards; their aim was to prepare a suitable leadership apparatus in case of a change of government.[41] A special force of 1,100 storm troopers was organized and trained, the staff reshuffled, and officers sent to Germany for instruction in SS tactics.[42]

The clerical camp did not like these innovations. Thus all Guardists were requested to join the Party and submit to its discipline.[43] The Party conducted courses for functionaries and installed reliable partisans wherever possible. The most important internal event was the aryanization of Jewish businesses. At the same time, fateful developments occurred beyond the borders. Slovak clericals watched with joy the downfall of heretical Yugoslavia, and they welcomed the establishment of Ustasha Croatia.[44]

When the German troops were concentrated in east Slovakia, the local citizens understood that the Soviet Union was Germany's next target. As early as May 2, 1941, General Čatloš approached the German military attaché in Slovakia, Major Becker, and offered Slovak troops in the event there was military action against Russia and a Hungarian involvement.[45] It is doubtful that Čatloš would have discussed such an important matter without the knowledge of the Party's hierarchy, or at least Tiso's. Then, on June 19, 1941, General Halder inquired, in the name of Hitler, whether the Slovak Army was ready to move against the Soviet Union. Ludin contacted Tiso and Tuka, and received an affirmative answer.[46] On June 22, 1941, Slovakia entered the war.[47]

In the trials after the war in Bratislava, numerous witnesses tried to place the sole responsibility for Slovak participation in the war on Tuka.[48] Given the documents, however, such an argument is hard to accept. It is more likely that Tiso and the clericals saw the war against the Soviet Union as a sacred fight against communism, in the same fashion that their superior spiritual leader did.[49]

Slovakia also fought the "Judeobolsheviks" at home. On September 9,

1941, the cabinet voted in favor of the so-called "Jewish Codex," which in its severity surpassed the notorious Nuremberg laws.[50] Much responsibility for this piece of legislation belongs to the Hlinka Guard and Tuka. Both the Catholic and the Lutheran churches and the Vatican opposed the racial paragraphs.[51] How far Tiso's personal opposition went can only be surmised.[52]

On February 16, 1942, at 4:30 p.m., the German Embassy received a telegram from the "Germany" section of the German Foreign Office. This wire stated that the German government was ready to accept 20,000 young, strong Jews, and thus contribute to the solution of the Jewish question. They were to be sent to the east where there was a shortage of workers.[53] Four days later, on February 20, 1942, at 3 p.m., Ludin replied: "The Slovak government eagerly seized upon the proposal" (. . . "Vorschlag mit Eifer aufgegriffen").[54] It took less than four days to decide the fate of twenty thousand human beings. The shortness of the time indicates that the Slovak statesmen displayed little opposition, if any. Was the German pressure so heavy that any reluctance would have been defied? It seems not.[55]

Dieter Wisliceny, while testifying at Bratislava at the trial of Dr. Anton Vašek,[56] said that according to his impression Tuka and Mach were eager to solve the Jewish question and thus obtain the confidence of Berlin. They knew of Hitler's interest in this question and wanted a radical solution to obtain his sympathies.[57] Such an explanation fits perfectly the situation in Slovakia at the time of the proposed deportation. What could have been a more welcome opportunity to the hard-pressed Tuka than the "ability" to solve the "Jewish question?"

Why was the deportation not opposed by Tiso? Years later he explained that nothing could be done because the state was endangered.[58] However, Tiso was highly regarded in Berlin,[59] and at the president's trial, Ludin stated that Tiso could have opposed Hitler without immediate danger to Slovakia.[60] It appears that the president was not interested in doing anything about the Jews but preferred instead to keep abreast of his struggle to remove Tuka. To intervene with Hitler for the Jews would have cost him not only his battle against Tuka, but also the confidence of the Fuehrer. Thus, involvement in the Jewish question did not seem worthwhile, especially when Ludin, in a speech, warned the Vodca not to remove Tuka. On March 28, two days after the first Jewish convoy left for the concentration camp, Ludin addressed a meeting of ethnic Germans and stated frankly:

I believe it is impossible to build a Fuehrer state here and to place it in the hands of priests. . . . [however] . . . the Reich does not care which men, or more precisely, which names, influence the developments because the German Reich does not tremble if Mr. X or Mr. Y directs this state.[61]

The president's decision was clear: to abandon the Jews to their fate.[62] Moreover, the Catholic Church provided Tiso with qualified support and Bishop Ján Vojtaššák urged the State Council to confirm the deportation.[63] The Catholic Press Agency published a statement about the deportation, proclaiming that "The Church cannot oppose legal actions of the government while it is taking steps to eradicate the evil influence of the Jews." The statement explained that the Jews themselves were to blame because of their not acknowledging the Messiah, and preparing him for a terrible and infamous death on the cross. It further claimed that they never changed their hostility toward Christianity, and even in modern times had played an important part in persecutions of the Christians in Russia and Spain.[64]

There were Catholic attempts to intervene. The Holy See protested the deportations; the protest was rejected.[65] The Slovak episcopate also intervened, but probably did not persist because Tiso had personally given his consent to the deportation.[66] However, the matter goes further than a simple lack of concern on the part of the Slovak leadership. Various sources had informed them that the Germans mishandled the Jews in Poland and the Ukraine, and that the very existence of these people was in danger. On a later date, in the summer of 1942, Tiso and his colleagues possessed irrefutable evidence that Germans had exterminated Jews. Nevertheless, the deportations were not discontinued until October 1942, after the combined efforts of the local Jewry, Jewish organizations in the free world, the Vatican, and persons in the Slovak political and religious elite succeeded in stopping them.[67]

Tuka had no advantage over Tiso and could not use the Jewish question as a pretense to attack Tiso.[68] The current crisis between the two was a repetition of the old personality clash which had to be solved sooner or later. The president cherished a hope that Germany would let him depose his rival.[69] Tiso had the right strategy, but the wrong tactics. Berlin was not about to abandon Tuka, who, in spite of his weaknesses, was still needed.

Thus, matters stood unsettled until von Ribbentrop intervened, through his envoy Ludin, before the session of the Party presidium took place. Ludin was instructed to quell the dispute. Because of the war, there were graver problems than this "nonsensical personal quarrel." As von Ribbentrop put it in his instructions to Ludin:

I think it is important for you to make clear your position concerning the dispute between Tiso and Tuka. In the interest of the foreign policy of the

WHO IS THE MASTER IN THE HOUSE?

Reich, continuation of the contemporary composition of the Slovak government should by no means be endangered. In other words, Tiso obviously has to remain the State's President and Tuka the Prime Minister.

And, elsewhere:

At that time, only this settlement can be found, because right now we have, as you can imagine, more important things to do than to deal with such a crisis in Slovakia. You had stated your opinion, saying that the interpolitical construction, as created at Salzburg, was not the best; however, one has to remark that this was the single possible solution in accordance with our interest, and this is still true as it was then. The proper time for starting a fruitful and reasonable development for the future of internal affairs in Slovakia has not yet arrived.[70]

The president made an attempt to overrule Ludin's prestige by appealing directly to Hitler, but failed to find a mediator.[71] The German minister talked to Tuka and sent a letter to Tiso.[72] In the next session of the Party's presidium the matter was settled. No further changes took place.[73]

Thus the last major encounter between the two Slovak leaders apparently ended in a stalemate. However, the events had made it clear to everyone that only German interference had saved the prime minister. Tiso finally gained the upper hand, and no one could shake his position thereafter. The Nazis had no illusions about it.[74]

Party and State After Salzburg

Finally, the state's fathers returned to their work and began to strengthen the Party's organization. They thought that only a firm Party could be a reliable tool to fight the influence of foreign and internal forces.[75] So Party reconstruction was begun at the local level. Over the whole country, branch meetings were held with an emissary of the secretariat present. The local leadership was based on the fuehrer principle with the chairman, aided by four advisers, holding sole responsiblity for local activities.

Indoctrination in "Slovak, national, and Christian spirit" ranged from lectures and festivities through distribution of newspapers to issuing licenses for dance parties. Besides the flood of political "education," the Party carried out many functions, especially in the rural sector, where schooling for improvements of such things as agriculture, hygiene, and medicine were held. Obviously, the Ludaks honestly wanted to raise the standard of living of the backward Slovak countryside.

The chief task of the appointee for social questions was to run the so-called Winter Relief. A campaign for contribution was conducted to help the needy. The Winter Relief, in spite of its pretense as a great Slovak social achievement, was organized on Nazi lines.[76] Actually, it was another tool to terrorize the population. While striving to abolish all existing charitable organizations and concentrate their functions in the Party,[77] the Winter Relief did not intend to help all the people in need. Party membership was one of the prerequisites for help.[78] The appointees for social and economic matters were to control prices and wages. In addition, the man dealing with economic life was to help to distribute Jewish property.

The need for jobs and benefits caused many to join the Party, or at least to manifest loyalty and reliability. Men who received help, and members of their families, could easily be turned into sympathizers of the regime. Their ranks swelled especially when Jewish property became available for the taking. The Ludaks were aware of people who joined for opportunistic reasons, and efforts were made to milk the opportunists financially.[79] Yet the slogan "Slovaks, get rich" exceeded in efficiency all political slogans of the Party.[80] *Arizators*[81] were among the firmest supporters of the regime, almost to its very end.

One of the Party's most important ways of gaining physical control over the population was supposed to be by the so-called *dôvernici* ("trustees') system. Attempts at its implementation failed in 1941, 1942, and 1943.[82] According to the plan, local branches were to be divided into cells, with a trustee supervising the "ideological training" of the entire population of his district. The failure of this plan testified to the lack of cadres and the unpopularity of the Party.

Indoctrination and the cult of Tiso's personality held an important place in the Ludak rule. The cult of the Vodca was one of the more successful Party undertakings because Tiso steadily rose to the status of a truly charismatic leader.

Serious attempts were made to present HSL'S as an equivalent to NSDAP. While depicting Tiso as the supreme leader, the Party claimed to be the exclusive and single speaker for the Slovak nation. It demanded absolute control over all channels of information and publishing, and asked for obedience from everyone.[83] Yet articles published by the Party's regional chairmen on March 14, 1941,[84] and careful reading of *Organizačné Zvesti* reveal that on the local level there occurred (1) clashes between the branches of HSL'S and HG; (2) clashes between officials, municipal and state, and Party officers; (3) nepotism and favoritism; and (4) miscellaneous local disturbances such as personal quarrels, passivity of appointees and members, and intrigues.

The leadership tried several ways of fighting this. It emphasized the need for discipline, periodic visits to branches, threats of expulsion, and the promise of privileges including monopoly to influence state affairs, recommendations, appointments, "interventions." and spoils of Jewish property.[85]

In spite of these efforts, the branches were in poor shape. The German adviser to the Party drew a gloomy picture, based on a sample of three hundred yearly reports.[86] The average branch held five meetings a year. Topics of discussion were aryanization, land reform, public works, prices of agricultural products and wages. Less than 40 percent of the members read the Party's papers. The recommendations consisted of the main administrative agenda.[87]

In the early months of 1941, the clerical camp was at its lowest ebb; Germany's interference reversed the situation, and by the spring of 1942, Tiso could celebrate a personal victory. His people reached the height of their power that year.

The ideology of the *Ľudové Slovensko* ("People's Slovakia") crystallized during the course of the struggle with the radical HG wing. The Party's
fathers grasped the need for an offical theory which would equal the stature of National Socialist, Fascist, or other ideologies of the time.

While the Guardists borrowed heavily from the National Socialists, the
clerical camp emphasized the originality of the HSĽS doctrine. Štefan
Polakovič, the Party's leading theoretician, explained that the local ideology was *analogata* to Nazi teaching. National Socialism was *princeps ana-
logon,* and local similarities were *per analogiam.* Imitation was a sign of
inferiority, said Polakovič; adaptation meant wisdom.[1]

Four basic interrelated elements composed HSLS ideology: religion,
nationalism, consideration of socioeconomic questions, and right-wing
authoritarianism.

Religion

The religious (Catholic) element of the ideology included a conservative
Weltanschauung and an application of neo-Thomism and Christian solidarism. One of the fundamental Party slogans was "For God and Nation."
The Catholic religion was viewed by the Ludaks as the essence of Slovakhood; an attack on one was also considered an attack on the other.

The conservative outlook of the Ludaks was reinforced by Catholic
dogma, an outlook less evident in the political than in the social sphere.
The Ludak government wanted to undo not only the damage done by the
modern and secular Czechoslovak Republic, but also that caused by the
liberal legislation of 1894-1895, promulgated by the Royal Hungarian
Government. Separation of church and state was abolished, and the
Church, with the help of the state, kept strict vigilance over the moral conduct of the population. Believing in the mission of Christianity and Catholicism, the rulers of the state voluntarily surrendered many of their prerogatives to the church.

Tiso claimed he rejected the idea of the church's supremacy in the
state;[2] nevertheless, he was convinced that "religion can be influential in
politics only as far and as long as politics does not make religion its servant
but acknowledges its supremacy and religious orders as its guide."[3] There-

fore Tiso assigned to the church and Catholicism the task of a spiritual leader, because "the Lord is a higher force than a man, the Church is more than a state."[4] Furthermore, he added, "In Slovakia, Catholicism is influential in politics, and is ready to carry responsibility. It is even ready for martyrdom."[5]

The Ludaks declared that Christianity gave the Slovak people the stamina to suffer and survive.[6] The prayer in Slovak rescued the language which, in turn, saved the Slovak nationality. Therefore, Catholicism evidently safeguarded Slovak nationality and the two were seen as inseparable.[7] Tiso explained that both nationalism and Catholicism were the Lord's creation, so they did not contradict each other.[8] Since the Slovak nation was created by the Lord's will to fulfill a special mission,[9] it followed that the togetherness of Catholicism and Slovak nationalism was a national condition. Moreover, there is room to question whether the Ludaks did not see in Catholicism an almost biological national characteristic.[10]

According to the Ludaks, Catholicism was responsible for the differences between the Slovak people and their neighbors. The Magyar cult of St. Stephen was a tool to dominate other nationalisties; the Hussites corrupted Czechs, presumably through opposing the Roman Church. Only the Slovaks kept the pure, pious faith.

Nationalism

Recognition of the role of religion in the Ludak *Weltanschauung* is essential to an understanding of Slovak clerical fascism and nationalism. Slovak nationalism began before the twentieth century, but only after World War I did national consciousness spread among the masses, and only then did it take the form of a fight for self-determination. The unpopular doctrine of the "Czechoslovak nation" boosted the fortune of the HSLS and presented it with the opportunity to pose as the foremost fighter for the nation. Thus, it seems that creation of the Slovak state meant the victory of Ludak nationalism, and, hence, the Ludaks were obliged to identify and clarify other elements in their national theory.

The need to oppose the doctrine of the "Czechslovak nation" forced the Ludaks to search into the Slovak past. The Slovaks were a people without a political history. In spite of their participation in the life of Hungary for some eight hundred years, no prominent figures or events were connected solely with the Slovak name. To fight the image of *homines novi* on the European stage, and to build a more respectable name for the nation, the Ludaks created their own version of Slovak historiography. They wished to destroy the notion that Slovak Catholics were more backward than the Protestants. The Ludak version of Slovak history revolved around two premises: the antiquity and quasi-messianic vocation of the Slovaks, and the Catholic faith as the soul of the nation's tradition. The Ludaks wanted not only to justify their possession of power, but also to strengthen the self-consciousness and nationalistic passion of the Slovak people. In order to prove the antiquity of the Slovaks, they characterized the entire Slavonic population which lived at the end of the first millenium in the territory of Hungary, Slovakia, and Moravia as Slovak.[11] The Great Moravian Empire was simply appropriated for Slovak history and its name changed to "The Slovak Empire." The Ludak court historian, Dr. František Hrušovsky wrote "Svätopluk[12] . . . in leading his Slovak troops, made efforts to acquire *životný priestor* ("a living space") for the Slovak nation, where it would be able to find living conditions for ever."[13] Given this type of historical writing, there is a basis for Polakovič's conclusions that "We are not of today, and not a nation without history."[14]

Yet Ludak theoreticians went further and elevated the Slovaks to the status of the founders of the oldest state in the area. According to Polakovič, the crown of Svätopluk, the symbol of Slovak independence, was some fifty years older than the crown of St. Wenceslas and 150 years older than that of St. Stephen. "Therefore, all of us are turning into fanatical believers of the idea of Svätopluk's crown."[15] Additional arguments are tied in with the Reich. German missionaries and past military alliances were used as examples to support the argument that Slovakia's well-being in the past was only due to its relations with Germany.[16]

The area's first Christian church, in the city of Nitra, and the activity of Sts. Cyril and Methodius were used by the Ludaks to claim that the Slovaks were the *Kulturtraeger* (culture bearers) of Central Europe and of the Slavs.[17] According to the Ludaks, the Slovak nation had for them, just as it had had for their forebears, a mission bestowed upon it by the Lord.

The Slovak episcopate voiced this idea in a letter to the faithful: "We are convinced that our small nation, being a creation of God and placed in the heart of Europe, has an important and honorable objective, or maybe many objectives, determined for it by the Lord."[18] Prime Minister Tuka also professed his belief in the Slovak mission: "Slovakia, in her innocence and receptivity, is almost destined by the Lord to accept from the regenerating new worlds what has to be appreciated; and so to serve as an example of a small but healthy state."[19]

Tiso described Slovakia as Benjamin among the nations, whose voice is the sound of justice.[20] The president thought that the national mission had two goals: to prove that there could be a just arrangement for cooperation among the minorities in Slovakia, according to the *voelkisch* principle; and to demonstrate that there was no contradiction between National

Socialism and Christianity.[21] Behind such concepts lay the idea that the Nazis could be "Christianized" and a form of synthesis achieved between Christianity and "modern political science."[22]

The leaders of the Hlinka Party believed that the Slovak nation suffered from an inferiority complex,[23] which they tried to counteract with an image of superiority. The more fortunate nations had the "something," others had to create it., as was the case with Slovakia.[24]

The story of the national Slovak revival of the nineteenth century was also modified in order to create a more favorable background for the Ludak movement. Special care was taken to diminish the memory of Czech influence on Slovak patriots. Prominent Catholics of the past were extolled as important patriots and the participation of many active Protestants was obscured. By stressing the part the Catholics had played in the national revival, the Ludaks intended to present their movement as the legitimate successor and heir to nineteenth century patriotism. As Polakovič put it, "Ľudáctvo ("Populism") is the word which best reveals the content of our [Slovak] political tradition."[25] According to Ludak historiography, the Slovak people had been involved in a constant struggle for higher goals from the dawn of their history to the present day.[26]

Socioeconomics

Ludak ideology also permeated the realm of sociology and economics. The Ludaks preached social peace. "The leader of the workers must not be Lenin but Christ," said Tiso.[27] Slovakia was a poor nation, and, as such, Tiso felt, Christian love should reign among its various groups.

The Catholic thinkers dreamed of the *Orbis Christianus* of the medieval period when man's place in the society was determined by his vocation. They wanted the harmonious social peace which supposedly existed in the Middle Ages, and the corporate system was considered the proper way to return to that social peace. The right of the individual to own property was strongly guarded by the Hlinka Party and was codified in the constitution.[28] Catholic theoreticians, however, despised "extreme capitalism" in the same manner as had Romanticists and neo-Romanticists earlier.[29] Such extreme capitalism caused an unjust trend in the social order, but it was believed that when limited through social institutions, it was able to support economic and cultural progress.[30] Marxist socialism and other materialistic ideology were rejected completely because they disregarded the human spiritual life.[31] The Slovak capitalist held money and property only as a trustee of the public, and it was his responsibility to use them for the common welfare. Attacks, overt and covert, against capitalism, were prohibited; the Slovak worker was not to regard the Slovak capitalist as an enemy.[32] Only the Jews, according to the Ludaks, represented the evil capitalism rejected by Catholic thought.

Different socioeconomic groups within a profession should cooperate for the sake of society, not compete. The corporate bodies created by the different economic groups should be independent but yet under the guidance of the church and the state. This Catholic doctrine paralleled the anti-plutocratic (i.e., anti-capitalist) drive of German National Socialism, which claimed it also could improve the lot of the poor, fight the egoistic rich, and establish social peace.

Socialists endangered the society no less than plutocrats, for they tended to split the nation and, being internationalists, were ready to cooperate with the nation's enemies.[33] In contrast to the peasant, the worker had no roots in the fatherland. Separated from the land, he became part of the proletariat and an easy prey for Marxism. The leftist worker movement not only undermined the nation's unity and its social peace, but also the very spiritual soul of the Slovak people—its religion.[34]

Jews were portrayed by both the Ludaks and the Nazis as the "egotistical rich." They became convenient "scapegoats" to be blamed for the economic ills; the fight against them did not divide the nation. The Jews were also depicted as the virus of the socialist plague, another common theme the Ludaks shared with the Nazis.

Slovak nationalism had deep roots in the socioeconomic structure of the country. In the past, the Party had nurtured itself on the feelings of discrimination of the Slovak people. The spearhead of the hatred was particularly directed against Czechs and Jews. The Czechs had already been partially expelled in 1938-1939, and in a process of "nostrification," much of their property had been transferred into Slovak hands. The Jews were stripped of their property much more thoroughly, Aryanization was described as a patriotic obligation;[35] its proclaimed aim was to create a solid stratum of middle class which, together with the rich peasantry, would comprise the backbone of the nation.[36] As Polakovič defined it, "Our nation must be economically satiated."[37]

Even though social questions played an important role in Ludak ideology, reality fell short of the theory. Opportunistic motives were the basis for many of the acts. Reforms took place primarily when they benefited those in power, or when the interests of those people were not adversely affected. Land reform, Aryanization and the nostrification of Czech property were the best examples of these reforms.

Authoritarianism

To understand the hostility of many clericals toward nineteenth-century liberalism, it is necessary to remember the Catholic approach to the period of Romanticism and its later influence.[38] Catholic thinkers rejected the idea that the public authority is only a sum of the rights of the individual and these rights should be asserted vis-à-vis the state. Consequently, they rejected the concept of a state as merely a watchman, called only when the personal security of the citizen has been encroached. Instead, the Catholics championed the common good of the human community, as represented by the state. The common good of the state and the private good of the citizen were interdependent.

The teaching of St. Thomas Aquinas provided the basis for the modern Catholic theory of the state. There were two important schools of neo-Thomism. The Dominicans pursued a conservative path; the Jesuits chose a more up-to-date version.[39] While the Jesuits thought mankind mature enough to manage its own business and accepted the ability of the people to bear the state's power (the *delegatio* theory), the Dominicans argued that only he who had power directly "by the grace of God" (the *designatio* theory) should rule.[40] The Dominican school had many followers in Bavaria and Austria who influenced neighboring Catholic nations, and an Austrian social scientist, Othmar Spann, who followed the Dominican school, elaborated the authoritarian concept. His philosophy had a strong appeal in Slovakia.[41]

Tiso rejected pluralistic democracy because "the majority could be stupid and may be wrong."[42] He wanted democracy built on quality,[43] a government by the elite. The Ludaks never failed to remind the people that the church was constructed on an authoritarian basis and was ruled by a hierarchy.[44] On one occasion Tiso told his audience: "Thank God there are no parties in Slovakia."[45] The democratic system should be replaced by an authoritarian one; only such a system would be able to install corporatism and break resistance.[46]

An observer of Slovak affairs might see that the Catholic leaders dealt more with politics than with religion—"political Catholicism." Mention should also be made of the similarities of the authoritarian approach of the Slovaks with that of fascism. The rejection of democracy, liberalism, and of representative government, in addition to the demand for hierarchical rule by the elite and a strong-arm regime all were basic elements of the state theory of the extreme right. Tiso was well aware of this when he said, "The premises of the Encyclicals of the popes, and particularly the foundation of their social teaching, and the foundation of national socialism are the same."[47] Even if Tiso paid only lip service to the Nazis, the effect of such a statement on the population was to make national socialism become more familiar and likeable, while encouraging the people in Catholicism.

Contemporary Catholic theoreticians have not failed to see the danger inherent in some schools of thought in their religion. Heinrich A. Rommen, a Catholic social thinker of German descent, warns that if the significance of the liberal ideas were not understood,

we will experience the sorry spectacle of the conservatives, who, having lost the *distinctio Christiana*, will uncritically accept any political doctrine and regime because it calls itself anti-democratic, anti-liberal, authoritarian, as it was in our time with uncritical praise for the different Fascist regimes.[48]

The Slovak leaders certainly lost the *distinctio Christiana*. They, similarly to the Austrians,

simply picked out whatever seemed the most effective anti-republican and anti-democratic argument, and were little concerned with the question of compatibility of Roman and Catholic ideas they used in indiscriminate fashion.[49]

Ludak Ideology

For a long time the Ludaks asserted that "the nation is more than a state."[50] This maxim had been born in Czechoslovakia, when the state was so dear to many Slovaks. The Ludak problem of how to attack the state without being considered disloyal was solved by elevating the nation over the state. While describing the nation as sanctified,[51] and love of it prescribed by the fourth commandment (love of parents),[52] Tiso also rendered the state sacred. He explained that only by the Lord's order could the Slovaks gain a state. For a nation not to be independent meant death. Since the Lord wanted the Slovaks to live, he wanted them to be independent.[53]

Therefore, we Slovaks, Catholics, we have no reason to justify ourselves in the face of the world, that the Slovak nation, when the historical opportunity arrived, created its state. This was our obligation.[54]

In Tiso's mind the genuine Slovak nationalist was probably identified with Catholicism, and thus the state must be Catholic also. The essence of Slovak history demanded connections of nationalism with principles of the Catholic doctrine.[55] The Slovak state was not a result of the *right* of self-determination; the Slovaks took only a *gift* when the historical opportunity arrived. The independence was indeed a gift, not of a free will of the people, but as compensation for true believers. Therefore the state ought to base its foundation on Christian (i.e., Catholic) thought.[56]

IDEOLOGY OF THE PEOPLE'S SLOVAKIA

The Party also received a place in the semi-sacred area of the Ludak ideology. Tiso proclaimed, "It is a biological fact in the life of a nation; it is here, and as long as the nation exists, the Party will exist also."[57] Polakovič went a step further and elevated the state, the nation, and the Party into a trinity: "The Party, the state and the nation today are an entity. The Party and the state serve the nation. Whoever loves the nation, belongs to the Party and is delighted with the state."[58]

The local brand of totalitarianism arose from this very concept. Following Catholic tradition, the Ludaks denied the state the right to interfere in many fields of human activities. Nevertheless, the desire to keep public and private life under control was expressed in the proclamation of the "totality of the nation":

If one talks about totality, one talks only about the totality of the nation. . . . We have to create the unity of the people under the slogan "Everything for the nation," which means a disciplined organization of all parts of the nation working for its happiness.[59]

Consequently, the secretary-general of the Party, Dr. Gejza Medricky, was correct in his demands that, "Every Slovak must be placed under its [Party's] discipline in such a way that nothing should be done in the state without knowledge and approval of responsible Party representatives."[60]

The Party, as the representative of the totality, requested control of every segment of life. "The Party gives the framework," said another secretary-general, Dr. Aladár Kočiš; "it not only guides the external life of the nation, but the spiritual creativity also."[61]

The authoritarian Ludak doctrine was a combination of Catholic and temporal elements. Exploiting the similarity of various aspects of the Catholic state and social theory with national socialism, the Ludaks tried to combine both, accepting pure totalitarian principles. Consequently, the ideology of Ludak Slovakia was a mixture of traditional (both Catholic and secular) and modern (fascist) elements.

In his trial after the war, Tiso acknowledged his appreciation of Nazi principles, explaining that they fitted the teaching of encyclicals. He saw four points of similarity: (1) the ethnic principle *(voelkisch)*, (2) the common good before selfishness, (3) social standards for workers, and (4) family wages.[62]

Ludak ideology accepted racism and took an undeniably biological approach. Expressions such as "race," "ethnicism," and "biological source" were frequently used in essays of politicians and scholars. Psychology, sociology, anthropology, ethnology, ethnography, economics, and other sciences reflected biological and socio-biological theories. The character of the Slovak people was measured with biological yardsticks: for example, Polakovič wrote that "The Slovak nation developed originally from a single biological source and did not unite with the blood of other nations."[63]

President Tiso spoke of the "Slovak race"[64] which, according to him, was rooted in the psychology and biology of the nation.[65] In his analysis of the characteristics of the Slovak national psychology, the leading Ludak psychologist Anton Jurovský found that the Slovaks had "deep-rooted religiousness" and "a natural talent for the mythical world." The Slovak, he continued, had a heroic mentality, faith in justice, courage, and stubbornness.[66] In the Nazi psychological anthropology, these were the characteristics of the Nordic type (the I-type);[67] the opposite was the S-type, characterized by the Jews.[68] One would not be mistaken, then, to conclude that the Ludaks had a concept of the biological-spiritual substance of the Slovak nation.

The racial approach by the Slovaks toward the Jews was fully developed only after 1941. However, as early as November 1938, Tiso approved the preparation of anti-Jewish laws, based on Nuremberg legislation. The work was to be done by Dr. Jozef Falath, a fanatical Slovak anti-Semite, in cooperation with the SS *Hauptsturmfuehrer* Adolf Eichmann.[69] It is not clear why the plans were cancelled. For a long time the Church held the opinion that once a Jew was baptized, he should be considered a Christian, regardless of his origin.[70] However, on March 23, 1941, *Slovák* published an editorial saying:

It is only natural that the Church will never make any disturbing influence on the solution of the racial Jewish problem. On the contrary, it will appreciate the opinion of objective science, which had to be recognized by our, as well as any, national legislature. In the definition of the racial question, one must not raise religious motives where there is no room for them, and which the Church rejects also.[71]

After the "Jewish Codex" was proclaimed in the fall of 1941, a racial approach toward the Jews became the official policy of the Slovak state.

While accepting biological standards toward Slovakism and Jewry, the Ludaks were forced to reject a similar racial approach toward Slavism. This rejection reflected the German hostility for such a concept, as well as their own disgust with what was called Czech and Polish treachery. Party officials tried at various times and in different ways to sever Slovak from Slavs or at least from Pan-Slavism.[72] Yet, when Slovakia began closing ranks with Croatia and Bulgaria (as well as with Rumania) against Hungary, and when the popular sympathy for Russia could not be repressed, the Party adopted a new theme: that the Slavs were good, Bolshevism was evil, and the Jew infected this pest. They interpreted the participation of Slovakia in the war against the Soviet Union as the liberation of a sister nation, Russia, from the Jewish enemy of Christianity and Europe.[73]

Geopolitics and the *Lebensraum* problem were closely tied to the ethnic *(voelkisch)* principle. Following their Nazi teachers, the Ludaks began to talk about living space. These writers not only claimed for Slovakia all territories settled by Slovaks, but also demanded recognition of the Slovak state as "the coordinating factor" in the Danube basin. Such a recognition would be a continuation of the "historical cooperation" between the Germans and the Slovaks.[74] (Magyars, who were not Aryans, should be denied the task of "coordination.")

The Slovak leaders did not neglect other parts of the fascist outlook. The Ludaks made efforts to boost the martial spirit of their people. On March 14, 1941, Tiso declared that "the characteristics of our times, the spirit and command of these days strengthen our consciousness that our Slovak reality demands military qualities. . . ."[75] Education and propagandistic campaigns were expected to fulfill this aim. The war, despite being an evil, was the natural condition of contemporary international relations.[76] It was an apocalyptical show which purified mankind. From the ashes a new Europe would be born.[77] In their attitude toward the army and war, the Ludaks followed the standard fascist stereotype.

Peasants stood very near to the Ludak heart. The Party drew significant support from villages and paid much attention to them. Tiso described the peasant as the source of Slovak nationalism and faithfulness to the fatherland, the rural society as the source of rejuvenation of the country's life.[78] In order to give the peasants a share of the fruits of the regime, land reform was introduced,[79] actually but another type of aryanization. The law made some of the distributed land hereditary; the plots could not be divided or sold.[80] This provision was another imitation of the Nazi methods (of the "hereditary estates"). The reforms aimed at treating an independent farmer "who is the best supporter of nationalism, the state and the genuine holder of the fatherland tradition."[81]

The Ludaks felt uneasy because of some of the contradictions between Catholicism and Nazism. To smooth the passage between these doctrines, the Ludaks made significant efforts to demonstrate similarities. They compared national socialism with "natural law."[82] The achievements of Hitler, according to Tiso, were due to this law.[83] Saints were honored as forerunners of Nazism. A poet, who belonged to the Franciscan Order, Rudolf Dilong, called St. Francis of Assisi the first Nazi and drew a protest from the Germans.[84] Other contradictory elements between Christianity and Nazism were obscured.

Ludak ideology showed strong influence of Catholicism. This was demonstrated not only in the values themselves, but also in the manner of their presentation. The Ludaks manifested appreciation for the unreal, spiritual world, the world of sacrifices and ideas. Speeches and writings were interspersed with expressions from the theological vocabulary and the spiritual realm.[85] The religious conviction was very clear in every part of the Ludak catechism.

The ideology of Ludak Slovakia was basically a mixture of four different elements. Yet each one of the four elements—religion, nationalism, socioeconomic elements, and authoritarianism—consisted of a traditional layer and a modern one. The tradition drew from the years before the creation of Czechoslovakia, and from experiences gained during the existence of the fallen Republic, as well as from the strong influence of the Catholic conservative tradition. Such a moderating impact should be attributed to the conservative outlook of veteran Party members. They influenced both ideology and actions.

The unmistakable influence of Nazi ideology may be partially explained in the character of life in the Reich orbit. The clerical Ludaks had no intention of blindly accepting national socialism; it would mean betrayal of their own beliefs. The differences were obscure and deemphasized, not surrendered. Yet Ludaks learned from the Reich as much as they could, from genuine interest and it was only natural for the Slovaks to look with veneration on their great patron.

The needs and feelings of the contemporary era, and the impression which Italian and German fascism made on the local people, created the modern layer of the ideology. In the last analysis, clerical fascism was a combination of Catholic, national, social, and authoritarian elements. In other words, local, genuine Slovak parts combined with a rather cosmopolitan teaching and gave birth to a new quality. The ideology of the "People's Slovakia" was a theory in flux. In its elaborated form the ideology of the "People's Slovakia" resembled a mosaic whose cementing factors were very flimsy.

Thus the sociologist Štefánek described the scientific activity of the Slovak state:

Many scholars, writers, and politicians approach falsely the principle of positive science. They do not admire reality. They prefer the addition of colors, tendentiously covering the reality by strong words, and not refraining from fabrications either. They regard this practice as a service to the State and to the Nation. Examples may be found in geopolitics, patriotic historiography, tendentious philology, and ethnography. No doubt pseudo-science and propagandistic scholarship can be of great assistance in political battles; its value, however, is slight and it compromises the young Slovak science at home and abroad.[86]

Štefánek's caustic remarks serve to characterize a large part of the Ludak ideological endeavors.

After the crisis of the spring of 1942, Tiso never again had to wage a major battle with Tuka and the Hlinka Guard. There were more clashes, but they are best described as unsuccessful attempts by Tuka and Mach to prevent a further loss of ground.

The period between April 1942 and August 1944 can be divided into three parts. The first terminated with the German defeat at Stalingrad and should be called the major period of Slovakia's clerical fascism; the second extended from the battle of Stalingrad to the surrender of Italy, when the ruling caucus worked hard to prevent the deterioration of the country; and the third was marked by a gradual, continuous loss of power by the leadership and the disruption of order in the country over a nine-month period, culminating in the National Uprising on August 29, 1944.

Tiso's regime was strong in 1942 for several reasons. That year witnessed Hitler's greatest expansion: from the Volga to Egypt, German soldiers were on their victorious march. While the mood of the anti-fascists was at its lowest ebb, supporters of the Reich felt triumphant, and Slovakia reflected this situation. The years 1941 and 1942 were the period of heaviest persecution of the regime's opposition. The Communist Party was beaten and shattered. Democratic elements either kept quiet or through their economic activity indirectly supported the system.[1]

The "Final Solution"

Another reason for the regime's strength was bribery of the population —predominantly Slovak, with Jewish possessions—on a scale never before seen. In 1942 all debts to Jews were wiped out. Their real estate was transferred to "Aryan" ownership. Much space in *Organizačné Zvesti* in 1942 was filled with articles, instructions, and advice on how to acquire houses and other valuables, and it urged the government to speed up and make more efficient the process of distribution. Although the government did not succeed in efficiently processing appropriated property—a failure due to nepotism, bribery, and corruption—the regime nevertheless gained many thousands of new supporters and satisfied the old ones.

The Jews, rich and poor, were deported to the east with barely seventy-five pounds of baggage per person, leaving behind their homes which were important assets in this spoil system. Guardists and ethnic German storm troopers (FS, *Freiwillige Schutzstaffeln*), who were instrumental in the deportations, looted the homes immediately after they were vacated. Part of the portable goods were transferred to government warehouses, where high-ranking officials helped themselves, and the rest was sold at auction, on behalf of the government Treasury.

A wave of bribery flooded the country. A "phonogram" (the phoned order releasing one from deportation) meant liberty, and everyone connected with its dispatch had to be heavily paid. The conscious leveling of human and moral standards of the Slovak people added strength to the clerical fascist government, and it bears the chief responsibility for debauching the nation.[2]

However, not everything on the domestic front worked as smoothly or received such popular support as did the anti-Jewish activity. There were heavy losses in the fighting in the east; moreover, the great number of Slovak soldiers defecting to the Soviets caused numerous headaches at home.[3] The war, domestic troubles, and the influence of the broadcasted propaganda of the Allies strongly boosted animosity toward Germany (rather than against the local government), as reflected in SD reports.[4] The discomfort reached its peak when the fortunes of war turned against Germany. Axis defeats in Africa had already disquieted the public so much that the president was forced to admit in his speech in the city of Trenčin on November 16, 1942, that "Anyone who follows our life closely feels a certain ferment *(rozkvasenie)*."[5] The apogee of spiritual breakdown occurred only eight weeks later. Still, this year remains as the most successful in the annals of fascist Slovakia.

While Tiso failed to oust Tuka with one blow, he overpowered the HG camp through continuous action on a smaller scale. The operation against the Guardists took two directions. On the one hand, the president reinforced institutions faithful to him by adding his men and ousting adversaries; on the other hand, he planted friends in Guard offices while cutting the Guard's prerogatives.

In order to further tighten his grip over the Hlinka Guard, Tiso nominated a liaison officer to the body. Then the Party weakened the position of HG Chief of Staff Kubala by dismissing some of his ranking officers.[6] Eventually a "moderate Radical," Dr. Karol Danihel, replaced Kubala.[7] Milo Urban and other members of *Gardista*'s board of editors barely escaped the same fate.[8]

In 1942 Tiso reorganized the Party's presidium. The head of the Ministry of National Economy, who served simultaneously as the Party's secretary-general, was released from this post. His replacement was Dr. Aladar Kočiš, previously editor-in-chief of *Slovák*, who took over this office, on April 1, 1942, as a full-time job. Among the other changes was the ex-officio status of the prime minister's place in the presidium, thus taking away Tuka's elected status which he had held since 1939.[9] Tiso's influence prevailed even in Tuka's own offices, where undesirable elements were released at the president's request. Only the direct intervention of the German Foreign Office, through von Ribbentrop, saved the Radical Matúš Černák who served in the Slovak Legation to Berlin, as well as some other officials of the Slovak Ministry for Foreign Affairs.[10]

At the Pinnacle of Power

The progress of the clerical camp alarmed the HG Radicals and their SS benefactors, yet they could not do anything because the Reich's official policy was to support the status quo. The German Foreign Office understood only too well that the so-called status quo meant, in fact, complete loss of ground for the Slovak allies of the Nazis. Despite this, German policy remained the same: no staff changes in the Slovak government, a close watch over the country, and faith in Tiso's "realistic" pro-German approach.[11]

Apparently, Minister of the Interior Mach did not realize this, or else still hoped for German support to improve his fortunes, and tried in vain to enlist Nazi aid. When the Party received a new constitution,[12] Tiso's newly appointed presidium omitted Mach. Mach had hoped to occupy the presidium post rejected by Tuka, and was insulted when it was not offered to him. He went to Tiso and resigned from his post in protest. But the resignation was not accepted; Tiso told Mach he had been installed by the Germans and if he wanted to resign, he would have to submit his resignation to them.[13] The chief of the RSHA, SS *Gruppenfuehrer* Gottlob Berger, sent Mach a message saying that it was not difficult to resign, but resignation was not the way to victory.[14] So Mach rescinded his resignation, and admitted publicly the hopeless stand of his circle.

During the year 1942, other significant developments took place in the Party's organization and life. The leadership felt strong; therefore it had no further interest in increasing membership. Its aim now was to accumulate faithful adherents and reject the others. The presidium ordered a membership census accompanied by a collection of secret data about the value and loyalty of its supporters.[15] Reversing the previous policy which made joining easy and resigning difficult, the Party now adopted a new policy which restricted admission and facilitated withdrawal.[16] The doors remained open for only two kinds of people: (1) young men approaching their eighteenth year if their parents had demonstrated loyalty to the regime and if the young men were members of the Hlinka Youth (*Hlinkova Mladež*,HM); and (2) the district leaders could make exceptions to this rule if the person in question were recommended by the local branch.[17] In September the secretariat ordered a purge of the membership aimed at purification of the Party from "revenue seekers hungry for glory." The purge would strengthen Party discipline, the order explained, according to the policy of the modern leadership principle, which held that (1) the will of the leader (Vodca) is an order, and (2) the leader is always right. Every member of the Party had to realize that all orders given, or prohibitions made, had their origin in the leader's will.[18]

These actions were connected with the legalization of Tiso's leadership in the Party and the state. During 1942, the parliament approved a group of laws concentrating the reins of power in the hands of the Vodca. The first among the items of legislation was the "Law on the Slovak Working Community" of May 6, 1942,[19] whose purpose was to create a general framework for the corporate bodies established earlier. The so-called community was a kind of blend of the Nazi German Workers Front and the corporate system. It acted as a front organization for the Party, having a "leadership" structure with the Vodca at the top. Membership in its four branches was obligatory for everyone who met the requirements; therefore it was supposed to put under its supervision the overwhelming majority of Slovaks. The "Law on the Student Association," also accepted by the parliament on May 6, 1942,[20] was also tied to the Party. With the creation of this body, all student clubs, with the exception of religious ones, were obliged to disperse and their students to enter the new organization.

Two additional laws were intended to help to impose Party control on the country. The "Law on Social Institute" was to manage and guide all social and charitable activity in the state.[21] In practice, however, it imposed a strait-jacket on voluntary organizations and dictated in the social field.

More important was the "Law on Hlinka's Slovak People's Party" affirmed on October 22, 1942,[22] which marked the high point of Tiso's power and that of the Party's leading faction. This legislation established the Vodca as the Party's supreme institution, representative, and guide. He was to appoint almost every high-ranking officer of the Party and its organizations, and would himself be elected once for a five-year term by a convention. All other Party officers, except for the five elected members of the presidium, were to be appointed on the basis of the leadership system. The law also stated that citizens of Slovak nationality were to participate in the government through the Party, which was obliged to lead and to manage the state. The state, in turn, was pledged to perform services on behalf of the political movement. The Party's insignia was protected, membership dues could be collected by the arms of the administration, and the correspondence of its bureaus had official status. The Party's secretariat had the power of censorship of the press, broadcast media, and movies, and a monopoly in publication of political treatises. Transgression of the law was punishable. Various paragraphs hint that no firm boundary was set between the state and the Party. The latter was to dictate, the former to submit.

Thus, the president held in his hands all reins of influence as head of a "fuehrer-type" state.[22a] Indeed, Father Tiso could view the scene with a great deal of personal satisfaction: the international situation was bright, and he ranked with Hitler, Mussolini, Antonescu, and other chieftains of a new Europe.

The Decline

As in a classic tragedy, the *Wehrmacht*'s defeat at Stalingrad shook the self-confidence of the Slovak leaders just when they dreamed of reaching the pinnacle of power. A shaken General Čatloš addressed the state council on March 5, 1943, after the German retreat from the Caucasus, in which a Slovak Army division participated, barely escaping complete destruction:

Nobody should get out of balance because of the changes of the fortunes of war; nobody should make pessimistic speculations nor listen to the faint-hearted, the defeatists, or the malicious. Nobody should draw any negative conclusions about our rescuers and allies because friendship and devotion are best recognized when the situaton is at its worst. . . . The nation should not under any circumstances lose confidence in politics and in its representatives, and along with them it must rally around the Fuehrer and keep faith with him.[23]

An unidentified but keen observer of Slovakian affairs evaluated the situation from Prague at the end of 1943, on the basis of frequent visits to Bratislava, and warned that the country was facing a crisis, and singled out Stalingrad as the most serious shock for Slovakia's domestic life. Italy's surrender strengthened the effect.[24]

After the battle on the Volga, anti-Soviet propaganda about the Bolshevik threat was intensified. How much Tiso could count on fear of the Bolsheviks in rallying his allies can be learned from a discussion by an unidentified Slovak official which was reported by the SD. This man described the fears "of groups which can be regarded as rightist" about the internal situation in the country if Russia were not defeated. The threat of "a repetition of the year 1918" (when a social upheaval upset Slovakia) was acute. Only the strong authoritarian regime of the "highly regarded and beloved President," with the help of all responsible elements, could save the country. These words were pronounced as early as the end of May

1942.[25] They were repeated in essence a year and a half later in a lecture in Vienna by the second in command of the German Embassy in Bratislava. Dr. Hans Gmelin. He, too, emphasized that the acute danger of communism could serve to strengthen the pro-German camp in Slovakia. On the other hand, Gmelin virtually supported the elimination of the HG from any public influence.[26]

Indeed, after 1942 the Hlinka Guard ceased to have any influence on the public. Its last massive appearance was during the deportation of Jews. Later its members grew softer and lost interest in politics. On September 21, 1943, following the decision of the Party's presidium, the headquarters of the Guard were transferred into the house of the Party. The Party press syndicate took over the *Gardista*, and the editor-in-chief, Milo Urban, was forced to resign.[27] "The last bastion of National Socialism had fallen, and nothing more stood in the way of Slovak unity," wrote the SD reporter.[28]

Curiously, the victory of the clerical camp resulted not only from its own determination and toughness, but also from the competition between the SA and SS, which had much to do with the Guard's misfortune. (While instruction and supervision of the Guard was in SS hands, the majority of the German Embassy's staff, from the Minister Ludin down, belonged to the SA.) The animosity between these two camps not only caused a lack of interest in the fate of the extremists by the legation, but also led to the direct undermining of SS activity in Slovak affairs.[29] In the light of that animosity, it is not surprising that the dreams of the HG Radicals, echoed in Mach's words about a "new Salzburg which will again elevate the Guard," were compelled to doom.[30] Ludin's stand was that the HSĽS was the single spokesman of the Slovak nation, and he would not interfere in the internal questions of the state as long as the interest of the Reich was not endangered.[31] Consequently, the avenue left for the SS was to support and groom the *Náš Boj* circle, which it did intensively.

The nation was never particularly enthusiastic about the war and its participation in it. As early as January 15, 1942, the German military attaché reported to OKW, "It is impossible to speak about a general fighting mood of the Slovak nation."[32] The objections to fighting, the desertions to the Soviet Army and partisans, and the fraternization of Slovak soldiers with the local population made the position of the government extremely painful. Thus it was decided to ask Germany to transfer the Slovak troops to the west. Bratislava tried to explain that the soldiers had to be located in places where they would find no common language with the population. When the request was presented to Hitler, he refused to send the Slovaks to the west or to the Balkans.[33] An explanation for his refusal can be probably found in the exchange between two ranking SS officers, which said: "As a Slavonic State, Slovakia's first and main task is to shatter the united Slavonic front."[34]

The government's troubles continued to increase and almost led to a showdown with Germany. On September 4, 1943, General Čatloš demanded that all Slovak soldiers return home; Germany would have to be content with a symbolic participation. The troops' situation provided too much material for the enemy's propaganda, the minister said, and the people at home would not understand why the sole military power of the state had to perish. The German general who transmitted the demand to the Germans advised a refusal, saying that since the Slovaks no longer believed in the possibility of a victory, they did not want to make any more sacrifices. Other likely reasons included fear of internal-political results, which could shatter the regime, and the desire of the state's leaders to loosen their ties with the Reich in its difficult hour.[35] But Germany was not ready to free the satellite. She continued to hold the troops and asked for additional reinforcements.

The stand of the Party fathers was significant. While originally they were happy to join the fight against communism, and to repay the Nazis in cannon fodder for helping to bring them to power, they now made great efforts to dilute their role. The gradual weakening of their grip at home, however, forced the regime's retreat in diverse fields, for the Ludak leadership felt that restricting their commitments in the war would improve their position at home.

The decision of the episcopate to reduce the number of priests in state and Party jobs also reflected the changing times. Although Archbishop Kmetko explained the act in terms of the overly large number of priests in secular offices [36] (a very significant explanation in itself), SD documents show clearly that this was not the case. The documents speak of the request of the clergy for retreat from "political life."[37] Obviously, when church leaders felt the state wavering, they preferred to diminish the clergy's official role in it.

In this atmosphere of poorly concealed nervousness behind a facade of "business as usual," a bombshell exploded—the deposing of Mussolini, *Nestor* and good father of dictators. Discrete remarks about false ideologies and governments not backed by the people appeared in the press.[38] The real shock came when Italy unconditionally surrendered. The reaction was both an outburst of mass joy and orgies of drinking, and panic running wild.[39]

When the atmosphere cooled down, the results became clearer. The basic result was a decline in the animosities between the various pro-German groups. Tiso and the HG Radicals started to cooperate more sincerely. The status of Mach rose, and he eventually became the number two leader of the state.

Another result was increased tension with Hungary. Since Italy, as a close ally of Budapest, was instrumental in the Magyar success in the Vienna arbitration of 1938, the Slovaks now dared consider the possibility of regaining lands they had lost to the Magyars. Although some of the regime's supporters also thought in terms of military action against Hungary, others, including Tiso, understood that such a step against the will of Germany was impossible. They regarded a show of loyalty toward the Reich, in competition with that of the Danubian kingdom, as more useful.

The policy of demonstrated hostility toward Hungary had an additional advantage. The leaders hoped to divert public attention from the blind alley toward which the state was heading with irredenta and anti-Magyar instigations that almost never failed to arouse the public—until now. The public instead continued to be concerned with the fighting and international situation. A telegram from Ludin, of March 30, 1944 mentioned his observation of the wane of Slovakia's lust for war in the fall of 1943.[40]

When German troops invaded Hungary in March 1944, the question of Slovak territories reappeared. Berlin was quick to warn Bratislava against any hasty actions. Ludin told Tiso and Tuka their reward would be given after the war. The warning was clear and they understood. "I got the impression," said Ludin in the telegram, "that what occurred in Hungary was a useful lesson which would have effective influence here. It forced the local alibiers to think it over."[41]

At the same time, qualitative changes took place in the state council and parliament. At midyear, 1943, the leaders felt that the time for reorganization had arrived. An internal committee, headed by the chairman of the council, Dr. Viktor Ravasz, was set up to prepare a new constitution. Although original plans were concerned with enlarging the council's prerogatives and giving it executive power, and granting parliament power to deal only in legislative matters,[42] the outcome was different. Not only did the council not obtain additional rights, it lost some of its previous ones and its membership was reduced in number. Documents do not reveal the reason for this change, but we know the chairman argued with Tiso and resigned.[43] It would seem that the president did not want to lose part of his power by creating a strong collective which could eventually oppose him.

Cancellation of the election of a new legislature was another move related to the parliament. According to the constitution, the present parliament had to be dissolved on December 31, 1943. An amendment to the constitution of October 27, 1941,[44] authorized the president to appoint new deputies to the house whenever such need occurred, an authorization Tiso used several times to pack the parliament with loyalists. Thus, no need for new election existed. Explained Mach: "Everything is in order. We have no reason to be afraid of elections. But now is a time of War; therefore, not a proper occasion. Besides, elections are only a waste of money, and they would direct the mind of the nation to superficial things."[45] At Tiso's request, the parliament's presidium was forced to expel some of its most honored members for their lack of discipline.[46]

At this point, the Party no longer possessed any effective power. Despite the routine life and work, an uneasiness existed. Great fluctuation among the numbers of appointees on the local level testified to the lack of interest in Party functions. In the spring of 1944 the Ludaks for the first time attempted to recruit some public support for the municipal administration. An article by Tiso in *Organizačné Zvesti*[47] revealed that the results of the experiment fell short of the expectations. Tiso's words also exposed the anger among citizens outside the Party about this additional attempt to monopolize public functions. The Vodca's hypocritical, nevertheless significant, reply was that hopefully, as a result of the municipal "elections," a greater interest in the Party would be aroused because it was the natural instrument of the nation's political will.[48] The Party was in grave trouble. The enemy was too close and everything the Party could give out had already been distributed. Furthermore, the Soviet Army was dangerously near: it was not worthwhile for the Party to become involved in political matters. A Hlinka Guardist described the HSĽS to Tiso in these words: "The Party is no longer able to lead the nation. One can compare it to an insurance company which once a year collects the premiums and otherwise does not bother its members."[49] This statement is clear enough: the Slovak National Uprising did not kill the Party, it only revealed it in its agony.

While in the first half of 1943, signs of the regime's disintegration were visible only to keen observers, later they affected everyone. Germans, both ethnic and citizens of the Reich, were insulted and beaten. Propaganda conducted by German and Slovak agencies fell on deaf ears. It was at this time that broadcasts of the Allies had their widest audience. Rumors, or the "whispered propaganda" used in those days, were rampant, creating much discomfort for the regime.

Significantly, as was the case with other dictatorial regimes, the churches served as a focus for the opposition. The Slovak Protestant Church took the lead in attacking the continuation of slaughter on the fronts, anti-Jewish measures, and other misdeeds. The pious elements in the Catholic Church also made themselves felt, particularly after the Vatican opened a peace campaign in 1943.

As never before, the officer corps, having indirect support from Čatloš, resisted the fascization of the troops. The troops were influenced by their commanders, and probably even more so by soldiers returning from the front. The veterans turned the army camps into spots of unrest, frequently conducting demonstrations and breaking discipline.

Anti-German demonstrations took place in Bratislava in the summer of 1943, during youth conventions held there. Efforts of officials and the press to calm the public were in vain; eventually, Tiso, Mach and others tried to follow the mood of the people. The president proclaimed that the state would gladly join whoever would promise and do more for Slovakia than Germany.(50) Still the Party continued to lose ground. Members quit; citizens, tired of war, became apathetic. Later, alibism spread to such a degree that an SD agent wrote to his superiors: "today in the country practically everybody has prepared a black list."(51)

The food supply improved in 1943 and 1944, yet the black market remained very strong. A Swiss journalist visiting the country described Slovakia as an "isle of plenty in the hungry Europe."(52) The economic situation later deteriorated as a natural result of war, but also because of intensive exploitation by the German war machine. Salaries did not match the inflation, and social unrest led to strikes and demonstrations. Finally, the only genuine friends the Hlinka Party had were the Aryanizers and others who had enriched themselves during these years. Other groups of the population were ready for withdrawal and for cutting off their ties from it. On the eve of the National Uprising, the internal disintegration was almost complete.

CHAPTER VIII

CLERICAL FASCISM AT WORK

For more than five years the Hlinka Party held supremacy in Slovakia. As Tiso put it: "For the first time we Slovaks have the possibility to execute our Christian-Social Program, because for the first time we hold in our hand the power."[1] The Party program was broadly designed. It had to create a new Slovak man, spur a new spirit in the economy and social life, and build a modern state of a new type; in short, the aim was a new Slovakia in a new Europe. Therefore, an analysis of the regime of the Slovak state ought to deal with many aspects. The government was not satisfied with power alone. It strove to influence the whole society in the spirit of Catholicism and authoritarian theories. Though the execution often fell short of its plans, the government's arms were still far reaching. Occasionally, the time was too short to realize the blueprint; in other cases there were too many obstacles to a successful fulfillment. Despite the shortcomings, numerous accomplished projects require evaluation, as do the failures. Four elements will be analysed in some detail: nationalism, the impact of religion, the government, and the socioeconomic structure.

Nationalism

Not as a mere collective self-consciousness, nationalism was a vital part of Ludak ideology. The education to aggressive and boasting nationalism began in the schools. Five years of education in an independent state was described proudly in this way: "The Slovak pupilhood was never as conscious, flaming with a sincere love for the nation, as today. This is desirable and necessary. Healthy nationalism, one should say even fanatical nationalism, cannot cause any damage."[2]

All levels of education revealed the emphasis on nationalistic indoctrination.[3] The new state began its publishing activity with history textbooks. Raised on these books, the high school student was compelled to participate in an annual competition of "patriotic consciousness."[4] This patriotism can perhaps be best illustrated by a credo taught to Slovak primary school students:

The solemn and sacred truth of the Slovak nation, in which I do believe, is . . . that the Slovaks are an individual nation, different from all others in their blood, language, spirit, culture, and peculiarity of country. The Slovak national roots remained undamaged from alien elements in their blood, spirit, and creation. All Slovaks in the whole world create a spiritual community of brothers in blood. . . . No other nation in the world resembles the Slovaks in honesty of heart, delicacy for understanding of beauty, and in creativity of mind. Throughout the whole world, a Slovak child has to be educated in the Slovak language. Whoever educates differently is a traitor to the Slovak spirit. Whoever takes the Slovak language from a Slovak child is a murderer of his nation.[5]

Classes of history, geography, language, and even music served as ground for indoctrination. Only religious instruction could compete in intensity with the education for nationalism.

In the years 1939 and 1940 the activities of the Ministry of Education and National Enlightenment included a nationwide course in Slovak history and a campaign of Slovakization of the annexed Polish territories. Next to the ministry was the propaganda apparatus of the Party, which controlled public meetings and national celebrations, and organized mass festivities on various anniversaries. The Party's Department of Culture selected the days, the ways of celebration, and gave ideological guidance. The Department of Culture of the HG high command had a similar task among Guardists. Many other organizations such as the Office for Propaganda, the radio, semiprivate institutions, and publishing houses, were involved in spreading nationalistic propaganda.

The emphasis on the Slovak language represented another sign of heated nationalistic fervor. All posters displayed in public were checked by chauvinistic linguists, so-called "purists," who tried to dominate and supervise all cultural life and artistic creativity. They wanted to "purge" the Slovak language of alien elements, particularly anything of Bohemian origin, and even expressions common to the Czech language.

The regime encouraged Slovakization of family names, and ordered government employes to use Slovak both in public and private life.[6] The great emphasis on the national language in a poly-linguistic country, as Slovakia was, is understandable; however, the chauvinism which accompanied the Slovakization drive resulted in discrimination toward the minorities. This campaign took place in the years 1940 to 1942, accompanied by intensive propaganda. Pressure was exerted on stubborn individuals to force them to Slovakize their names.[7] Special legislation was enacted to smooth the action.[8] The campaign drew a favorable response from patriots, careerists, and opportunists. Although aimed at Magyarized persons, Slovakization also hurt the ethnic Germans, and aroused anger from their leaders.

CLERICAL FASCISM AT WORK

In the summer of 1939, the parliament passed a new law regarding citizenship.[9] This "Law for Citizenship" divided the population into four groups, inequal in right to demand citizenship of the Slovak state: (1) The first group were the autochthones, whose ancestors had lived in the country at least between 1850 and 1871. If their origin was "obvious," citizenship was granted without documentation—as was the case with the great majority of the population: Slovaks, ethnic Germans, ethnic Magyars, and Ukrainians. (2) Those whose ancestors arrived in Slovakia after 1870, and had lived in the country at least three successive generations, composed the second group. The Ministry of Interior requested documentary evidence before granting citizenship to anyone belonging to this group. All Jews and Czechs were requested to submit documents. (3) The third group, employes of the government, whether Slovaks or not, received automatic citizenship. State legislation barred Jews from civil service; relatively few Czechs remained state employes after the wave of expulsions in 1938 and 1939. (4) All other inhabitants of the country formed the last group, which had to formally apply for citizenship.[10]

The Law for Citizenship was to be supplemented with another, the "Law of Defense for Nationality."[11] This act banned denationalization, and protected the property of individual nationalities. The law was not presented to the parliament, however, and some of its ideas were found in the "Law on the Political Parties of the National Groups" (i.e., minorities) and in the constitution.[12]

The political parties of each nationality were given broad rights, in order to be able to intervene and safeguard the interest of their co-nationals, whether or not the co-national was a member of the Party. The Party could likewise intervene in cases of a change of nationality; it could defend citizens against the administration, and it controlled the so-called "national cadaster," in which the population was listed according to its ethnic origins. The need for such a legislation testified to an internationality tension caused both by the aggressiveness of Slovak nationalism, and the arrogance of the ethnic Germans. Magyars and Ukrainians also added to the problems.

The census of 1940 provided an outstanding opportunity for national competition, accompanied by hatred and even the danger of riots. The Slovaks were particularly anxious to secure a clear majority in Bratislava to dominate the ethnic Germans there. In the eastern regions, the Slovaks aimed at decreasing the number of Ukrainians. On the other hand, the ethnic Germans were boosting their numbers in the population, anyone of Teutonic origin was required to declare himself German. In the county of Spiš (Zips), Magyars did their best to persuade Magyarized Germans to remain Hungarians.

This census supplied details of the national and ethnic composition of the Slovak state. The population included 2,998,244 Slovaks and Czechs, 128,347 Germans, 54,897 Magyars, 69,116 Russians and Ukrainians, and 3,849 Poles. While only 29,002 people described themselves Jews by nationality, there were 85,045 persons of Jewish religion.[13]

In the national question no difference existed between the clericals and the Hlinka Guard. Furthermore, neither Mach nor Murgaš was less ready to compromise in his attitude toward the ethnic Germans than were Tiso and his followers. The president's camp was trying to preserve a *modus vivendi* and not antagonize the local Nazis. The Guardists demonstrated rather ambivalent behavior in their aggressiveness toward Karmasin and his people; while flaunting close friendship with the Nazis, the Radicals were harming their allies. Accepted and groomed by the Reich, the Guardists enjoyed feelings of security, which may explain the ambivalence. The clericals, unlike the HG, lacked their sense of security, and therefore were more careful not to antagonize Berlin.

Pavol Čarnogurský, one of the leaders of the Hlinka Party, and for a long time the head of the Slovak League, outlined the national policy of the new state in an article published shortly after the proclamation of independence.[14] He told the ethnic Germans that the Slovaks would do their best to preserve a good relationship, warning that misunderstanding of the Slovak mentality might lead to friction. The ethnic Magyars could keep as many rights as they had had, but any extension would be a blow to the Slovak national honor. As for the Ukrainians, ("Russins"), Čarnogurský wanted to make clear that such a nationality would not be permitted to exist in Slovakia. "We have to prevent and destroy at the very beginning any idea, and even the smallest action, which could lead in Eastern Slovakia to any national symbol different from the Slovak double cross on Slovak hills."[15]

The line drawn here was broadly enforced through the whole period. The ethnic Germans were widely privileged, yet involved in continuous friction with the dominant nation. The ethnic Magyars were underprivileged, but actively supported by Hungary. In spite of an official recognition as a national group, the Ukrainians were oppressed and sometimes denied constitutional rights. The Gypsies fared somewhat better than the Jews; nevertheless, they were persecuted and victimized. The need for Czech skill made it possible for thousands of them to stay in the country, though they were constantly harassed. The government regarded the tiny Polish minority, created after the Polish-German War, as Polonized Slovaks with no particular privileges.

CLERICAL FASCISM AT WORK

Of all national groups, the Germans were in the best position. They had firm support from Berlin, and could parade their own sacrifices on behalf of Slovakia's independence. For a certain period after March 1939, these people demanded *Heim ins Reich* ("Home, to the Reich"). But Berlin turned a deaf ear to this slogan and to the modest request at least for the annexation of the district of Bratislava.[16] Until the end of the war, many among the ethnic Germans, not to speak of their leadership, regarded themselves as the forerunners of Nazism in Slovakia.[17]

The German minority enjoyed a number of privileges, unusual even for a democratic and liberal country. It had its own state secretary, army units, para-military troops, political organizations (on the same footing with those of the Hlinka Party), economic and health institutions; and a great number of voluntary or semi-voluntary groups and associations. Special legislation secured a broad range of privileges. Still, this group did not feel itself compelled to obey the country's laws if they clashed or appeared to clash with its own needs or prerogatives.[18]

The Slovaks and the ethnic Germans fought over three major issues (Slovakization versus Germanization, territorial expansion, and economic expansion) and numerous minor issues. The ethnic Germans intended to inflate their number, and do so quickly. The Slovaks worked hard not only to paralyze these efforts, but also to regain compatriots on the brink of losing their national identity. Schools and churches were the battlefield, with occasional interference or blackmail from the administration. The Ministry of Education opened Slovak minority schools in German villages; the Germans responded by luring Slovak pupils to their schools in the cities. For the first time German parishes witnessed Slovak chaplains celebrating Mass in their mother tongue. The government intervened against ethnic German agents, who sought to persuade individuals of Teutonic descent to join them.

However, the ethnic Germans were not to be pushed into a corner so easily, and tried to increase the number of the German minority by persuading Slovaks of German ancestry to emphasize their Teutonic kinship. The so-called "Chabans," the offspring of Anabaptist refugees from Germany, can serve as an example: during past centuries, the Chabans had been almost entirely assimilated and were regarded as Slovaks. The dispute over their national identity reached the highest levels of the government, where the Germans eventually lost. Nevertheless, this confrontation demonstrated the gravity of the problem.

The fight over territory was connected with the battle for national affiliation. The government and the Party encouraged the appearance and settlement of Slovaks in places known to have a German majority or a substantial minority. The administration made efforts to draw up borders for the administrative counties in such a way that the ethnic Germans would remain an insignificant minority. The Hlinka Party and the Slovak cultural organization opened branches in predominantly German localities. The planned Law for Defense of Nationality included also a provision banning legal or illegal transfer of land from one nationality to another.[19]

Ethnic Magyars could also rely on a friendly foreign government, in case of need. Hungary's relations with Slovakia were strained, however, and the Danubian Kingdom could not support its compatriots as effectively as did the Reich. The Slovak minority in Hungary also suffered under national oppression. Therefore, both sides had seen in the minority of the other side hostages for its brothers. Occasionally, Budapest and Bratislava sent complaints to Berlin, which exploited the issues skillfully, without satisfying either side.

The organization of the Magyar minority resembled that of the German, only on a much narrower basis. The ethnic Magyars had cultural, educational, and social institutions, even some economic undertakings.[20] Opportunities to acquire education in the mother tongue were relatively small. Red tape delayed the required registration of a Magyar Party and its front organizations. Ethnic Magyars were given only a minor part of Jewish property, if any. Conservatives of an aristocratic-traditional shade led this group. The Magyar leaders were in many political questions much more liberal than the Slovaks.[21] They were, however, hostile to Slovak independence, since they dreamed of the renewal of the kingdom of St. Stephen.

The Magyar Party enjoyed a monopolistic position among the ethnic Magyars. Besides safeguarding the rights of its people, the Party was active among the remnants of the Magyarones. Irredentist activity never did cease, and provided the Slovak government with excuses for various persecutions. Steps taken against the Magyar irredenta strongly hit the Ukrainians, since the government claimed that the "Russin nationality" was a trick of the Magyarones, directed against the state's unity.[22] In spite of the peculiarity of the Magyar case, there was enough in it to indicate the nationalistic patterns of the Ludaks.

Of all accepted and recognized autochtohone minorities, the Ukrainians fared the worst.[23] No sovereign state existed to safeguard and care for them, though the Reich made occasional attempts to secure their friendship. The local government did not allow the Ukrainians to create a separate party. The single Ukrainian deputy was compelled to serve in parliament as a member of the Hlinka Party. According to the results of the 1938 and 1940 censuses, the Ukrainians were the third largest national group in the country. Ukrainian nationalists argued that every Uniate

CLERICAL FASCISM AT WORK

("Greek-Catholic" in the local usage) was actually a "Russin." The government on the other hand, was of the opinion that a majority of the Greek-Catholics were Slovaks who were using the east Slovak dialect. On that ground, the officials during the census of 1940 registered many as Slovaks.

The religious question played the most important role in denying the Ukrainians an opportunity for self-identification. Only a small portion of the inhabitants of east Slovakia were Orthodox, the Uniates counting for some 183,000 persons.[24] Slovak nationalists held a theory that the Greek-Catholics were descendents of the ancient Slavs, Christianized by the Byzantine missionaries Sts. Cyril and Methodius in the ninth century. Only the Greek-Catholics had succeeded in preserving the original Slavonic liturgy and rite.[25] Following this theory, the Slovaks argued that the Ukrainians were trying to impose themselves on Slovaks and Ukrainize (or Russify) them. The government was therefore obliged to protect its nationals and help them to find their identity.[26]

A hard core of Ukrainians kept their identity in spite of the discrimination and the administration's blocking of repeated efforts to register a Ukrainian party. Quarreling among themselves over the question of denomination, the Ukrainians were an easy prey for governmental divide-and-rule. However, even a formal request, signed by representatives of all factions, had no better results.[27] During the time of the Slovak state, Uniate priests were requested to leave politics alone, and to concentrate on spiritual work—unlike the Roman Catholic clergy, which was immersed in politics.

In order to promote the Slovak culture among the Uniates, the government sponsored the so-called Institute of Sts. Cyril and Methodius, appointing a Roman Catholic professor of theology as chairman. The regime made efforts to substitute the Ukrainian service in churches with Slovak ones.[28] It also supported publication of new prayer books in the Slovak language. The Ministry of Education opened Slovak schools in Ukrainian villages, and denied citizens' requests to teach in their own language.[29] The Slovak League was very active in the east, promoting Slovak education and cultural activities.

The fate of the small Polish minority was similar to that of the Ukrainian. Poles could be found among the inhabitants of territories returned or received from Poland, after its defeat in the fall of 1939.[30] When Bratislava established a Slovak administration, it submitted all inhabitants, particularly the youth, to intensive brainwashing. Polish nationality was not recognized, and Polish clergy and teachers had to leave their parishes and schools and go to Poland.[31] The Slovak Roman Catholic Church discouraged religious services in the Polish language.[32] The northern districts served also as the ground for an intensive activity of the Slovak League. The Czechs, a persecuted minority with no organization whatever, were constantly watched and suspected. Lacking a legal collective status and the threat of expulsion never completely removed, many Czechs, in order to avoid expulsion, opted for German nationality. Much Czech hardship was a result of a general atmosphere and continuous harassment, rather than of formal legislation. Tuka's speech in the parliament on November 30, 1939, illustrates the attitude of certain segments of the population. The prime minister attacked mixed marriages, accusing Slovak spouses of Czechs of national treachery, and children of these couples of being of impure and unreliable blood. "These children will be the biggest enemies of the nation, when most needed."[33] The paper *Slovák* echoed Tuka immediately, in an article by the well-known woman journalist Žela Inovecká. Accusing Czech girls of immoral behavior while "hunting" the best Slovak men, she concluded that Slovakia needed a law against mixed marriages.[34] While many letters to the editor protested against the article,[35] the article nevertheless clearly shows the atmosphere prevailing in certain circles,

Together with the Jews, the Gypsies were at the bottom of Slovakia's society. Always a grave social problem, the Gypsies were treated in a manner typical of authoritarian regimes. They were subjected to a continuous persecution by different branches of the government, making their lives very difficult.[36] The authorities prepared plans for the forced separation of Gypsy families and for their confinement in labor camps.[37] In 1942, the government considered the possibility of expelling the Gypsies "to the territories in the East."[38] It is probable that the cessation of deportation of the Jews saved the local Gypsies as well.

The Ludak behavior in the realm of minorities was one of intolerance and aggressiveness. Though there were over- and under-privileged minorities, the overall picture demonstrates discrimination and often national oppression.

Religion

Religion played an important role in public life. In the Party's ideology, it presented the very soul of clerical-fascism. An extensive religious influence rather than direct command shaped Slovakia's daily life. The dream of Slovak political Catholicism was to build a God-fearing and God-obeying nation. Spiritual matters were to be handled by the clergy.[39] Although not many fields revealed a direct influence of the Church, indirect influence, through priests and laymen, and through the general prestige of the church and hidden intervention, was strong and widespread.[40]

The key importance of the clergy as spiritual leaders, politicians, managers, and administrators need not be repeated. Still, it must be remembered that personal ambitions and political aims placed the clergy in a variety of jobs. The churchmen were, after all, the most reliable and most important body of intellectuals available to the Hlinka Party. The priests were willing to hold unpaid functions and take responsibilities which laymen would not. The typical clergyman was still the village priest, managing together with the local teacher all the public affairs of his parish, duties far beyond his spiritual obligations.

The state's legislation reflected the heavy clerical pressure as did the army, culture, professions, corporations and associations, and many other fields. Religion was compulsory for soldiers, teachers, officials in several offices, and practically all pupils and students.

The soldiers were commanded to participate in religious services, observations, and exercises. Profanity in the army was strictly forbidden. Young people suffered from religious interference in their social lives. The organ of Catholic Action, *Katolické Noviny*, proposed the general prohibition of dance parties, believing them harmful to morality.[41] The administration also used morality as the criterion for the evaluation of cultural activities, criticizing even swimming because of the brevity of swimming outfits.

The Church imposed itself on cultural life with the same petty dictatorship. In discussing the status of the press, *Katolické Noviny* said, "The leadership principle requests also that the press subordinate itself to the national and Church interest."[42] These were not empty words: *Matica Slovenská*[43] came under heavy fire when it published "un-Catholic" or anti-Catholic literature.[44]

The Church diligently controlled the spiritual life of the citizens. It organized various religious activities, requesting believers to attend. Spiritual exercises were organized in professions. Ministers and the members of parliament had collective exercises as well.[45] Protestant sects such as Baptists and Adventists were outlawed and their followers persecuted.[46] The government demonstrated its revenge and hostility toward the old Republic.[47] A decree prepared during the period of autonomy appeared in the press on March 14, 1939: members of the so-called Czechoslovak church would either return to Catholicism or they would be regarded as atheists, a status almost equal to that of a Jew.[48]

The school system exhibited the strongest influence of the church. *Katolické Noviny* explained religious supremacy in education as being of basic spiritual and material interest to the individual. The interest of the nation and state were only secondary to the individual.[49] Parents were not to interfere with state-managed schools; such a situation could lead to a Europe with no culture and no Christianity, where the teachers would be free to tell their pupils that Christ did not exist.[50] Thus, although schools under the supervision of the church shielded the youth from an intensive Nazi propaganda, the pupils were given an indoctrination of another type.[51]

The law described the final objectives of primary education in this way:

The grade school educates on a Christian-national basis the children to be moral and faithful citizens of the Slovak Republic; it provides them, in the spirit of the national culture, with a basic general knowledge, in order to be able to fulfill the tasks of religion and citizenship.[52]

Minister Sivák characterized the state's aim as: "... we want to raise a moral, pure, refined, deeply religious, Christianly thinking youth. ..."[53]

Under these preambles Slovak young people lived and studied. The Ministry of Education made instruction in religion compulsory for every child, independent of the will of his parents.[54] School regulations obliged the students to go to church every Sunday, and the teachers were requested to check the attendance of their pupils.[55] The same was true with other religious activities. A law forbade the teachers to be members of any anti-religious organization, or the schools to employ an educator not married in a church.[56] School supervisory boards had to include a priest or minister; if the church also owned the institution, a clergyman had to be chairman of the board. The church had the right to introduce into schools some rules of its own, with the consent of the Ministry of Education. In matters of religion and its instruction, the church was completely autonomous. These rules applied to schools of any faith.[57]

Though the direct influence on high schools was not as strong as on the elementary, the church was able to introduce many changes, comparable to the period before Munich. Some of the high schools were taken over by religious orders. In all institutions, the curriculum put more emphasis on the humanities and on instruction of Latin. Theistic interpretations were required both in sciences and the humanities. Regulations regarding religious instruction were similar to those for elementary education.

College students were the hardest to influence, yet attempts were made. The law instituted compulsory instruction of religion for all vocational and other types of schools.

Abolition of coeducation in high schools was one of the most significant attempted changes in education under pressure of the church. The Ministry of Education explained the change with moral, ethical, pedagogical, and didactic reasons,[58] yet the real reason may be found in the words of Minister Sivák, who told the protesting public:

CLERICAL FASCISM AT WORK

I beg the Slovak public to stay calm. I want to make it sure, that only our best wishes, and the supreme good of woman's dignity, value and honor, led to our decision to abolish co-education. In our mind there was only the single right and genuine cult of a Christian woman, the cult of a life-giver, for which we intend to prepare [the girls] already in schools.(59)

Ludak journalists accompanied the abolition of coeducation with a wave of attacks on "the emanicipation of women, another innovation of the Judeo-bolshevistic agents."(60) New high schools for girls were only supposed to prepare their students to be "dignified matrons, nationally conscious and unselfish mothers, and good educators of their children!"(61) Graduates of the girls' high schools were not to have the matriculation examination (*abituriat-maturita*) necessary for entrance to any school on an academic level. The legislators expected the girls not to continue in studies unless they took special courses after graduation. To complete the restriction, a numbers limitation was set on women in universities; the regulations permitted no more than 105 new women students to enroll annually at the University of Bratislava, beginning with the school year 1941-1942.(62) These plans caused such alarm among the parents, however, and such a public outcry, that the Ministry of Education was forced to suspend the plans temporarily.

In extracurricular activities, the Hlinka Youth was supposed to educate its members to the same ideals that the schools did. Various organizations connected with the Catholic Action had equal objectives. Membership in the Hlinka Youth had a value similar to a genuine Catholic organization. There were only a few Protestant members of HM.

When a child wanted to do some reading for pleasure, the school libraries could furnish him with descriptions of lives of saints or other books "which will convince him, that everything that happens, happens only through God's guidance."(63) Such "nasty" literature as *Robinson Crusoe* or *The Children of Captain Grant* had no place in school libraries;(64) for a while, even Pushkin's works were on the Index.(65)

In spite of the deep involvement in spiritual matters, the material side of the world was not forgotten. The clergy took an active part in the "gold rush" of the leadership, and so did the church as an institution. Numerous priests took positions on boards of trustees and became managers of private firms. Some of them were famous for their collections, such as the already-mentioned Monsignor Karol Koerper, or the mayor of Bratislava, Dr. Belo Kováč. When accused of seeking wealth, the priests defended themselves, saying that the income was spent on charity.

The priests were invited to take such positions because of their influence in the government, and because of the desire to please the clerics. But some of the clergy, including Bishop Ján Vojtaššák, also participated in aryanization.[66] The *Naboženský fond* ("Religious Fund") of the Catholic Church, which handled its business, got expensive presents from the State Land Office (*Štátny Pozemkový Úrad*), valued in the millions of Slovak crowns.[67] Jews, baptized in a desperate hope to save their lives, endowed money to various Slovak churches and to many clergymen. The economic situation of the Catholic Church in Slovakia improved enormously during these years; new churches and the renovation of the old ones, as well as the construction of new buildings for institutes and monasteries, marked the boom.[68]

The Catholic Church played an essential part in the life of Ludak Slovakia. For its good services, the church was richly rewarded in the spiritual as well as in the temporal realm.

Authoritarianism

Authoritarianism was the third feature typical of Slovakia under clerical fascism. The Party was supreme in the state and ruled through the government. The regime dominated the population in two ways: through the administration directly, using modified traditional tools inherited from the old Republic; and through various front organizations, institutes, and auxiliary corporations. Some parts of the population could withstand the pressure better; others were weaker. The Hlinka Party never did gain complete control over the nation. Its success varied in different periods and in different social strata.

The Party had four basic levels: the local and the county branches, the district committee, and the national leadership which was divided into the presidium and the central secretariat. With the exception of the local branch, all levels were divided into a "voluntary" part (technically representative, appointed, and unpaid); and that of paid secretaries hired by the secretary-general. The local branch had only the "voluntary" officers. Paid directly from Bratislava, the secretaries were rather independent of the local "representative" officers. They were, however, superior to unpaid officers on the lower levels.

Members of parliament had a somewhat autonomous status, as had the specially appointed political trustees attached to counties with no parliament member in residence. Both the parliament members and political trustees served as a "forum" for complaints and as mediators for interventions. If the county chief (*okresný nacelník*) and the district lieutenant (*župan*) were members of the Party, as was the case in the overwhelming majority, they had *ex officio* seats on the county or district committee. In several cases, these officials held county or district chairmanships in the

CLERICAL FASCISM AT WORK

Party, but it was not a rule. The parliament members, political trustees, and chairmen of Party front organizations were also *ex officio* members of the respective committees.

The secretary-general headed the central secretariat. This was a powerful position. His post somewhat resembled that of the chief party treasurer of the NSDAP.[69] He was responsible for the smooth performance of the Party's political and administrative activities, and supervised front organizations and acted as chairman of some. The secretariat was composed of two parts: one for political and administrative work, the other for interventions. The secretariat assigned a group of so-called central secretaries to various ministries and independent central offices, where they acted as agents for interventions in the highest echelons of the government. Only the secretary-general could contact a minister personally.

The leader, the presidium, and the convention created the representative upper stratum. Though the statutes of the convention were written and rewritten, the Slovak state saw only one such assembly, in the fall of 1939. Special courts were to watch discipline and behavior of the members. There were county courts, district courts, and a supreme court, headed by a judge of the state's supreme court. Since the days of Dr. Kirschbaum's secretaryship, several minor and few major alterations had occurred in Party organization. Among them were the reconstruction of the secretariat and manipulations with the presidium. Yet, these moves were insignificant insofar as the Party's work was concerned.

Front organizations such as the women's branches, corporations, and youth groups helped the Party in dominating the country. Though the Party was a male organization, membership in women's branches was highly encouraged. The women were to deal with charitable work, such as the Winter Relief.

The Party's life during the Slovak state can be divided into three stages. During the first stage, it was a mass party, possessing an authoritarian approach but with a leadership concept still underdeveloped. There were only a few structural changes from the days of the democratic Czechoslovak Republic. This period terminated with the elections of Tiso for president and chairman of the Party, an elevation which created a sort of Caesaropapism.

The next stage lasted until the middle of 1942. The leadership concept continued to crystallize during the struggle with the Hlinka Guard. Any adult Slovak could join or leave the Party as he pleased. The secretary-general appointed local and district leaders from a list presented by the branch.

The last stage was marked by a thoroughly totalitarian set-up. The clerical wing defeated the Hlinka Guard and became the unchallenged master of the country. The Party reflected this situation. According to the wish of its Fathers, the Party had to be an elite body, well disciplined and always reliable. Strict regulations made membership difficult. The last remnants of democratic choice in local officers evaporated completely. *Vodca* became an official title. In theory, this period lasted to the end of the Slovak state. Practically, it did not really survive the surrender of Italy.

The regime subdued non-Ludak organizations either by replacing elected officers with Party members, or by withdrawing authorization from the organization altogether. Additional legislation tightened the control. The corporations were the last word in regimentation of the society. A member of one corporation was excluded from membership in another, and from membership in any political organization apart from the Party. If the Party disagreed, he was barred from accepting a function in any association.[70] Monopolized trade unions were the forerunners of corporations, but they failed to control the population efficiently. The Ludaks hoped that the corporations (*stavy*, or "estates," in Slovak) would manage better. The monopolizing right of association had a double purpose: to paralyze eventual opposition, while spreading Party influence, and to increase its ranks. Members of the Party were expected to monitor the population, propagate Ludak ideals, and help to awaken the nation's enthusiasm.

In spite of high hopes, the Slovak state could not be completely dominated for structural reasons. The Catholic Church did not agree to surrender to the Party, and was not asked to do so. The national minorities were a further obstacle to complete domination. The ethnic Germans opposed and prevented the single state party wished by the Slovak leadership,[71] a party in which the minorities would have their own branches.

The policy of regimentation ruined voluntary action in public life. Slovak papers and writers often complained about the spreading selfishness.[72] Instead of the celebrated idealism, the country was overwhelmed with unprecedented materialism.[73] The citizens tended to be apathetic, particularly after the war took a turn for the worse. Only those activities directed from above were fulfilled, but even then, orders were often sabotaged or neglected. It seems that acts of protest based on voluntary participation increased. The Lutheran Church presents a good example. Thanks to wide support from its believers, it was more active than ever.[74] Similar rejuvenation could be observed in the Hungarian and Ukrainian minorities. The efforts of the remnants of the Jewish community, after the deportations of 1942, were impressive. The Jews tried to revive all traditional institutions, and to build new ones. They tried also to help Jews in Poland, Greece, and Hungary.

While Tiso described the Party as the oil and brains of the state, the administration was the mechanism for carrying out policy.[75] The constitution accepted on July 21, 1939, laid down the basic principles for the way in which the state should function. In spite of the changes parliament imposed on the constitution at various times, it remained a document that men and institutions did not feel bound by.

Special legislation defended the republican form of the state.[76] The office of president was the highest function in the Republic, with other top administrative functions being held by the prime minister, as head of the administration. This division of authority in the Constitution can be attributed to the strong influence of the democratic world outlook, still alive among the people. In the final form of the constitution, the president became highly influential, free from any formal responsibility for the "odious steps" of the government.[77] The powers and prerogatives of the prime minister were controlled and restricted, at least theoretically, by the parliament. Since the Slovak wish to elevate Tiso to the supreme position in the state clashed with German intentions to see Tuka there, creation of two supreme offices seemed to settle the conflict.[78]

Although the prime minister led the council of ministers, he was lacking in the ability to direct it, and his repeated efforts met with no success. A prominent Ludak emigrant, Konštantín Čulen, wrote that the ministers would hardly get a vote of confidence in a regular parliament, either.[79] That such a government could still govern the country can be explained only by the confidence and backing of the Party and its leader. Also, Germany's support, and the policy of her minister to Slovakia, Hans Ludin, which prevented any changes in the state, contributed to the cabinet's stability between July 1940 and September 1944.[80]

The district was the next administrative level under the government. According to *Slovák,* districts were created to act as mediators between the country and the central administration.[81] The SD agents reported, however, a strong opposition among top executives afraid of over-bureaucratization. According to SD reports, the district administration was to satisfy the demands of some Sidorites and provide jobs for additional politicians.[82] A district lieutenant's chief responsibility was to carry out orders coming from Bratislava. Still, he was powerful enough to persecute opponents of the regime, send them to prison, or fire officials on his own responsibility.[83] He could initiate and perform anti-Jewish policy in his district, independent of the central government. These and similar prerogatives made a district lieutenant a powerful personality in an authoritarian system.

The districts were divided into counties, headed by county chiefs. These men were to preserve public order and civil peace in their territory, and to represent the central government. In most cases the local councils were dissolved, and the government installed commissars in their stead.[84]

THE PARISH REPUBLIC

If one applies the classic concept of division of power in Slovakia, the president, along with the government on the central and local level, represents the administration; the parliament and the state council correspond to a legislature; and an elaborate structure of justice represents the judiciary branch. Yet, the reality was quire different. First, the Party broke the model. Second, the administration was stronger than the other two branches, and was able to act independently of the legislature, and occasionally even to dictate to it. As for the judiciary, both the Party and the administration could—and did—influence its decisions. Many Ludak politicians wanted to establish a strict legal order and saw the Republic as a state of law. The legislature of the Slovak Republic, particularly while dealing with Jews, took measures, however, unthinkable in any liberal and democratic state. It violated not only the rights of personal freedom and private property, granted by the local Constitiution, but basic human rights.

An interesting question for the student of the Slovak legislature is whether the laws were promulgated to retain norms of legality or to explain and put order into obviously illegal acts. It would seem that the legislature intended to prevent the public from destroying property while it canonized robbery. Anti-Jewish legislation presents examples of legislative steps taken in order to perform non-normative behavior, and for carrying out injury within formal laws. This legislation openly erased the borders between the executive and judicial branches.[85] Three types of legislation were known in Slovakia's jurisprudence. A law passed by the parliament ostensibly had the highest ranking. An order with force of law could be issued by the cabinet and renewed periodically. Simple orders of the cabinet, and of individual ministers had the lowest ranking. All three types were issued and enforced. In reality, however, it so happened that an order of the cabinet could suspend laws passed by the parliament.[86] Laws were frequently manipulated, changed, "plastered," or annulled. The Constitution was "plastered" four times between July 1939 and August 1944. On some occasions, the government asked for retroactive legislation to condone as legal acts already carried out. An outstanding example was the law regarding deportation of Jews,[87] passed by the parliament after many of the victims had already been deported.

It would not be a mistake to conclude that the Slovak state was far from being a state of law. Such an image was preserved, however, and its creators made efforts to keep the image of legality, and of separation of power. The *Snem* (Parliament) did not have a monopoly on legislation, yet continued to function in spite of the anger of Slovak Radicals and German Nazis. *Snem* legislated occasionally under order,[88] or bestowed part of its prerogatives on the government.[89] It also occasionally professed disagreement with acts of the administration.[90] In any case, the parliament granted the regime some sort of legitimacy that was appreciated by the people. The population could forget neither the Czechoslovak democracy nor the Ludak struggle for a local diet. Therefore, the *Snem* had to be preserved.[91]

Unlike the Fuehrer, the Vodca had no formal legislative power of his own.[92] But his influence was immense, and through letters he was able to change the text of laws or participate personally in their formulation.[93]

The Party was the strongest authority in the state. Yet while the Party was the chief power, it tried to enhance its superiority along normative patterns. Collision with the bureaucratic structure broke the normativeness, and emphasized the Party's superiority over the law. Nevertheless, in spite of the autocratic rule, it would be unjust to accuse Party fathers of a lack of concern for the well-being of their people. In general the relations between ruler and ruled were in the nature of a priest-shepherd. On the other hand, the Party's discipline methods toward its people illustrate this feeling of superiority over the law. Tools of coercion, such as secret police and harsh prisons for political delinquents, as well as two kinds of regular police and armed units were on hand. The prisons were never empty of political delinquents.[94] The secret police used German Gestapo methods against people suspected of being subversive.[95] Many political delinquents were delivered directly to the German security agencies, never to be seen again. The Jews were particularly harassed. The secret police placed many of the government's former adversaries in "protective custody" in the notorious prison of Ilava, among them politicians, functionaries of trade unions, Catholic and Lutheran clergy, and many others. The physical terror slackened only in 1944.

Propaganda, or violence against the soul, in Franz Neumann's expression, was another feature of terror. Local institutes and Germans conducted propaganda in Slovakia. The Office of Propaganda published booklets, wall papers, posters, and the like. It provided the press with information for publication. As the official censor, the Office of Propaganda could also influence the press indirectly. It controlled radio, cinematography, cultural events, and publishing houses.

The direct activity of the Party and its front organization, as well as the Catholic Church, opened additional avenues for influencing the mind. The Ministry of Education and various cultural organizations were also active in the field of propaganda. In addition, German agencies worked in Slovakia. In spite of the efforts of these organizations to propagandize the populace, the people seemed to have developed an effective immunity, and to have successfully resisted the propagandistic efforts.[96]

The Ministry of Education conducted a purge of the libraries, removing books "politically defective, Czech, and progressive."[97] The Party encouraged what it called "the national art." "Tendency [i.e., political-ideological] in art," argued a Ludak writer, "not only does not kill the creativity, but refines the creation."[98] The emphasis was on historic, patriotic, or religious motives. The Ludaks scorned and censured modern art; " . . . the art appears in decadent forms, described in foreign terms such as *futurism, dadaism, cubism.* It seems as if the art has to mark the moral decay there, where the various ideologies, helped by politics, failed. The [Slovak] art has to shape the *materia* along the Slovak imagination."[99] (Italics added). Literature witnesses similar tendencies. Critics conducted heavy attacks on so-called "progressive" poets and writers. Under fire was the surrealistic school, popular with poets of communist and clerical leaning. Publishers presented the public with works of dubious value, since the authors previously "were oppressed, being Ludaks." Meanwhile, some well-known veterans were forced into silence.[100]

Interestingly the Party's attacks on art and literature were not as rigidly pressed as its attacks in the political realms. Known communists and "Czechoslovaks" held exhibitions, published books, and were stage directors and actors in spite of the criticisms. Slovakia granted much more freedom to the artist than Germany did. In spite of retreat in some fields, the period of independence was not a lost time for Slovak arts and letters. Indeed, great progress could be witnessed in music, theater, and playwriting, for example. The regime endorsed such creativity, which dealt with beloved personalities and topics. Theology, of course, fared better than ever. In regard to science, one had to accept the following: "There is only one truth. Science has to serve only this truth. It should be its maid, worshipping it in religion as well as in research."[101]

The Party badly needed leaders in every sphere of life, yet a great portion of the intelligentsia lined up with the opposition and was either hostile, or at least passive, and was not ready to give support. Appeals and threats to the intellectuals were frequent in the daily press.[102] The regime's sympathizers wrote proclamations and periodically set up new institutions to supervise and to guide, all of which failed in their purpose. Slovak totalitarianism, according to Vlado Clementis, a communist writing in London during the war, was multicolored.[103] The Office of Propaganda, the Ministry of Education, and indirect German influence, competed with each other in guiding the cultural life. While the competition went on, the intellectuals were relatively free of control.

It is also important to remember that the hard core of Ludaks included only an insignificant number of lay-intellectuals. The majority of the scholars and artists, who had chosen to cooperate with the regime, did so by their own free will. The ultramontane attitude of the Ludaks did not help them to widen their circle of friends. Young intellectuals, who otherwise willingly accepted totalitarianism, disliked the clerical guidance. Instead of loyalty, they had chosen opportunism. In such an atmosphere, a rigid totalitarianism in the intellectual sphere could not exist. Moreover, Minister Sivák and other clericals of his type, with a background of lifelong activity in Czechoslovakia, were not willing to use harsh methods in order to oppress intellectual opposition.

Slovakia reflected authoritarianism in political and social life. In spite of failing or badly executed plans, the intentions of the planners were clear: to dominate the population, and to direct its activity.

Socioeconomics

In economic and social matters, the official policy of the Party was denunciation of the liberal laissez-faire system, as well as of the "materialist socialism oppressing the individual." The Ludaks inscribed on their banners "Solidarism" and "Common Good Before Selfishness."[104] Or as an economist put it, the national socialist economy, which served as the model for Slovakia, had only one principle: the welfare of the nation as a whole,[105] a theme constantly reiterated. Again in reality, however, the actual situation was different. Slovakia had an almost free and unaltered market economy, in spite of labor market and price control, food rationing, and government and Party sponsorship of monopolistic trade companies. While prices squeezed the small producer, larger manufacturers made a better profit than ever.

The regime preferred and supported Ludak entrepreneurs in their drive against the veteran capitalist groups. The real essence of "anti-capitalism" became evident as anti-Semitism, aryanization, and nostrification (i.e., transfer of property from foreign into national hands).

The slogan of solidarism, so often used, meant in practice a justification of dictatorship by the wealthy against the poor. The government stripped employes of the right to bargain and strike, and put them under the supervision of officially sponsored institutions; the peasantry could deal only with the monopolistic companies and as a result lost its independent representation. Thus the middle class not only got rid of "alien" competition, but also appropriated Jewish and Czech property, and made money in the boom of the war economy and through the black market. The ranks of the local upper class swelled with newcomers, the people who profited from the new political system and the war. The nouveaux riches joined the veteran social elite: the few Slovak large estate owners, businessmen and industrialists, who lent at this time a considerable support to the Party. Yet the heavy industry of Slovakia, limited as it might have been, was never in Slovak hands. The German capital (particularly Hermann Goering Werke, a.G.) inherited the local Czech and foreign investments. Thus Slovak nationals benefited little from the profit of heavy industry. The Slovak share in ownership of the local light industry expanded, however, substantially; and the number of industrial plants in the country also increased.

When the Party came to power, it began to curtail and outlaw worker organizations and trade unions. Even during the period of autonomy, only the "Christian Worker Unions" affiliated with the Hlinka Party were allowed to exist. The regime put heavy pressure on the workers to join the Party and its trade unions.[106] In November 1940, the Christian Worker Union lost the rights to deal with social matters of the workers.[107] And when the Slovak Working Community came into existence, the last remnants of trade union autonomy withered away.[108]

The Slovak Working Community was composed of four corporations, each representing employes and employers, although the legislature took pains to prevent the workers from having any voice in these organizations. The employes had the corporate bodies only. The government dissolved the elected worker councils and prohibited any further elections. Municipal or state offices were in charge of appointing labor representatives in the plants.[109] No bargaining over salaries and wages was to be held, as the state prescribed both. An economist praised the authoritarian prescription of payments and the abolition of the "unhonorable" negotiations as one of the regime's greatest achievements in the field of economy.[110] A central and compulsory employment office took upon itself the task of finding jobs for the unemployed. It possessed the right to send people into forced labor.[111]

The government made major changes in the field of the social conditions. It introduced family wages, additional money aids for children, and paid holidays. It helped families of low income to acquire their own houses. The impact of these positive achievements was diminished when the government also cut compensation for the unemployed, curtailed social security, and transferred all social work to the Party's Winter Relief. Since the nature of the Winter Relief was one of charity, the workers thus lost an important social achievement.[112]

A check of managers and board members of monopolistic companies reveals the same names repeatedly appearing in key positions. These were the leading Ludak businessmen, their relatives, or close friends of the Peasant Bank, the leadership of the Corporation for Agriculture, the

Chamber of Agriculture, in the parliament, and in the Party's presidium.[113]

Agriculture and everything connected with it was the chief region of domination of the so-called Turček-Danihel group. The Ludaks succeeded in ousting and taking over not only Jewish and some foreign (mainly Czech) capital, but also a strong Slovak Lutheran group, connected with the former Agrarian Party. The Ludaks explained the expansion as having been carried out in favor of the Slovak peasantry. Speakers argued that the peasant had been exploited until now, and did not hold a share of the wealth achieved from his sweat. While conquering the sugar industry, Deputy Štefan Danihel made the following remarks to a reporter of *Slovák*: "A close group of political-economic representatives of the Party bought this industry. *Not for themselves, but for the whole peasantry.* Perhaps some peasants thought that peasantization of the industry should be done differently. They will see in the future that our way was the right one." (Italics in the source).[114] Four years later an economist, Professor Rudolf Briška, told a meeting of experts that the peasantry should be granted influence in the food industry, if economic effects were desired. At the same time he stated that the sugar industry served the capital more than agriculture or the consumers.[115] The sugar industry is an excellent example of the unselfish economic service done by the Ludaks for the Slovak nation.

Ludak strategy aimed to penetrate the economy through planting its own men as well as by take-over. A special member of the secretariat, holding the rank of a central secretary, was assigned to deal with economic matters.[116] He had to manage the Party's budget and its enterprises, and he was responsible for encouraging and directing its activity in the field of economy. A Party committee was supposed to guide[117] the economy according to the principles of solidarism.[118] How much solidarism was in the guiding is hard to measure, yet governmental influence was heavy.

The government interfered in both positive and negative ways; among the former were the promotion of new industries and the prohibition of the three-field agriculture. Numerous examples represent the negative. The government issued orders permitting those in charge of the economy to send trustees or provisional managers to any enterprise "if the public interest requires it."[119] Also, the state's Land Office could transfer lands without any rent from the owner to anyone else "if they are not cultivated."[120] The administrative interference in the financial life transgressed the monetary necessity. The Party's wish to nostrificate financial institutions and to strengthen its own enterprises inspired the governmental actions.

The Peasant Bank was the Party's leading financial enterprise. Tiso's personal circle sponsored and dominated it. The bank's founding was a significant departure from the past. In previous years, the People's Bank, founded by Hlinka, had had the Party's blessing. Located in the city of Ružomberok, the bank was staffed and managed by Sidorites. After the proclamation of independence, the bank steadily diminished in importance. The *Sedliacká Banka* ("Peasant Bank") was founded on January 1, 1941, with capital supplied by the previous Agrarian Peasant Cooperative Movement. In the year 1945, the bank was Slovakia's leading financial institution, with property worth one miliard Slovak crowns.[121] The growth of the Peasant Bank was due not only to the direct support of the administration, but also to nostrification of Czech property (actually of banks having their headquarters in Bohemia-Moravia), and aryanization.[122]

The Tatra Bank, with strong ties to the Hlinka Guard, competed in wealth and influence with the Peasant Bank. Ján Farkaš, chairman of its board of managers, was Tuka's personal friend, and Guardists staffed this bank and its affiliated companies.[123] Competition between the two institutions resembled the political competition of their sponsors.

The Peasant and Tatra Banks illustrate well enough Ludak interests in financial life and the firm grip they achieved. A similar situation prevailed in other sections of the economy, such as industry and transportation. Worth mentioning is the benefit gained by the lower middle class. This stratum supplied the Ludaks with many supporters and functionaries. The Hlinka Party rewarded them richly. Middle class gentiles had previously suffered from Jewish competition, and the gentile lawyers, physicians, and pharmacists were happy to be rid of their Jewish colleagues. In the retail trade, in handicraft, in shop- and tavern-keeping, the Jewish entrepreneur was even more significant than in the free professions. Thus anti-Jewish legislation affected about 11,000 small-size enterprises, which were either aryanized or liquidated before October 1, 1941. While local people aryanized about 1,800 stores and shops, the rest disappeared altogether. The owners or appointed trustees sold the goods and equipment far below the real price, closed the establishments, and quit.[124]. Thereafter the market was left to the gentile competitors and all sorts of newcomers.

The Slovak press reflected intensively the desire of the small businesses to eliminate Jewish competition. Especially vocal were individual shopkeepers and their organization: they constantly called for "christianization" of the trade, asking the public to support them exclusively and not the "exploiting aliens." The Jews were not the only target of these jealous creatures. In Bratislava, shopkeepers begged the municipal authorities to transfer Bulgarian vegetable growers to inferior trading locations in the marketplace. In the villages, they sounded a cry against co-op stores. Elsewhere, they asked the administration to give preference to Christian and

and Slovak bids. Interestingly enough, in many cases the government accepted and carried out these pleas.[125]

Historiographers in Czechoslovakia today usually speak about the "bourgeoisie" as *the* profiteers of the Ludak era,[126] when in fact, the benefit derived by the middle class was far bigger than that of "big business." Slovakia's townfolk, semi-intelligentsia, and rich peasantry should be counted as the long-term winners. The six years of Slovakia's independence facilitated a rise in their standard of living, and in their expectations and demands. They discovered new horizons and acquired incentives to strive for things not known previously. It is a fact that many of the men managing contemporary Slovakia made the great jump in the days of the Slovak state, either through themselves or through their parents.

The medium-to-poor peasantry was less fortunate. According to a Czechoslovak historian, only a minor part of lands predestined for reform was actually divided.[127] The large estates were not allocated for reform, in order not to endanger the economic interest and food supply of the country.[128] The law requested the receiving peasants to pay half the land price in cash, and it also provided long-term loans for the poor, because, as the first chairman of the state's central Land Office put it, "bolshevik principles have to be excluded."[129] Other officers of the Party later criticized this blunt statement, but the peasants were made to pay. The *Organizačné Zvesti*, in reflecting on the machinations and intrigue which marred the reform, counted preference for Party members, nepotism, and bribery.[130] While the peasantry waited nervously, bureaucratic procedures slowed down the actual allotment.[131] When the Law on Land Reform passed in the parliament in 1940, *Slovenská Politika* stated proudly: "Slovakia took with distinction a place in the category of socially-just states."[132] Two years later, *Organizačné Zvesti* warned, "Not everybody can be satisfied. If nothing would be divided, all people would be happy with their possessions, because they understand that nothing is served on a silver plate."[133]

The village presented its own kind of jealousy. The peasants visited the officials to slander their neighbors, but particularly the few Jews who still lived in the villages, or the trustees of Jewish fields, in a hope of having plots transferred into their hands. The general impression is that the countryside, where the majority of the population lived, had considerably less good fortune in the Slovak state than the middle class in the cities.[134]

In the economy, as in other sections of Slovak life, the Ludaks enjoyed a privileged position. They exploited their advantages for personal enrichment and for strengthening the Party's hold on the country. During the first years of independence, Slovakia's economy witnessed severe weaknesses. The situation improved much in the following years. Though

THE PARISH REPUBLIC

severely undermined by Germany's exploitation, Slovakia succeeded in establishing a fairly sound economy, and benefited from the opportunities presented by the war.

Various parts of Slovakia's life reflected the rule of the Hlinka Party. The Slovak clerical fascist practice did not leave any section of society free of its influence. The state was able to control many of the local activities. Arbitrary guidance, even if inefficient, still remained an important element in the citizen's life.

On August 20, 1944 *Slovák* published an article calling on the population to close ranks around the government. "Let's increase the flame of love for the Slovak statehood! Let's help the ones losing the faith! Let's spread more propaganda of our spirit!"[1] This threefold appeal contains in essence all the domestic problems facing the regime on the eve of the National Uprising: lack of public support, escapism among the least faithful, and disintegration of institutions charged with guiding the population.

The Regime and the Resistance

The first half of 1944 was a period of relative plenty. Yet while calmness prevailed in Slovakia's domestic affairs, the war deeply affected local life. First came the German occupation of Hungary; then the Allies started to bomb that Slovak industry important to the Nazi war efforts; and finally, guerilla activity increased. Minor partisan troops, consisting chiefly of escaped Russian POWs, communists, and Jews, appeared in remote places early in 1943, and in some cases, even earlier. At the end of 1943, "regular" Russian partisans entered eastern Slovakia and were quickly reinforced by local citizens. These troops developed intensive activity which later spread into other regions. The underground—consisting of army officers, Czechoslovak loyalists, and communists—increased in force. Meanwhile, cannon already were roaring in neighboring countries.

Internal disintegration and demoralization, the partisan activity, and the proximity of the front disquieted both the Germans and the regime. When the Nazis began serious consideration of sending troops into Slovakia, the Ludaks were disturbed by this and by the dim outlook of the future. Forces such as the radical elements of the Hlinka Guard, long believed to have faded from the scene, appeared again. After August 1944, the Guardists consistently gained the upper hand in clashes with the last active members of the Party. Significantly enough, the "Young Generation" was faithful to the Party to the end, while only a few of the Old Guard remained with Tiso, who continued as Germany's ally to the bitter end. Interestingly enough, only the Slovak forces responsible for the "independence" (i.e., Tiso, the Hlinka Guard, and the young generation led by the Nastupists), remained Germany's loyal, lasting supporters. The army, *l'enfant terrible* of the regime, stabbed the state in the back, and so caused its final breakdown.[2]

On August 8, a group of Guardists conferred with the president and informed him of the grave situation prevailing in the country.[3] They particularly pointed out suspicious elements in the army, the failure of the Party, and the corruption and inefficiency of the parliament and administration, and presented several suggestions for correction. Tiso raged when he was told about the "conspiracy in the army," and promised to take steps to correct the situation. The Guardists told him that this was the last opportunity to do so without German interference.[4] To Ludin's offer to bring in German troops "to order Slovakia's conditions," the president answered that the proposal was tempting, but he was wary of creating a stand for a *kuratische Zustaende* ("trusteeship") in the country.[5] Although Tiso took various steps in order to improve the internal condition in the state, giving special attention to the army, Ludin still felt alarmed. On August 24, 1944, he sent a telegram to the German Foreign Office, proposing the use of German troops against partisans in Slovakia.[6] Three days later he requested Berlin' opinion on a reshuffling of the government, emphasizing the unquestionable loyalty of Tiso and Mach. (Tuka's poor health prevented his participation; Čatloš was considered unreliable.) Ludin proposed to include Ďurčanský in the new cabinet, in spite of the latter's doubts about Germany's victory, because he thought cooperation with the Reich a guarantee for Slovakia's independence.[7] Again von Ribbentrop proved his notorious lack of common sense: he not only rejected Ludin's suggestion, but proposed to imprison Ďurčanský at a suitable opportunity. He did agree to the reshuffling and to the ouster of Čatloš, but asked to preserve Tuka's position.[8]

Von Ribbentrop's reply was too late. On the day it arrived, Slovak soldiers, the civilian population, and partisans took arms against Bratislava's ruling clique and the Germans. The Slovak National Uprising saved the honor of the nation, destined by its clerical fascist rulers to remain the last ally of the Third Reich. It was a resounding vote of no confidence in the government.

Two dominant forces staged the Uprising; the Slovak Communist Party, supported by the Soviet Union and various sympathizers inside the country; and by a non-communist coalition of anti-fascist bourgeois elements allied with important segments of the Slovak army and with the Czechoslovak government in exile. On the civilian side the communists made serious efforts, by no means unsuccessful, to gain popular support. The popularity of the Soviet Union as a great Slavonic and anti-fascist power grew steadily. Some social maladies particularly felt by the workers and poor peasantry, and decades of socialistic propaganda, also helped the communists. Above all, a lack of sympathy for the Nazis and for Nazi Germany, the changing fortunes of war, and the often comic setting of the "Parish Republic" made the people receptive to propaganda hostile to the Ludaks.

The bourgeois elements naturally could build on the same conditions. The fear of socialist experiments, the sympathies for the Western Powers and for the Czechoslovak government in exile also boosted the non-communists. Young Agrarians, Protestants, and some Catholics composed the basis of the group. While the non-communists enlisted support of sympathetic army officers, including several generals, guerillas under Russian and Slovak command strengthened the bargaining abilities of the communists.

Both groups formally agreed to cooperate against the Ludak regime in a clandestine meeting on Christmas Day, 1943. They created the so-called "Slovak National Council," and decided to assume all powers in the country at the propitious moment. The conspirators aimed at a renewal of the Czechoslovak Republic.

After the meeting both groups began preparation for open resistance against the Bratislava government. In their activities, the non-communists enjoyed the assistance of—though not always unconditionally—the exile government in London. The communists were less fortunate, since they lacked direct communications with Moscow and with the Czechoslovak leaders in exile. Nevertheless both partners in Slovakia proceeded with their underground activities. They coordinated their labor, although when the explosion erupted in the summer of 1944, many pilot plans were not finished. The eruption began about August 28 and 29, but evidently not in the way the army officers would have liked. Apparently premature and irresponsible actions by the guerillas invited German intervention thus forcing the uprising on the slightly reluctant army. Moreover, some of the officers failed to fulfill the directives given them in advance, consequently hampering the success of the undertaking.

In retrospect, it seems that even more than domestic failures, the calculations and anticipations of the Great Powers brought about the bitter conclusion to the National Uprising two months later. To the Western Powers, Slovakia was in the Russian sphere of influence, so they were reluctant to assist without an agreement with Moscow. Furthermore, the Anglo-Americans perhaps were not too eager to get much involved in a project organized partially by communists. Difficulties of a technical nature also prevented extensive western assistance to Czechoslovakia.

Though the initial outbreak of the uprising resulted from actions of Russian-commanded partisans, Moscow probably was only a little interested in Slovakia's front. The Slovak communists certainly were in the dark about the Soviet plans. The Soviet Union supplied Slovakia with war

THE PARISH REPUBLIC

materials and men, but not in quantitites sufficient for a prolonged stand. It ordered an assault on Dukla Pass in eastern Slovakia, but the attacking troops did not advance far against the stubborn German defense. Nowhere else did the Soviet Army try to break through the German lines, nor did any high-ranking Soviet officers reach the capital of the liberated territory, Banská Bystrica. The highest-ranking Soviet officer in Slovakia was a second-grade colonel, a drunkard and fanatic. Moscow could have done much more for her Slovak ally than she did. As for local fighting, contemporary Slovak historians have "discovered" much more glory in the National Uprising than the participants usually witnessed.

Under German Occupation

The Slovak National Uprising caused a profound soul-searching in the Ludak leadership. The Old Guard in particular realized that the fight was over, and tried to adjust,[9] while the Young Generation, the Hlinka Guard, Jozef Tiso, and several of his veteran friends refused to accept the situation. Instead, they accused the nation of betraying its own interest. Durring the uprising and even after the war, Tiso continued to claim that the Slovaks were the only people who had risen against their own state.[10] He reflected on the days of 1938-1939, and argued that his co-nationals did not appreciate enough Slovakia's independence because they had achieved it too easily, while they were not yet ready for it.[11]

Another argument developed then, and still maintained by the Ludak emigrants in the west, claimed that the Uprising was the work of Russians, Jews, communists, and a small band of Lutheran traitors.[12] The Young Generation and the Hlinka Guard did not just confine themselves to a display of bitterness, but got involved in political struggles over the future of the state.[13] The Catholic Church was eager to appear as inconspicuous as possible; most of her bishops were anxious not to commit themselves to either side. Important defections occurred in the administration, while only a very few army units remained faithful to Father Tiso.[14]

Thus, on August 30, 1944, Ludin reported Tiso's invitation to the German troops, and the president's proposal to disarm Slovak units. The minister described the Vodca as "completely loyal, however, thoroughly afraid and overly nervous."[15] The entrance of the German Army ended the semi-independent rule of Ludaks. From that time on, the Slovak government was but a front for open Nazi supremacy in the country.

SS General Gottlob Berger was the first commander of the German units. A short time after his arrival, he visited the president and initiated the creation of a new government.[16] Berger particularly pressed for the appointment of Kubala as commander-in-chief of the HG and the police.[17]

Subsequently, the Guard regained an importance it had known only in March 1939. The Guardists were armed and participated in security service actions against partisans and Jews.

Dr. Štefan Tiso, (not a relative of the president), previously chief justice of Slovakia's Appellate Court, accepted the premiership of the new government. He, rather than the ailing Tuka, who had been dropped by the Germans, was the president's personal choice.[18] Other members of the cabinet were unimportant, excepting the new head of the Ministry of National Defense, Štefan Haššik, who was a long time die-hard Ludak and pioneer of anti-Jewish legislation.

Slovak parliament deputies were ordered to meet to hear an exposé by the new prime minister, denouncing the National Uprising and praising Slovak-German friendship.[19] On October 27, 1944, parliament legislated itself out of business by passing a law transferring the right of legislation to the cabinet and the president.[20]

The question facing the Germans about the Party was whether to revive it and to what degree. All German observers agreed that the Party had declined to the point where it was contributing nothing.[21] On September 26, 1944, the commander of *Einsatzgruppe H*, SS *Obersturmbannfuehrer* Dr. Witiska, dispatched by Germany to deal with Slovakia's affairs, prepared a plan for the reorganization of Slovakia. In it he stated that the fiction of the Slovak state had to be preserved. The corporate organizations could be considered the only useful bodies and should be put to work in the social field. His suggestion was accepted.[22]

Still, the Ludaks did not intend to vacate their former powers entirely. An angry Tiso threatened to disperse the Party if it did not become quickly organized. Suddenly there were again struggles in the caucus, even though the Party had no followers. The renewed Hlinka Guard, in addition, was unhappy with the revival of its ancient foe and began an open battle against it.[23]

The main fight developed around the position of the secretary-general. Among the several candidates for this post, Ďurčanský was the outstanding one; he was also Tiso's choice. However, the Germans had mixed feelings about their old adversary, and when it appeared Ďurčanský was not interested, his candidacy was dropped.[24] Nevertheless, he remained one of the most influential members of the Ludak leadership.

After Ďurčanský's name was eliminated, the competition was between the veterans versus the Young Generation. Eventually, an Old Ludak, Dr. Pavol Oplustil, deputy speaker of the parliament, was chosen. The Young Generation and the HG accepted his nomination, which was anticipated by an appeal to Tiso, known since as the "Memorandum of the Young Generation."[25] The memorandum, presented by a delegation

including Ďurčanský, on September 20, 1944, opened with the words
Vodca náš! ("Our Leader"). It introduced the slogan "back to March 14th,"
which indicated the need for reorganization of the state, as though it had
just acquired independence and the preceding five years had not transpired.
Slovakia, it said, had to acquire a "decisive authoritarian government."
The Party, its institutions, the legislature, and state and municipal administrations should be purged of cowards and unreliables. A final solution of
the Jewish and Czech question was requested. Obviously, they demanded
punishment for the men of the coup.[26]

The Party was divided as in the "good old days," into a Young Generation, a veteran group (the *staroľudaci*), and the HG. The two extreme
wings were particularly aggressive; fighting each other violently, they both
attacked the center and the administration. At that time, testified Sokol,
the Party had no unifying force. The men were dealing with problems
each according to his best understanding.[27] Yet the president was still
struggling to keep his authority. Did Tiso still believe in Germany's victory,
or at least in a miracle? It must be assumed that such was the case.

The last action of the Ludaks, on a somewhat larger scale, was a convention of the Young Generation at the spa of Piešťany, on January 4,
1945. Here a formal organization for the group was created. A manifesto
accepted by the convention insisted upon an independent Slovakia.[28]

The commander-in-chief of the HG, Kubala, vehemently attacked the
Young Generation as a propagandist attraction of useless people who
spoke instead of fighting Bolshevism with arms in hand. Only the HG contained the idealists who could revive Slovakia's life, according to Kubala.
He complained in a letter to the Germans that the Reich did not grant its
whole support to the Hlinka Guard, the single ever-faithful force in Slovakia.[29] This was the swan song of political strife in the "Slovak State."

The last stage of "independence" was under complete German domination. Nevertheless, Hitler decided to keep Slovakia afloat as long as it completely supported the Reich. Since Slovakia had to provide its share of war
needs, the full cooperation of the Hlinka Party, the Hlinka Guard, and the
Catholic Church was requested. The special comrade relationship with the
Slovaks had to be somewhat limited and these organizations would have to
be under strict German control.[30]

This stand, supported by the German Foreign Office and other agencies,
was never carried out, for the *actual* rulers of the country were neither the
Slovaks nor German diplomatic personnel, but the SS. Himmler visited
Bratislava, Kaltenbrunner had been there, and above all, the commander-
in-charge belonged to this unit. Himmler, answering von Ribbentrop's request for a milder approach in Slovakia, wrote brusquely that he under-

stood that the Reich's foreign policy needed Slovakia independent. But privately the Slovaks had to be spoken to in no uncertain terms *(Fraktur gesprochen)*. Himmler considered it an exaggeration to grant Slovakia an imaginary status as a genuine authority and sincere ally.[31] Himmler later responded to Ludin's request to see him, saying that when the situation in the Reich was consolidated, he would again come to the *southeastern part of Germany* (emphasis mine) for as such he considered Slovakia.[32]

After the fall of 1944, the Soviet Army gradually advanced into Slovakia. The Nazis squelched the uprising in blood. Deportation of Slovak soldiers, surrendered fighters, and the civilian population followed. Mass executions took place in the country; the Jews were the main victims, but many others were murdered as well.[33]

While the surviving victims of the Nazi and clerical fascist regime enjoyed the first days of freedom, a mass exodus of Ludaks followed the retreating Germans. Dr. Jozef Tiso first sought asylum in a monastery in Austria, and later surrendered to the United States Army. With his surrender all legal remnants of Slovakia's "independence" ceased. However, it was to be one of the ironies of the Ludak destiny that Sidor, Slovak envoy to the Vatican, would remain the last official representative of the deceased state.

CHAPTER X
SUMMARY AND CONCLUSIONS

The independent Slovak state was a product both of the radical nationalism of the newly awakened people and of Nazi aggression. To describe it as merely a creation of Hitler's intrigues and as a tool of Germany would be as much a mistake as considering the local separatist aspirations alone.

There is still some doubt of whether there would have been an opportunity for Slovak independence had the Czechoslovak Republic survived Munich. The Ludaks never were able to produce a majority among the Slovak people, yet the HSL'S was a genuinely local movement, with all the traditional ethnic elements. It truly represented the backward, reactionary conservatism of the Catholic clergy of former upper Hungary. Even if the Hlinka Party had had no connection whatever with foreign radicals, it still should be described, at least in the last year of Czechoslovakia and during the period of Slovak independence, as a rightist party of the "mass" type, rather than a traditionally conservative one.[1] Skeptical of achieving an independent Slovakia through other means, strongly nationalistic-minded Party youth (the Young Generation) adopted and cherished totalitarian theories. When the time came, they shifted from theories to action, joining with the Nazis to destroy the Republic and create their own state. Hitler's pressure, in March 1939, was welcomed by a small and arrogantly aggressive minority composed of a few clerics and an efficient group of Radicals. Granted power and support by Berlin, which preferred indirect rule to a complete takeover, this minority was able to draw to itself a large number of citizens and take control of the state.

The state not only brought great economic profit to many but emotional and social satisfaction as well. Slovaks gained national self-consciousness and pride. They became convinced of Slovakia's ability to manage its own matters. Consequently, partisans of the fiction of the "Czechoslovak nation" lost ground and turned into an insignificant minority in the population. The Party established itself as the single power of the country, with a monopoly over governmental functions. It worked hard to spread its influence through the various sectors of the social life by means of oppression, changes of personnel, rewards, legislation, indoctrination, and ideological manipulation.

During its six years of domination the Party passed through four major stages corresponding in part to stages in the internal life of the country.

SUMMARY AND CONCLUSIONS

In the first stage, which lasted from March 1939 to July 1940, the Party concentrated its efforts on its own internal consolidation, as well as on control of the state. However, continuous internal strife marred its existence. Sidor and his group were the first victims; during this time the clerical group emerged as the major power. Conservative elements comprised the largest segment of this group, yet it was influenced strongly by modern Catholic social theory. The clericals formed a loose association with young intellectuals who contributed chauvinistic nationalism and authoritarianism to the *Weltanschauung* which, together with the values of the clericals, gave the "clerical fascist" color to Slovakia's politics.

The Hlinka Guard opposed the main bulk of the ruling force. Officially an organic part of the Party, the Guard strove for primacy, with some help from the Reich. Ideologically, the Guardists stood nearer to German National Socialism than their foes, yet they too found it impossible and undesirable to reject all local values. After Dr. Jozef Tiso, himself a cleric, was elected president and leader of the Party, an open competition developed between the movement and its para-military troops. The elections were Tiso's personal victory, due to his firm ties with the clericals and with the Young Generation. Moreover, he could also count on the support of the Guard and so unify the majority of the Party, a task impossible for any other leader in Slovakia. Jealousy, lust for power and German intrigues ruined this unity, pitting the HG against all the other factions. Following the Salzburg meeting of the Slovak leaders with Hitler and von Ribbentrop, the chief representatives of the Young Generation lost their position and direct influence in the life of the country. Moves on both sides created a situation favorable to German intervention, the action which terminated the Party's first stage, and which led to a new series of struggles for supremacy in the state and in the Party.

In the second stage, the fight raged from the Salzburg meeting to the spring of 1942. Tuka and Mach, the chief representatives of the HG Radical wing, tried unsuccessfully to change the state's and the Party's institutions to suit themselves. The tension reached a climax in January and February of 1941 when a plan for a coup d'état was uncovered. Germany wished the strife to end and compelled the Radicals to submit to Tiso's authority. Subsequently, the tide turned against the Hlinka Guard, which lost ground as the clericals gained it. In the spring of 1942, Tiso regarded the situation as ripe for the complete ouster of Tuka, then prime minister. Again, German influence prevailed, and Tiso was unsuccessful. The Germans felt that they needed the HG Radicals (i.e., Tuka) to check Tiso's otherwise unlimited powers. Slovak Guardists also served Berlin's interests, fulfilling its requests and controlling the other camp. Nazi pressure compelled the president to retreat formally; this cost him considerable influence.

THE PARISH REPUBLIC

The year 1942 gave the clericals the opportunity to try to realize their social utopias. They failed, and the subdued society became unreliable, leading to the stagnation and gradual collapse of the regime the following year. Though it attained internal unity of opinion, the Party machinery nevertheless began to disintegrate. After Mussolini fell, the leadership of the country began losing its grip. Simultaneously Czechoslovak resistance increased. These two events coincided during August 1944, when the Slovak people rose and the National Uprising terminated the third stage of the Party's life.

In the fourth stage, from August 1944 to the liberation of the country by the Soviet Army, the Slovak government exercised only de jure power in close cooperation with its German masters. Factionalism in the Party revived briefly when the Hlinka Guard was reconstituted, and the clerical camp split again into Party veterans versus the Young Generation.

Perhaps the gravest shortcoming of the Hlinka's Slovak People's Party was its lack of internal unity, an imperfection which manifested itself in many circumstances. The HSL'S was a spokesman for heterogeneous elements united only by their opposition to the previous regime. The strong, authoritarian personality of Father Andrej Hlinka held these elements together and successfully led them. When Hlinka died, only a short time before Slovakia achieved autonomy and independence, the Party had no decisive guidance and only a limited opportunity for internal crystallization and for the selection of a new leader. While trying to achieve mastery of Slovakia, the Party was forced, at the same time, to endure the the internal contest of a three-way leadership battle between Tiso, Tuka, and Sidor. The consequences of this unfortunate situation became apparent after the proclamation of independence. The Ludaks were able to appear as guides of the state thanks only to the emergence of Tiso, who proved to be shrewd and decisive, ready to form all kinds of temporal coalitions to stay in power, and to German interference and pressure which also contributed to the consolidation of the center of the political power.

Dr. Tiso was not only Party leader (Vodca), but also its ideologist. Since it was not easy to find a common denominator for a polygenic society such as the HSL'S, Christian solidarism fitted Party ideology well. As it happened, however, Slovak life was not conducted in a manner compatible with solidarism.

A regime based on social demagogy, and preventing the free play of socioeconomic forces, could not reside within a democratic system. A strong government was required to enforce an aritifical structure, which intended to discriminate against and to suppress whole social strata. A successful corporatism depended on an authoritarian regime. Slovakia demon-

SUMMARY AND CONCLUSIONS

strated that an authoritarian Christian government could not even tolerate Christian social trade unions.; while the employers and businesses were left with their own institutions, rigid control was imposed on labor. "Christian solidarism" enabled Tiso and his friends to overcome the social heterogenity of the Hlinka Party.

The Slovak state had an outspoken authoritarian regime. The Ludak *connubium* which the Nazis enlarged the authoritarian approach inherent in corporatism, as members of the Nastup group interpreted and adjusted modern authoritarianism and totalitarianism to suit local conditions. They, together with the interpreters of solidarism, crossbred the two schools, resulting in the ideology of *Ľudové Slovensko, ľudactvo* (the so-called "People's Slovakia"), which included such modern elements as extreme and aggressive nationalism, and the single party system—in short, the characteristics of an extreme rightist dictatorship.

The Catholic Church had a cosmopolitan rather than nationalistic outlook. The Church required its believers to act in accordance with its doctrine of brotherhood and love. The hatred, encouraged by the Ludaks against the national minorities, and particularly against the Jews, and the racial approach toward the nature of the Slovak people had nothing in common with the teaching of the Gospel. Nor would anybody be able to discover in Catholic thought a proposal for the rule of a single party. But the Ludaks did use some Catholic doctrines to justify their authoritarian concepts. These were the general components of HSL'S ideology.

Slovakia's clerical fascism was nourished from local sources and developed according to the country's peculiarities. The priest was the traditional leader of the Catholics of upper Hungary, and remained so in Czechoslovakia. If the Slovak was passionate in his religious belief, so was the Party, in which religion played such an important role. Hlinka accused the Czechs, who wanted to raise the level of the long-neglected masses of Slovakia, of attempting to deprive the people of their religion.[2] Party theoretician Polakovič viewed religion as an accomplished fact and explained it as a mystical connection between the cosmos, the world, mankind, and the Slovaks. The Lord had created this nation, as it existed, because he expected the Slovaks to fulfill a mission.[3] Therefore, the Catholic religion and the church had an outstanding position in clerical fascist ideology, and the church acquired unprecedented influence over public life. To anchor this historical mission of the nation, and to prove its traditional Catholicism, historiography was manipulated accordingly. The "Slovak mission" added a new dimension to religion, as well as to Slovak nationalism. It supported the continuation of the regime which strove to fulfill the vocation.

THE PARISH REPUBLIC

The Hlinka Party was created during the first Czechoslovak Republic. The accomplishments of the Republic had been such that its former Hungarian subjects could not have dared dream of. Since it would have been improper to attack this state, the Ludaks instead pressed for "changes" on behalf of 'the "nation." The "nation" was not the community of Slovaks living in their own land, but a metaphysical term, a symbol detached from the material reality, and the Ludaks developed their doctrine of the state as a tool in the service of the nation's well-being. Though this interpretation was not an original one, it admirably fit the needs of a party in opposition, and would not be abandoned even during independence.

The Slovak Christian mission and the supremacy of the nation are essential to an understanding of Ludak clerical fascism. These phenomena could not have developed elsewhere and can only be explained against the background of Slovak history and tradition.

Slovakia's regime has already been described as authoritarian. The leadership certainly had intended to make it so. The wish to "guide" every aspect of life, the efforts to control all organizations, the gradual disappearance of voluntary activity, and the need for governmental or Party initiative to boost all kinds of activities were the signs of an expansive totalitarian rule. [4] However, these wishes were not realized. Instead, the Party's biggest success was to monopolize political institutions. Even in this area it had to share its power with the German Party and, to a lesser degree, with the Magyar Party. In other areas, the Party's position in the sphere of security was challenged by the Slovak Army, the Hlinka Guard, the semi-military ethnic German organization, and the Reich; the Catholic Church was the Party's main competitor in the social area, as well as in cultural activity, and foreign affairs were conducted under the close surveillance of the Wilhelmstrasse. While banning all competing political forces, the clerical camp discovered that the Hlinka Party was far from unified. Finally, the short time the Ludaks were in power did not allow them to reeducate the bulk of the nation. They remained a minority which was restricted from omnipotency by its own limited membership.

One of the factors preventing realization of Ludak aspirations was the existence of additional parties in the country, particularly the German one, which forced the Ludaks to act in ways contrary to their own wishes. The ethnic Germans, backed by the Reich, competed with the Ludaks as an autonomous element; they could act with impunity and on several occasions served as a rallying point for the opposition. Slovakia thus proved that a truly totalitarian government could not allow the existence of independent political forces and survive, especially if those forces were supported from outside.

Party efforts to enforce control and influence through physical power were shattered by the existence of an independent armed center. The army put obstacles in the way of the government, and was not under its political control. In the final analysis, the National Uprising demonstrated the Party's lack of adequate coercive power.

In spite of the great friendship among the political and religious organizations, the Catholic Church should be classified as *the* power which prevented complete *Gleichschaltung*. The church wanted to enforce *Gleichschaltung* of its own and the secular leaders were only too anxious to help her. In this way, however, parts of the population and of various organizations were freed from the Party's direct surveillance.

While unity of Slovaks was hailed as being above class and social differentiation, the introduction of religion into public life created new divisions. In many ways the church appeared as an obstacle to the totalitarian trends in the culture. Opinions of the clergy differed from those of the administration in several respects. Even those laymen who were ardent believers could not go along with the domination by priests. Nazi-minded intellectuals found it easier to communicate with anti-Nazis than with clericals. Thus, instead of a rigid dictatorship in the cultural sphere, chaos emerged, making possible the existence of non-Nazi intellectuals. Such trends could be observed in many fields. In spite of the proclaimed friendship and brotherhood of the regime with religion, which was demonstrated by the abolition of separation between the state and the church, the goals of the two institutions were not identical, and occasionally clashed.

Lack of unity was a progressive cancer to the Party. It would be wrong to compare the HG to the SA or the SS. While German semi-independent bodies recognized the supremacy of the Fuehrer, nothing of this kind existed in Slovakia. Tiso was never accepted as an omnipotent leader, and the HG Radicals posed an effective opposition. Even later, when common danger and need of mutual help drove the HG closer to the president, the relationship was more on a voluntary basis. The structure was not, in this case, based on a hierarchical principle. After all, Hitler held the actual supremacy in Slovakia, and both camps knew this very well. The HG Radicals tended to apply for help from the Reich through the ethnic Germans or directly. On several occasions they received positive replies. A regime which could not be sure of complete supremacy in its own territory and over its own subjects, could not impose its will on the population at large. Thus Nazi interference in Slovak internal affairs made Slovak totalitarianism an illusion. Although Berlin would have appreciated a full-fledged totalitarianism in Slovakia, it was caught in a dilemma: should it support a totalitarian regime which could endanger its supremacy in Slovakia, or should it prevent its establishment?

The battle between Tiso and Tuka further illustrates the lack of Party unity. Tuka skillfully presented his own grievances as political issues. Tiso understood the prime minister's intentions well and used the very political principles against Tuka which the prime minister claimed to defend. By copying totalitarian methods from Germany and using Nazi phraseology, the Vodca worked hard to overrule his adversary and to impose Party domination over the Hlinka Guard. In this case he succeeded, thanks in part to the fact of the Reich's bad luck in having its most faithful Slovaks of such a poor quality.

Finally, the lack of cadres and the hostility of a large part of the intelligentsia to the Party prevented more rigid regimentation of the country. The Party was in power too short a time to train a sufficient number of technicians and implant its creed deeply among the population. Only relatively little support came from the country, because of the unpopularity of the Party among people of ability and professional skill. Therefore, the regime was forced to modify its beliefs and goals to such an extent that they no longer resembled the original intentions.

When speaking of clerical fascist rule in Slovakia, it is necessary to differentiate between what was intended and what was accomplished. The intentions were to establish a kind of theocracy in modern totalitarian dress. Instead, the outcome was a clerical authoritarian system using, more or less efficiently, several totalitarian methods. Nevertheless, the Slovak statehood had an appeal to certain parts of the population. The shortcomings did not prevent those who would have liked to have seen more fulfillment of the design nor those who opposed it from liking their own state.

The example of Hlinka's Slovak People's Party proved that no uniformity existed among the movement of the extreme right. The HSL'S, like the Croatian *Ustasha* or the Rumanian Iron Guard, grew out of the peculiarities of its own country. In certain circumstances, there were no contradictions between the totalitarian right and religion; they were able to cooperate successfully. The study of such political phenomena as the Hlinka's Slovak People's Party may contribute to an understanding of other extremist movements. In its life, the Party and country reflected the varying fortunes of the Third Reich and of the Axis. Nevertheless, the political life of Slovakia during the Second World War demonstrated a great deal of independence and ingenuity, and has been discussed in these terms. In Slovakia, the HSL'S established a Parish Republic: a unique combination of a parochial state and an authoritarian structure.

NOTES

CHAPTER I

1. The majority of Protestants(Lutherans) in Slovakia are in the Evangelical Church of the Augsburg Confession.

2. According to the first Czechoslovak census of 1921, of 3,000,870 inhabitants of Slovakia, 650,547 were Magyars, 145,844 were Germans, 88,970 were Ruthenes and 73,628 were Jews. (Method Bella, "The Minorities in Slovakia," in R. W. Seton-Watson, ed., *Slovakia Then and Now,* (London, 1931, p. 337.) The same census found that 70.9 percent of Slovakia's population were Roman Catholic, 6.5 percent Greek Catholic (Uniates), 17.6 percent Protestant (various), and 4.5 percent Jewish. *Aperçu Statistique de la République Tchecoslovaque* (Prague, 1930), p. 10 (hereafter cited as *Aperçu Statistique*).

3. Bohemia-Moravia is settled by the members of the Czech language group.

4. Robert J. Kerner, ed., *Czechoslovakia,* (Berkeley, Calif., 1949), p. 85. Milán Ivanka, *Proti tajnej iredente* (Bratislava, 1928), pp. 4, 26, 27 (hereafter cited as *Proti*).

5. *Ibid.*, p. 26.

6. *Kresťanska Slovenská L'udová Strana.* From the word *L'udová* ("People's") was derived the nickname Ludak. In 1925 the Party officially took Hlinka's name as its title, and began using the initials HSL'S (*Hlinková Slovenská L'udová Strana*).

7. See Jozef Materna, *Minulost' a prítomnosť slovenských autonomistov* (Bratislava, 1923); Iván Dérer, *Slovenský vývoj a l' udacká zrada* (Prague, 1946), pp.348-345.

8. *Pravda* (Bratislava) 17 January 1947, p. 2, trial of Tiso, Mach, and Ďurčanský (hereafter cited as Trial T-M-D).

9. *Čas* (Bratislava), 8 January 1947, p. 2, Trial T-M-D.

10. Daniel Rapant, "O dobréj a zléj propagande" [About a good and bad propaganda], *Slovák* (Bratislava), 7 March 1944, p. 4.

11. Konštantín Čulen, *Boj Slovákov o slobodu* (Bratislava, 1944), pp.161, 162 (hereafter cited as *Political Parties*).

12. L. G. Faguľa, *Andrej Hlinka* (Bratislava, 1943), p. 78.

13. Chmelař, *Political Parties*, p. 60.

14. Juraj Krámer, *Iredenta a separatizmus v slovenskéj politike* (Bratislava 1957), pp. 62-74, 131-151, and copies of document nos. 2, 3, 9, 12, 19, 20, 21 (hereafter cited as *Iredenta*).

15. *Aperçu Statistique*, p. 265.

16. *Statistisches Jahrbuch der Čechoslovakischen Republik* (Prague, 1936), pp. 269-270.

17. Jozef Lettrich, *History of Modern Slovakia* (New York, 1955), pp. 80, 81 (hereafter cited as *Modern Slovakia*.

18. Jörg K. Hoensch, *Die Slowakei und Hitlers Ostpolitik* (Koeln-Graz, 1965), p. 34 (hereafter cited as *Die Slowakei*).

19. U.S. Legation, Prague, Correspondence, 800 Slovakia, 1938 (Department of

NOTES

State, Washington, D.C.), Vol. IX, dispatch, Wilbur J. Carr to the secretary of state, June 10, 1938 (hereafter cited as U.S. Legation, Correspondence, 800.).

20. František Vnuk, "Slovakia's Six Eventful Months (October 1938-March 1939)," *Slovak Studies, Historica*, 4 (1964) p. 23 (hereafter cited as *Slovakia's Six Months*)."

21. Ľubomír Lipták, "K česko-slovenským vzťahom," *Historický časopis SAV* 15 (1961): 563. Cf. Milan Strhan, "Živnostenská banka na Slovensku 1918-1938," *Historický časopis SAV* 15 (1963): 177-218.

22. It was assumed that the Slovaks were branches of one Czechoslovak nation. This erroneous concept caused much harm to the common life of these kindred people. Living under the threat of a German minority, three-million strong, the Czechs could not afford any Slovak regional autonomy, otherwise they would have to grant the same rights to the Sudeten lands. A nation of eight million Czechoslovaks facing three million Germans was far better off than six million Czechs facing three million Germans. Hence many a Slovak felt that he had to pay the price of the national survival of the Czechs, presumably by extinction of his own particularity.

23. Of forty Slovak deputies in the Revolutionary National Assembly, the first Czechoslovak parliament, only six had any parliamentary experience whatsoever, Compare this with the 55 Czech veterans of the Viennese Imperial Council out of 214 deputies. For these numbers, as well as for details about the unfortunate activity of the Slovak deputies before the first Czechoslovak elections of 1920, see Ladislav Lipscher, "Klub slovenskych poslancov v rokoch 1918-1920," *Historický časopis SAV* 16 (1968): 133-168. For the persecution of the Slovak national and political life in Hungary, see the classic by R. W. Seton-Watson, *Racial Problems in Hungary* (London, 1908).

24. The lack of understanding of political realities was demonstrated in the demands to nominate Slovak bishops, including Hlinka, instead of the Magyars. Inasmuch as such a step was a prerogative of the Pope, and furthermore, since there was tension between Prague and the Vatican, the central government could not possibly comply with the Slovak plea. See Juraj Krámer, *Slovenské automistické hnutie v rokoch 1918-1929* (Bratislava, 1962), pp. 21-35.

25. In the first program of the Christian Slovak People's Party, accepted on 19 December 1918, about 70 percent of the request had economic and social connotations, including such demands as land reform, taxation of luxury goods, progressive income tax, and free medical care for the poor. *Boj Slovákov*, pp. 154-156.

CHAPTER II

1. Hoensch, *Die Slowakei*, p. 103.
2. Čulen, *Boj Slovákov*, p. 213.
3. Vnuk, *Slovakia's Six Months*, p. 32
4. Čulen, *Boj Slovákov*, pp. 218-221.
5. Ladislav Lipscher *Ľudácká autonomia, Iluzie a skutočnosť* (Bratislava 1957), pp. 131, 141 (hereafter cited as *Ľudacka autonomia*).
6. Vladimír Záděra, *Děset let parlamentní retrospektivy, 1935-1945* (Prague, 1948), p. 76 (hereafter cited as *Děset let*).
7. Vnuk, *Slovakia's Six Months*, p. 31.
8. Záděra, *Děset let*, p. 76.
9. Hoensch, *Die Slowakei*, p. 135.

NOTES TO CHAPTER II

10. These two men were similar in many ways. Both had leftist leanings. Indeed, there were rumors that Murgaš had fought on behalf of the Magyar Soviet Republic. Mach preserved relations with some leftist intellectuals to the end of his political career. Both were radical nationalists; both had literary aspirations, and both were engaged in journalism. They resembled each other in ambition and in the unscrupulous methods which they used in obtaining their goals. Mach was the more intelligent, the more idealistically minded, and was somewhat more effective as an organizer than was his counterpart. Competition between these two was to affect the Hlinka Guard for a long time.

11. Vnuk, *Slovakia's Six Months*, pp. 30, 80; *Ľudácka autonomia*, pp. 148-153.

12. *Ľudácka autonomia*, p. 168.

13. *Ibid.*, p. 157; Vnuk, *Slovakia's Six Months*, p. 80; Lettrich, *Modern Slovakia*, p. 114.

14. Lettrich, *Modern Slovakia*, p. 114.

15. Jozef Paučo, ed., *Dr. Jozef Tiso o sebe* (Passaic, N.J., 1952), p. 43 (hereafter cited as *Dr. Tiso*); *idem.*, *Tak sme sa poznali* (Middletown, Pa., 1967), p. 233 (hereafter cited as *Sa poznali*).

16. U.S. Legation, Correspondence, 800, Vol. III, dispatch, George F. Kennan to the secretary of state, 4 January, 1939.

17. *Ibid.*, p. 22.

18. U.S. Legation, Correspondence, 800, Vol. IX, dispatch, George F. Kennan to the secretary of state, 8 November, 1938.

19. *Die Slowakei*, pp. 130, 131; *Sa poznali*, pp. 172, 180.

20. Lipscher, *Ľudácka autonomia*, p. 274; Paučo, *Sa poznali*, pp. 177-201; *Trials of the Major War Criminals before the International Nuremberg Military Tribunals* (Nuremberg, 1946-1949), Vol. XXXI, pp. 118-119, document PS-2790 (hereafter cited as *IMT*).

21. George F. Kannan, *From Prague After Munich* (Princeton, N.J., 1968), p. 7. excerpts from a personal letter of 8 December 1938 (hereafter cited as *From Prague*).

22. Vnuk, *Slovakia's Six Months*, pp. 96, 100, 101.

23. Hoensch, *Die Slowakei*, p. 211; "Československá otázka v diplomatických spisoch horthyovského Maďarska 1936-1938 do Mnichova)" [The Czechoslovak question in the diplomatic documents of Horthy's Hungary (1936-1938 until Munich)], *Historický časopis SAV* 15 (1967): 110-134 (hereafter cited as "Horthy's Hungary").

24. "Horthy's Hungary."

25. Hoensch, *Die Slowakei*, p; 211.

26. *Ibid.*, p. 212.

27. *Ibid.*, p. 221-224.

28. Záděra, *Děset let*, p. 41.

29. *Ibid.*, pp. 77, 78.

30. U.S. Legation, Correspondence, 800, Vol. IX, dispatch, George F. Kennan to the secretary of state, 8 November 1938.

31. U.S. Legation, Correspondence, 811.11, Vol. III, dispatch, Wilbur J. Carr to the secretary of state, 25 January 1939.

32. Vnuk, *Slovakia's Six Months*, p. 66; Lipscher, *Ľudácka autonomia*, p. 25; Ivan Kamenec, *Židovská otázka a spôsoby jej riešenia v čase autonomie Slovenska* [The Jewish question and its solutions during the period of Slovakia's autonomy], Manuscript, Bratislava, 1968, p. 26.

33. T-120 R-1141, 442375, report, von Druffel to the Foreign Office, 26 January 1939. German documents are arranged by the collection number (T), roll of the microfilm (R), and frame number.

34. Kennan, *From Prague*, p. 18, report on conditions in Slovakia, written in January 1939; Zadera, *Deset let*, p. 76.

35. Hoensch, *Die Slowakei*, p. 237.

36. *Ibid.*, pp. 228, 233; Vnuk, *Slovakia's Six Months*, p. 102.

37. Hoensch, *Die Slowakei*, p. 226; Lipscher, *L'udácka autonomia*, p. 274.

38. The previous secretary, Dr. Martin Sokol, one of the leading Moderates, claimed in a trial after World War II that his dismissal came to his attention via radio while he was walking in the streets of Bratislava. [*Pravda*((Bratislava), 13 February 1947, p. 1]. Dr. Kirschbaum denied this charge in letters to me, of 11 September and 20 October 1965,

39. U.S. Military Tribunals, Nuremberg v. Ernest von Weizsaecker *et.al.*, Document NG-5356, telegram, von Druffel to German Foreign Office, 10 March 1939 (cited hereafter as *USMT*).

40. Hoensch, *Die Slowakei*, pp. 222-225.

41. Pauco, *Sa poznali*, pp. 172, 178. Dr. Josef Pauco belonged to the Nástup group, and as such partipated in the meetings with Tuka. His reminiscences, published in the above mentioned book, should be used with extreme care because of their bias and bombastic character.

42. Hoensch, *Die Slowakei*, pp. 222-225.

43. Josef Danáš, *L'udácky separatizmus a hitlerovské Nemecko* (Bratislava, 1963), p. 122; Bohuslav Graca, *14 marec 1939* (Bratislava,1959), pp. 93, 94.

44. Karol Sidor, *O vzniku slovenského štátu* (Bratislava, 1945), p. 7 (hereafter cited as *O vzniku*).

45. *Ibid.*, p. 15.

46. *Ibid.*, p. 17.

47. *Documents on German Foreign Policy, 1918-1945*, Ser. D, Vol. IV (Washington D.C.), pp. 243-245 (hereafter cited as *DGFP*).

48. Ferdinand Ďurčanský, "Mit Tiso bei Hitler. Die Entstehung der slowakischen Republik," *Politische Studien* 7 (1956): 1-10; Pauco, *Dr. Tiso*, pp. 185, 186; *USMT*, Official Record, Case No. 11, Vol. 31, p. 12910.

49. Joseph M. Kirschbaum, "Facts and Events Behind the Scenes of Slovakia's Declaration of Independence," *Slovakia* 9 (March 1959): 3.

50. *Čas* (Bratislava), 17 January 1947, pp. 1,2. Witness of Čatloš in trial T-M-D. Tiso's public pronouncements during and after the war are contradictory, and should be understood in light of the objective circumstances. Living in the Nazi orbit Tiso must have spoken publicly about "Hitler's generosity" in establishing the Slovak state. Nor would an accused defendant praise the Fuehrer in 1947. Therefore second hand witnesses are more reliable in this case than Tiso's own statements. Cf. Čulen, *Po Svätoplukovi*, pp. 235-249,

51. USMT, Official Record, Case No. 11, Vol. 31, p. 12910.

52. Hitler complained that Sidor described himself as "a soldier of Prague," evidently a mistake. Cf. *Supra* p. 38f.

53. Vnuk, *Slovakia's Six Months*, p. 120.

CHAPTER III

1. *IMT*, British Exhibit, D-572, dispatch, Consul P. Pares to Mr. Newton, 20 March 1939.

2. T-175, R-518, 9385708, memorandum of an unknown SS *Sturmbannfuehrer*, 23 March, 1939. On the day of its founding, the territory of the Slovak state was 37,284 square kilometers and its population amounted to 2,656,426. This number included 2,260,894 Slovaks, 128,347 Germans, 77,488 Czechs, 6,966 Ukrainians (or Russians), 57,897 Magyars, 28,763 Jews, 26,265 Gypsies, 3,848 Poles, and 3,818 others. By religion, the population was divided into 1,956,233 Roman 183,736 Greek Catholics, 412,584 Protestants of various denominations (including 387,677 Lutherans or Evangelics), 85,045 Jewish people, 5,778 Greek Orthodox, and 9,994 without a confession. [Štátny štatistický úrad, *Územie a obyvateľstvo Slovenskej republiky* (Bratislava, 1939), pp. 10-16].

3. *IMT*, document R-100. Information given by the Fuehrer to the chief of the German High Command, 25 March 1939.

4. *Documents on German Foreign Policy*, Ser. D, Vol. VI, p. 70, document No. 61, memorandum by the foreign minister, 21 March 1939 (cited hereafter as *DGFP*).

5. For the German and Hungarian interference in the life of the new state, see particularly Hoensch, *Die Slowakei*, pp. 315-356, and František Vnuk, "The German Zone of Protection in Slovakia, A Study in Slovak-German Relations in March August 1939," *Slovakia* 9 (1959): 7-23. See also Hans Dress, "Die Stellung des sogenannten slowakischen Staats im Rahmen der faschistischen Neuordnung Europas (1939-1945)," *Zeitschrift fuer Geschichtswissenschaft* 15 (1967): 659-670; and Jörg K. Hoensch, *Der ungarische Revisionismus und die Zerschlagung der Tschechoslowakei* (Tuebingen, 1967), pp. 269-289.

6. On 18 April 1939.

7. T-120, R-336, 248210, telegram, the German consul in Bratislava to the German Foreign Office, 6 June 1939; T-120, R-1141, 44204-05, dispatch, the German consul in Bratislava to the German Foreign Office, 16 June 1939.

8. T-77, R-878, 5626052, meeting in the Office of Army Intelligence, 30 May 1939; 5625965, *ibid.*, 14 June 1939.

9. T-120, R-1141. 442396, telegram, the German consul in Bratislava to the German Foreign Office, 18 May 1939. Cf. Paučo, *Tak sme sa poznali*, p. 784.

10. T-120, R-114, 443404-05, telegram, the German consul in Bratislava to the German Foreign Office, 16 May 1939.

11. T-120, R-280, 208111, memorandum, Hans Bernard—German minister in Slovakia, 25 June 1940.

12. T-175, R-524, 9394712, memorandum, SS *Unterscharfuehrer* Dr. Ofczarek, SD branch, Vienna, 25 September 1939.

13. T-175, R-524, 9394649, report, SS *Unterscharfuehrer* Dr. Ofczarek, SD branch, Vienna, 31 October 1939.

14. T-175, R-531, 9394649, report, SS *Obersturmfuehrer* Dr. Chlan to the Supreme Office for Security of the Reich (*Reichsicherheithauptamt*, RSHA) 31 October 1939.

15. T-175, 9383976-884, report, SS *Obersturmfuehrer* Dr. Chlan to RSHA, 6 October 1939.

16. Several clues reveal that the Moderates had misgivings about Čatloš' role in the participation in the war against Poland.

17. U.S. Legation Correspondence, 800, Vol. III, dispatch, George F. Kennan to the secretary of state, 14 January 1939.

18. Dr. Gesa Szuello, previously a member of Prague's parliament, was well acquainted with Slovakia's concerns. T-120, R-1139, 443100, dispatch, the German minister to Budapest to the German Foreign Office, 3 May 1940.

19. T-77, R-879, 5626994, *Grenzbote* (Bratislava), 30 July 1940, p. 1.

20. Joseph A. Mikus, *Slovakia, A Political History 1918-1950* (Milwaukee, Wis., 1963), pp. 134, 135 (hereafter cited as *Slovakia*); T-120, R-1318, D498579-597, report from an unknown provenance, 19 June 1940.

21. Vnuk, *Slovakia's Six Months*, p. 133; Lettrich, *History*, p. 163; Mikus, *Slovakia*, p. 130; Ferdinand Beer *et. al.*, *Dejinná križovatka* (Bratislava, 1964), p. 65 (hereafter cited as *Dejinna križovatka*).

22. T-120, R-1301, 479847, dispatch, the German minister in Bratislava to the German Foreign Office, 3 July 1940; Mikus, *Slovakia*, p. 130; Lettrich, *History*, pp. 163, 164,

23. T-120, R-1279, 484564, report of a secret agent, 19 May 1939.

24. T-77, R-878, 5626113-118, dispatch, Bernard to the German Foreign Office, 10 January 1940. "Dr. Ďurčanský had the steady impression that his task was to defend Slovakia's life and interests. Thoughts of the need of 'defense' dominated all his deeds."

25. *DGFP*, Ser. D., Vol. IX, p. 16, no. 2, report, Wilhelm Keppler, 18 March

26. T-120, R-280, 208111, memorandum, German Minister Bernard, 25 June 1940.

27. T-175, R-524, 9394684-85, report, SS *Obersturmfuehrer* Dr. Chlan to RSHA 18 October 1939.

28. Štefan Polakovič, *K žakladom Slovenskeho štátu* (Bratislava, 1939).

29. *Slovák* (Bratislava) 30 March 1940, p. 1.

30. Joseph M. Kirschbaum, *Náš boj o samostatnost'* (Cleveland, Ohio, The Slovak Institute, 1958), p. 103.

31. Karol Sidor, *Šest' rokov pri Vatikane* (Scranton, Pa.: Obrana Press, 1947), p. 26 (hereafter cited as *Šest' rokov*).

32. *Nástup* (Bratislava), 1940, no. 1, p. 1; *Gardista* (Žilina), 6 January 1940, p. 1; *Slovák* (Bratislava), 28 January 1940, p. 4; Sidor, *Šest' rokov*, p. 89; T-175, R-516, 7383167, report of the Guardist Ctibor Pokorný about his discussion with several leaders of the Nástup group. Dr. Kirschbaum, although consulted several times, failed to provide additional details.

33. T-77, R-878, 5626203, dispatch, German military attaché to German High Command (*Oberkommando der Wermacht*, OKW), 9 January 1940.

34. T-175, R-518, 9386464, report of SD agent Kuno Goldbach, 3 March 1940; R-533, 9404922, report, SD branch Brueck-on-the-Leitha to SD branch Vienna, 10 February 1940; T-77, R-878, 5626108, report of an agent of the Army Intelligence of February 1940.

35. T-175, R-517, 9384325, report, SD branch Brueck-on-the-Leitha to SD branch Vienna, 15 January 1940.

36. The reports of one Eduard Frauenfeld, who came to organize the Slovak Office for Propaganda in April 1940, but found internal politics more interesting, were essential in the formation of German attitude.

37. T-120, R-1307, 489799, report, Wuester to von Ribbentrop, 22 January 1940.

38. *Slovák* (Bratislava), 25 January 1940, p. 1.

39. T-120, R-326, 248346, report, SD branch Bratislava, 27 February 1940.

40. T-120, R-1307, 489758, dispatch, German Minister Bernard to the German Foreign Office, 23 February 1940.

41. This took place during a session of the government on 19 April 1940, T-120, R-1450, D588115, report, Frauenfeld to the German Foreign Office, 7 May 1940.

42. *Ibid.*

43. T-120, R-336, 248378, telegram, German Minister Bernard to the German Foreign Office, 21 May 1940.

44. T-120, R-1307, 489825-28, secret dispatch, Bernard to the German Foreign Office, 21 May 1940.

45. T-77, R-878, 5626643, dispatch, German military attaché to OKW, 22 May 1940.

46. *Čas* (Bratislava), 21 August 1946, p. 3, trial of Otomar Kubala.

47. T-120, R-336, 248379, telegram, Bernard to the German Foreign Office, 22 May 1940; 248383, memorandum of Under State Secretary Woermann, 23 May 1940.

48. T-120, R-1307, 489825−28, secret dispatch, Bernard to the German Foreign Office, 21 May 1940; cf. T-120, R-1450, D588211-215, Information Service of the German Foreign Office, 27 May 1940; T-175, R-524, 939492-408, report, SS *Untersturmfuehrer* Urbartke, 13 June 1940.

49. T-120, R-336, 248387, telegram, Bernard to the German Foreign Office, 24 May 1940.

50. T-120, R-336, 248398, dispatch, Ringelmann to Woermann, 30 May 1940.

51. T-120, R-280, 208145, telegram, the German Embassy to the German Foreign Office, 1 June 1940.

52. T-120, R-336, 248394, memorandum to the files, Under State Secretary Woermann, 25 May 1940.

53. T-120, R 280, 208155, dispatch, the chamber of the Reich's foreign minister to the state secretary, 28 May 1940.

54. *DGFP*, Ser. D., Vol. IX, p. 537, memorandum, von Killinger to von Ribbentrop, 9 June 1940.

55. T-175, R-541, 9415049-51, memorandum to the files, SS *Oberscharfuehrer* Pamer, 2 December 1940; T-77, R-879, 5627012, memorandum to the files, Army Intelligence, 11 July 1940.

56. *DGFP*, Ser. D., Vol. IX, No. 40, p. 537, memorandum, von Killinger to von Ribbentrop, 9 June 1940.

57. The editor-in-chief of *Grenzebote*, the mouthpiece of the German party.

58. T-175, R-524, 9394392-408, report, SS *Untersturmfuehrer* Urbartke, 13 June 1940.

59. T-77, R-879, 5627621, dispatch, the chief of the German Military Mission in Slovakia to OKW, 17 January 1941. Cf. L'ubomír Lipták, "Príprava a priebeh Salzburgských rokovaní roku 1940 medzi predstaviteľmi Nemecka a Slovenskeho štátu," *Historický Časopis* 13 (1965): 357 (hereafter cited as *Príprava a priebeh*).

60. Beer *et. al., Dejinna križovatka*, p. 65.

61. U.S. Department of State, 740.011 European War 1939/4928, telegram, Montgomery to the secretary of state, 30 July 1940; *Čas* (Bratislava), 3 August 1946, p. 1, trial of Tuka.

62. *Slovák* (Bratislava), 17 March 1939, p. 1.

146

NOTES

63. František Vnuk, "Dr. Jozef Kirschbaum ako generalný tajomník Ľudovej strany," in Jozef Pauco, ed., *Pätdesiatnik Dr. Jozef Kirschbaum* (Middletown, Pa., 1963) pp. 52-57 (hereafter cited as Pauco, *Pätdesiatnik*).

64. *Slovák* (Bratislava), 29 September 1939, p. 3, an interview with Kirschbaum.

65. *Ibid.*, 3 December 1939, p. 3.

66. *Nástup* (Bratislava), 15 April 1939, pp. 93, 94.

67. Jozef Kirschbaum, "Strana a Štát" [The party and the state], *Nástup* (Bratislava), 15 September 1939. I am indebted to Dr. Kirschbaum, who provided me with a copy of the article.

68. *Slovák* (Bratislava), 15 April 1939, p. 1.

69. The Catholic Action, a frame organization for the Catholic laity.

70. *Slovák* (Bratislava), 24 May 1939, p. 3.

71. *Ibid.*, 20 May 1939, p. 1; 1 June 1939, p. 3; 3 October 1939, p. 5.

72. *Ibid.*, 3 October 1939, p. 5.

73. Juraj Gajdoš-Breza, *Dni obrody* (Prešov: Nakl. J. Stanovského, 1940), p. 75.

74. *Collection of Slovak Laws* No. 245/1939.

75. *Ibid.*, No. 185/1939.

76. Solidarism is the social system whose governing principle is the solidarity of the community to its members and of the members to their community [Gustav Gundlach, "Solidarismus," *Staatslexikon, im Auftrage der Goerresgesellschaft*, 5 vols. (Freiburg i.B.: Herder & Co., 1926-1931), IV: 1612]. Martin Vietor, "Prispevok k objasneniu fašistického charakteru tkzv. slovenského štátu," *Historický časopis* (April 1960): 483 (hereafter cited as *Príspevok*); cf. T-135, R-518, 9385778.

77. Vietor, *Príspevok*, p. 484.

78. *Ibid.*; cf. Karol Mederly, "Zásadné smernice slovenskej ústavy" [The basic directives of the Slovak constitution], *Slovák* (Bratislava), 7 June 1939, p. 4.

79. *Slovák* (Bratislava), 23 May 1939, p. 4; *Pät' rokov slovenského školstva* (Bratislava: Štátne nakladateľstvo, 1944), p. 510 (hereafter cited as *Pät' rokov*).

80. Vietor, *Príspevok*, p. 483; cf. *Slovák* (Bratislava), 7 June 1939, p. 3 and 25 July 1939, pp. 4, 5. Indeed, there was nothing new in this idea; Tiso had already proclaimed it during the period of Slovakian autonomy.

81. T 175, R-518, 938561, report, SD branch Vienna to RSHA. The letter was mailed on 24 September 1939.

82. Juraj Kráľ, "Pohľad na socialnu politiku Slovenskej republiky," in Mikuláš Šprinc, ed., *Slovenská Republika, 1939-1949*, (Scranton, Pa.: J.J. Lach, 1949), p. 141 (hereafter cited as *Slovenská Republika*).

83. Sidor, "Šesť rokov," pp. 60-63. T-120, R-2198, 338151-338156, dispatch, Ludin to the German Foreign Office, 4 February 1941; Secretaire d'état de Sa Sainteté, *Actes et Documentes du Saint Siège relatifs à la Seconde Guerre Mondiale*, Vol. IV (Città del Vaticano, 1967), p. 115, Document No. 51, Footnote No. 2 (hereafter cited as *Actes et Documentes*). Cf. *Actes et Documentes* Vol. IV, p. 102, Document No. 40, p. 316; Document No. 212, p. 507; Document No 368, pp. 597, 598.

84. Juraj Kráľ, "Pohľad na socialnú politiku slovenskej republiky," *Slovenská Republika*, p. 142,

85. See the proclamations of tavern keepers, *Slovák* (Bratislava) 25 May 1940, p. 4; of architects, *ibid.*, 1 May 1940, p. 9; of railroad workers, *ibid.*, 13 June 1940, p. 3.

86. T-81, R-524, 5295170, a copy of letter, the state secretary for affairs of the German Ethnic Group to the legislative branch of government's presidium, 22 December 1939.

87. Letter, Dr. Kirschbaum to me, 11 September 1965.

88. T-175, R-514, 9380705, dispatch, SD branch Vienna to RSHA, 10 October 1940. *Schuschniggiade* was the nickname used by the Nazis for the regime in Austria between 1934 and 1938. They labeled the corporate system in Slovakia similarly.

89. Pavel Kukliš-Kunovský, *Ako je na Slovenska?* (Pittsburgh, Pa.: 1940), p. 28. *Slovák* (Bratislava) 21 June 1939, p. 3.

90. *Ibid.,* p. 22; T-175, R-514, 9381061, report of an SD agent, 5 June 1939.

91. Kukliš-Kunovský, *Ako je*, p. 4.

92. *Slovák* (Bratislava), 23 May 1940. p. 1.

93. T-175, R-514, 9381069, dispatch, SS *Hauptsturmfuehrer* Dr. Chlan, of SD branch Vienna, to RSHA; the letter was sent on 14 March 1940. Tuka had hated the Protestant bishops since his trial in 1929.

94. Among other reasons, it was because of a dispute about a paragraph on the marriage of divorcées. T-175, R-514, 9381178, German investigation of Bishop Osuský, November 1944. Cf. Vilém Prečan, *Slovenské Národné Povstanie, Dokumenty*, (Bratislava : Vydavateľstvo politickej literatury, 1965), Document No. 55, report on Slovak internal affairs, p. 185 (hereafter cited as *Dokumenty*).

CHAPTER IV

1. In the city of Trnava, on August 13, Tiso said, "We do say frankly, we do not apply for your votes. . . . We say, thank God that there are no more parties here." *Slovák*; (Bratislava) 15 August 1939, p. 5.

2. "Kritika spojujúca" [The unifying criticism], *ibid.*, 28 January 1940, p. 1, editorial.

3. T-120, R-336, 248516, Tiso's address to the Party secretaries, 20 January Cf. Polakovič, *Tisová nauka*, pp. 222, 333.

4. Joseph N. Moody, ed., *Church and Society; Catholic Social and Political Thought and Movements, 1789-1950* (New York: Arts, Inc., 1953), p. 506 (hereafter cited as *Church and Society*).

5. For Austria, see Diamant, *Austrian Catholics*, pp. 193, 194.

6. T-120, R-1450, 588242-54, list of the members of parliament.

7. T-81, R-527, 5294541, newspaper clipping, *Frankfurter Zeitung*, 8 August, 1940.

8. T-175, R-531, 9402998-99, list of the leaders of regional organizations, 15 October 1940.

9. Vladko Maček, *In the Struggle for Freedom* (New York: Robert Speller, 1957), pp. 233-236. Ivan Mestrović, *Uspomene na politicke ljude i dogadjaje* (Buenos Aires: Knižnica Hrvatske Revije, 1960), p. 318.

10. "Čo urobili katolickí kňazi za slovenský národ a štát" [What have the Catholic priests done for the Slovak nation and state], *Katolické Noviny* (Bratislava), 7 November 1940, p. 2; "Vysviacka biskupa Škrábika v Nitre" [Annointment of the Bishop Škrábik in the city of Nitra] , *Slovák* (Bratislava), 19 September 1939, p. 2.

11. *Čas* (Bratislava), 8 January 1947, p. 2; cf. Kmeťko's address to the elected president, in the name of the Collegium, *Slovák*,(Bratislava), 15 November 1939, p. 2. p. 2.

12. T-120, R-1318, D498510, Tiso to the pro-Nazi Dutch priest, van den Bergh; dispatch, RSHA to the German Foreign Office, 9 September 1940; T-175, R-524, 9394551, report, SD branch Vienna to RSHA, 10 December 1940.

NOTES

13. T-175, R-514, 9381509, the case of Viliam Ries; T-175, R-533, 9404923, the case of Fraňo Boháč.

14. Letter, Dr. Kirschbaum to me, 11 September 1965.

15. U.S. Legation, Prague, 1938, Vol. IX, Correspondence 800, dipatch, Wilbur J. Carr to the secretary of state, 7 September 1938. Cf. T-175, R-524, 9394816, SD description of Tiso's personality, no date, approximately December 1938.

16. Jozef Paučo, ed., *Dr. Tiso o sebe; obhajobná reč pred tzv. Narodny'm súdom v Bratislave, 17 a 18 marca 1947* (Passaic, N.J.: Slovenský Katolický Sokol, 1952), p. 101 (hereafter cited as *Josef Tiso*).

17. Konštantín Čulen, *Po Svätoplukovi druhá naša hlava* (Middletown, Pa.: Prvá katolická jednota, 1947), p. 32 (hereafter cited as *Po Svätoplukovi*); Milan S. Ďurica, *Die slowakische Politik 1938-1939 im Lichte der Staatslehre Tisos* (Bonn, 1967), p. 20.

18. Čulen, *Po Svätoplukovi*, p. 46.

19. At his trial, Tiso attributed his appreciation of military terminology to his study of the work of St. Ignatius Loyola during his training for the priesthood. (Paučo, *Jozef Tiso*, p. 194). However, General Čatloš testified about the president's manifested interest in military matters [*Čas* (Bratislava), 17 January 1947, p. 2] and Tiso's sorrow that the Czechoslovak army did not recognize his military rank from World War I [*Čas* (Bratislava), 16 January 1947, p. 2, trial T-M-D]. Cf. *Čas* (Bratislava), 5 December 1946, trial T-M-D.

20. "Tiso . . . we personally considered him as a priest who was willing to permit everything—a hypocrite, and the worst you could expect. He did everything against his preaching, and we, our so-called 'working group' [the clandestine leadership of Slovakian Jewry], did not even consider him too much, because any time something we tried to achieve through Tiso it did not work . . . because nothing happened, what we tried to achieve through the connection with Frieder [Dr. Armin Frieder, the chief rabbi of the Slovak state], and Tiso, we completely dropped it." The Hebrew University of Jerusalem, The Institute of Contemporary Jewry, *Oral History Division Catalogue No. 2*). The interview was held in the English language.

Ludak emigrants in the West often argue that Tiso supported the persecuted Jews as he himself claimed during the trial.

21. T-175, R-119, 2643751-66, report, SS *Gruppenfuehrer* Gottlob Berger to Himmler, 19 February 1943; *USMT* Nuremberg, Official Record, Case No. 11, Vol. XXVIII, p. 11514. A testimony of Ernst Woermann, under state secretary of the German Foreign Office.

22. *Pravda* (Bratislava), 22 January 1947, p. 2, trial T-M-D.

23. T-175, R-524, 9394782, Karamasin's oral report in the Institute for Germans Living Abroad (*Deutsches Auslands-Institut*) of Stuttgart, June 1939. Cf. T-77, R-878, 5626203, dispatch, German military attache to OKW, 9 January 1940; *DGFP* Ser. D, Vol. XI, p. 693, No. 393, protocol on Tuka's visit to von Ribbentrop, 26 October 1940; T-120, R-341, 249643, personal telegram, Ludin to von Ribbentrop, recommendation for granting of Germany's highest decoration to Tiso, 5 August 1942.

24. Paučo, *Jozef Tiso*, pp. 40-42; cf. *Čas* (Bratislava), 4 March 1947, p. 2, trial T-M-D. Witness of Sivak.

25. *Pravda* (Bratislava), 11 March 1947, p. 1, trial T-M-D; cf. T-175, R-524, 9394407, report SS *Untersturmfuehrer* Urbartke to SD branch Vienna 13 May 1940 (Tiso to Slovak journalists Tido J. Gašpar and Aladar Kočiš); T-120, R-1138, D-49857, SD description of F. Ďurčanský, contained in the files of German Foreign Office, recalls Tiso's enthusiasm while speaking about his meetings with Hitler, as opposed to the coolness of the Slovak minister for foreign affairs.

26. I did not find any proof that Tiso ever seriously tried to contact the Allies. Dr. Jozef Lettrich, wartime leader of the pro-Western underground in Slovakia, confirmed this impression during a personal discussion in October 1965 in Washington, D.C.

27. T-175. R-524, 939420, report, SD branch Prague to RSHA, 27 March 1943.

28. T-175, R-533, 9405291, report, SD branch Vienna to RSHA, 2 May 1941; cf. "Politicke publikácie" [Political publications] , Slovák(Bratislava), 24 March 1941, p. 3.

29. Milan S. Ďurica, "Dr. Joseph Tiso and the Jewish Problem in Slovakia," Slovakia 7 (September-December, 1957): 4 (hereafter cited as Dr. Joseph Tiso).

30. Ibid.

31. N. S. Timasheff, "Totalitarianism, Despotism, Dictatorship," Totalitarianism, ed. Carl J. Friedrich (Cambridge, Mass.: Harvard University Press, 1954), p. 46. Hereafter cited as Timasheff, Totalitarianism.

32. Carl J. Friedrich and Zbigniew K. Brzezinski, Totalitarian Dictatorship and Autocracy (New York: Frederick A. Praeger, 1961), p. 3. Cited hereafter as Friedrich and Brzezinski, Totalitarian Dictatorship and Autocracy.

33. Ibid.

34. "A society is totalitarian if the number of the auxiliary functions of the state is so high that all human activities are regulated by it," Timasheff, Totalitarianism, p. 43.

35. Friedrich and Brzezinski, Totalitarian Dictatorship and Autocracy, p. 18.

36. Ďurica, Dr. Joseph Tiso, p. 4.

37. Slovak term for Fuehrer, used since 14 March 1939. Slovák (Bratislava), 14 March 1939, p. 2.

38. Collection of Slovak Laws No. 225/1941 granted the president the exclusive right to appoint new members of parliament to fill vacated places. Law No. 105/1943 enlarged the president's prerogatives in the state council. Law No. 165/1943 set the last day of the present house at 31 December 1946.

39. Ibid. No. 215/1942.

40. Ibid., No. 70/1942.

41. Edward L. Delaney, "I was in Slovakia," Slovakia 2 (March 1952): 32; USMT, Nuremberg, Case No. 11, Official Record, Vol. XXI, p. 13088, testimony of Dr. Edmund Veesenmayer.

42. Cf. Friedrich and Brzezinski, Totalitarian Dictatorship and Autocracy, p. 26.

43. Čas (Bratislava) 4 November 1947, p. 1, trial of the members of the Slovak government.

44. Supra, pp. 13, 26.

45. T-175, R-520, 9388820, letter of the ethnic German representative in the Association of Distilleries to the German party, 24 November 1940; cf. ibid., pp. 36-37.

46. Turček and Danihel contra Grenzbote; Slovák (Bratislava), 19 January 1941, p. 3, HG Radicals and German Party accused the leading Ludak businessmen of enriching themselves and supporting the Jews.

47. Speaking about the elections of 1925, a Slovak pro-Ludak author did not count communist voters as Slovaks. Joseph A. Mikuš, Slovakia, A Political History, 1918-1950 (Milwaukee, Wis.: Marquette University Press, 1963), p. 20 (hereafter cited as Slovakia).

48. Slovák (Bratislava), 26 May 1940, p. 1, editorial; Gardista (Žilina), 27 November 1943, p. 3.

49. Husák, Svedectvo, p. 73.

50. T-175, R-531, 9303066, address to the Party's secretaries, 20 January 1941.

51. T-175, R-533, 9405005-009.

52. T-175, R-518, 9385985-89. This memorandum does not bear a date, but an analysis leads to the conclusion that it was prepared no later than October 1941 and not before the end of 1940.

53. Infra, Chapter VI.

54. Čas (Bratislava), 7 December 1946, pp. 1, 2, trial T-M-D, 12 December 1946, pp. 1, 2. Cf. letter from Dr. Kirschbaum to me, 20 October 1965.

55. T-175, R-518, 9385991, report of SD agent Bloechl, 4 March 1943.

56. T-175, R-524, 9394597, report, SS Untersturmfuehrer Urbartke to SD branch Vienna, 16 April 1942.

57. T-175, R-516, 9383835, protocol from a meeting of the High Command of the HG, 8 August 1939, delivered by Murgaš to SD.

58. T-120, R-1307, 489799, report, Wuester to von Ribbentrop, 22 January 1940; cf. ibid., 9 August 1940.

59. T-175, R-518, 9386775-82. dispatch, SD branch Vienna to RSHA, sent on 21 August 1944.

60. Pravda (Bratislava), 5 June 1946, p. 3. Cf. T-175, R-119, 2643767, note to the files, SS Obersturmbannfuehrer V. Nageler, 10 February 1943.

61. T-175, R-516, 9383627, note to the files, SS Hauptsturmfuehrer Dr. Bohrsch, 3 December 1943.

62. Most books describing the modern history of Slovakia deal with Tuka. There is much material in the proceedings of the National Court in Bratislava between the years 1946 and 1948. Besides Tuka's own publications and speeches, the German documents contribute much to our knowledge. However, no adequate study has been done concerning Tuka to date.

63. Infra, p. 73.

64. I read Tuka's Die Rechtssysteme (Berlin, A. Limbach, 1941); an abstract of his first work, A szabadsag [The liberty], in Jan E. Bor [Ernest Zaťko], Vojtech Tuka, úvod do zivota a diela (Turčiansky Sv. Martin: Kompas, 1940); and several articles.

65. Vojtech Tuka, úvod do života a diela, pp. 41-42

66. Ibid., p. 130.

67. Tuka, Die Rechtssysteme, p. 121.

68. Ibid., p. 160.

69. Ibid.

70. Ibid., p. 40.

71. Ibid., pp. 41-42.

72. Ibid, p. 118.

73. Ibid, p. 121.

74. Ivan Dérer, Slovenský vývoj a ľudacká zrada (Praha: Kvasnička a Hampl, 1946), p. 57. Tuka missed Hitler and met only a few of his followers.

75. Ibid. p. 58. The storm troopers were called Rodobrana.

76. Slovák (Bratislava) 2 December 1939, p. 4.

77. Tuka explained the imprisonment as a Czech vendetta for his demand for an independent Slovakia, and not punishment for high treason.

78. Slovák (Bratislava) 2 December 1939, p. 4.

79. Grenzbote (Bratislava) 31 July 1940, p. 1.

80. The German minister, Ludin, testified about Tuka: "While talking to him, I had unpleasant feelings that he was using Slovakia as a pedestal for his own personality," Pravda (Bratislava), 4 March 1947, p. 2, trial T-M-D.

81. *DGFP*, Ser. D, Vol. XI, p. 693, No. 393; protocol of meeting of von Ribbentrop and Tuka, 26 November 1940.

82. *Ibid.*

83. T-120, R-341, 249425, memo from Weizsaecker, Hungarian minister in Berlin, Sztojay to Weizsaecker, 11 October 1941; Sztojay complained of the Slovak anti-Hungarian propaganda.

84. Husák, *Svedectvo*, p. 164.

85. T-77, R-879, 5627801, dispatch, the German military mission in Slovakia to German Army Intelligence, 28 November 1941; Field Marshall Keitel decided, because of the war needs, not to insist on the removal of the legionnaires.

86. Dr. Kirschbaum told me in a discussion in Toronto, Canada, in April 1965, "We did not like to get orders from these hoodlums [*chrapúni*] such as Murgaš or Múťhanský [another dubious character prominent in HG]."

87. T-175, R-518, 9386526, *Grenzbote* (Bratislava), 20 November 1940.

88. *Slovák* (Bratislava), 3 December 1939, p. 3, Kirschbaum eulogized Codreanu in a student meeting. Professor Ďurčanský in a letter (3 December 1965) to me denied any relation with the Iron Guard.

89. This is similar to the Croatian *Ustasha*. However, while *Ustasha* was a violent, terroristic organization, the Nástup group, in spite of organization pogroms and occasional disorderly behavior in streets, was basically restrained.

90. Rosie Goldschmidt Waldeck, *Athene Palace* (New York: Robert M. McBride and Co., 1942), p. 300.

91. *Wer war Matuš Černak?* (Munich: Akademischer Verlag, 1955), p. 45.

92. *Slovák* (Bratislava), 10 March 1940, p. 3. In his address, Kirschbaum attacked the expansion of the ethnic Germans. Cf. Ľubomír Lipták, "Prípava a priebeh salzbursky'ch rokovaní roku 1940 medzi predstaviteľmi Nemecka a Slovenského štátu," *Historický časopis* 13 (1965): 343-345.

93. Waldeck, *Athene Palace*, p. 298.

94. *Ibid.*, p. 298.

95. *Slovák* (Bratislava) 29 September 1939, p. 4.

96. Alojz Miškovič, "Problémy nášho životného priestoru" [The problems of our living space], *Slovák* (Bratislava) 22 May 1940, p. 4. Jan Svetoň, *Slováci v europskom zahraničí* (Bratislava: Slovenská akademia vied a umeni, 1943).

97. Joseph M. Kirschbaum, "The Politics of Hlinka's Party in the Slovak Republic," *Slovakia* 1 (May 1951): 45. Cf. Konštantín Čulen, "Zdravica zaslužilému," in Paučo, *Pätdesiatnik*, p. 16.

98. "O novú duchovnú tvár slovenskej mládeže" [For a new spiritual face of the Slovak youth], *Slovák* (Bratislava) 9 July 1939, p. 1, editorial.

99. T-77, R-878, 56226049, note to the files of the German Army Intelligence, 1 June 1939.

100. Slovakia received territories which had been taken by Warsaw after Munich, and additional space held by Poland since the ambassadors' award of the so-called "Javorina dispute" in 1920. However, Slovak statesmen rejected Hitler's offers of pure Polish districts, such as Zakopané.

101. "Free masons" was another popular epithet for this group.

102. *Slovák* (Bratislava), 29 September 1940, p. 4; Gejza Medrický, "Poslanie HSLS v slovenskom národe" [The mission of HSLS in the Slovak nation], *Slovák* (Bratislava), 14 March 1941, p. 17. Cf. *Die Slowakische Republik: Rueckblick auf den Freibeitskampf und politisches Profil*, Blau Bucherei, Vol. III (Bratislava, Verlag Tatra, 1940), p. 64.

NOTES

103. Moreover, in the economy, they could not get rid even of Jews, especially when the Jews had influential friends and money with which to bribe.

104. Usually they enrolled in the Party.

105. Jozef Tiso, "Duch ľudácky sa nesie Slovenskom" [The Ludak spirit is moving upon the face of Slovakia], *Organizačné Zvesti* 3 (November 1942): 1.

106. One should remember that the need for armed forces stemmed from Slovakia's hostile attitude toward Hungary.

107. In Czechoslovakia, a teacher was usually an officer-reservist. Anton Rašla, *Civilista v armáde* (Bratislava, 1967), pp. 70-79. General Rašla gives an excellent account of the political and social atmosphere prevailing in the Slovak Army.

108. T-77, R-881, 5629599, memorandum, Čatloš to OKW, 8 January 1944. Prečan, *Dokumenty*, Document No. 6, report on Slovakia's internal affairs, 8 March 1943, pp. 61, 61; and No. 33, manifesto of the Slovak soldiers who joined the Soviet Army, 29 December 1943, pp. 127-131.

109. Some 800 young Jews owe their survival to the Army, which rejected the idea of having the enlisted men deported to Poland. Many of them later sacrificed their lives for the freedom of Czechoslovakia [The Hebrew University of Jerusalem, the Institute of Contemporary Jewry, Oral History Division, Catalogue No. 1 (Jerusalem, 1963), Interview No. 77].

CHAPTER V

1. T-120, R-280, 208085, internal report of German Newsservice, no. 212, 30 July 1940; T-77, R-87a, 5626991, report, German military attaché to OKW, 20 July 1940. Cf. letter of Dr. J. Kirschbaum to me, 11 September 1965.

2. T-77, R-87a, 5626991, report, the German military attaché to OKW, 30 July 1940.

3. T-120, R-1301, 479876, report von Killinger to the German Foreign Office, 19 August 1940.

4. Waldeck, *Athene Palace*, p. 229.

5. T-120, R-1301, 479876, report, von Killinger to the German Foreign Office, 19 August 1940.

6. T-580, R-877, *Berliner Dokumente, Slowakische Politik zu Anfang 1941.*

7. T 120, R-336, 248815, guidance for meeting of von Ribbentrop and Tuka, prepared by Under State Secretary Woermann on 21 November 1940. Cf. with the draft of the same guidance, prepared by Ambassador Wuester on 11 November 1940. T-120, R-280, 208064.

8. T-175, R-518, 9386487, dispatch, Nageler to RSHA, 1 October 1940.

9. *Ibid*

10. T-175, R-119, 2643751-60, report, Nageler to Himmler, 19 February 1943. Cf. with the report of Dr. Herbert Buchtala on racial examination (*militaeraerztliche Untersuchungen in rassischer Hinsicht*) of the Hlinka Guardists, 18 October 1940. (T-175, R-518, 9386497).

11. T-175, R-530, 9401405, report, SD Branch Vienna to RSHA, 28 May 1941; T-120, R-2198, 338763-338184, Ludin to the German Foreign Office, 28 January 1941.

12. T-120, R-1307, 489923, newsservice of the German Foreign Office, 9 August 1940.

13. Vietor, *Príspevok*, p. 488.

NOTES TO CHAPTER V

14. *Slovák* (Bratislava), 18 January 1941, p. 1, editorial: "Ľudové Slovensko."

15. Sidor, *Šesť rokov*, p. 293. Letter, Dr. Kirschbaum to me, 11 September 1965.

16. Vietor, *Príspevok*, p. 488.

17. T-120, R-336, 24894, telegram, von Killinger to the German Foreign Office, 27 October 1940, 248494, telegram, von Killinger to the German Foreign Office, 30 October 1940. Cf. Tuka's letter to Tiso, Tuka's trial, *Čas* (Bratislava), 5 November 1946, p. 1.

18. Konštantín Čulen, "Snem a vláda," *Slovenská Republika*, p. 119.

19. Vietor, *Príspevok*, p. 489. Cf. T-120, R-2198, 338157, 336158, dispatch, Ludin to the German Foreign Office, 5 February 1941.

20. Vietor, *Príspevok*, pp. 486-487.

21. Konštantín Čulen, "Snem a vláda," *Slovenská Republika*, p. 267. Cf. *Čas* (Bratislava), 15 February 1947, p. 4, trial Sokol and others.

22. Sidor, *Šesť rokov*, pp. 120-122. Cf. T-580, R-66, *Berliner Dokumente, Slowakische Politik zu Anfang 1941*.

23. T-77, R-879, 562603-05, report, the German Military Mission in Slovakia to OKW, 2 November 1940.

24. T-120, R-1301, 479882, dispatch, von Killinger to the German Foreign Office, 19 August 1940.

25. T-175, R-518, 9386437, dispatch, SS *Obersturmbannfuehrer* Dr. Boehrsch to RSHA, 20 October 1944.

26. *Čas* (Bratislava), 16 January 1947, p. 2.

27. *Ibid.*, 18 December 1946, p. 1, trial T-M-D; *Pravda* (Bratislava), 17 December 1946, p. 2; cf. T-175, R-541, 9415134, dispatch, SD branch Vienna to RSHA, 2 May 1944.

28. *Čas* (Bratislava) 20 August 1946, p. 3, trial of Otomar Kubala.

29. T-175, R-524, 9394535, report, SD on the internal situation in Slovakia, 29 November 1940.

30. T-580, R-66, *Berliner Dokumente, Slowakische Politik in Mitte Januar 1941*.

31. T-77, R-879, 5627575-583, report, German military attaché in Slovakia to OKW, 22 January 1941; cf. T-120, R-336, 248530, Woermann's note to files, 24 January 1941.

32. T-175, R-528, 9398002, memo to the files, SD branch Vienna, 29 January 1941.

33. T-77, R-879, 5627575-583, report, German military attaché in Bratislava to OKW, 22 January 1941; cf. T-175, R-531, 9403075, report, the German adviser for HSĽS, Hans Pehm, 23 January 1941; *Slovák* (Bratislava), 31 January 1941, p. 1, editorial: "Odpadol balast," and p. 4, Mach's speech on 28 January 1941 in the city of Banska Bystrica.

34. T-120, R-336, 248533, telegram, Endroes to Luther, 31 January 1941. Ludin later criticized this telegram bitterly.

35. *Ibid.*

36. T-580, R-66, *Berliner Dokumente, Der Reichsorganisationsleiter der NSDAP, Hauptschulungamt*, Munich, March 31, 1941; *Slowakische Politik*.

37. *Ibid.*

38. T-175, R-524, 9394462. An SD agent quotes a high-ranking official of the German Foreign Office, Gunther Altenburg.

39. For a better understanding of the German policy in the *Suedostraum*, I owe much to Prof. Miklos Nagy-Talavera of Chico State University, Chico, California, whose knowledge of Rumanian and Hungarian affairs was an invaluable help.

NOTES

40. T-175, R-530, 9401397, report, Gestapo Vienna, 15 February 1941; cf. R-514, 9380713, report, SD agent to SD branch Vienna, received here on 25 October 1940.

41. T-175, R-75, 2593697, report, SS *Obergruppenfuehrer* Gottlob Berger to Himmler, 2 May 1941.

42. *Ibid.*

43. T-175, R-518, 9386576, report, SD branch Vienna to RSHA, 2 May 1941.

44. T-81, R-550, 5324460. According to *Grenzbote* (Bratislava), 29 July 1941, p. 2, Čatloš stated that Slovakia was ready to send an army division to help the Croats in their fight against the Serbs.

45. T-77, R-879, 5627384-85, dispatch, the German military attaché to OKW, 2 May 1941. This proposal has to be understood in connection with the Hungary-Slovakia animosity.

46. T-120, R-336, 248625, telegram, Ludin to von Ribbentrop's Chancellery, 21 June 1941.

47. T-77, R-879, 5627266, dispatch, the German military attaché to OKW, 24 June 1941.

48. Paučo, *Jozef Tiso* , p. 272. Cf. *Čas* (Bratislava), 8 August 1946, p. 2, Tuka's trial.

49. T-120, R-783, 377024, the Spanish minister in Germany to Weizsaecker, 4 October 1941. The Pope's indirect message to the Fuehrer, praising the Germans for fighting Bolshevism.

50. *Collection of Slovak Laws*, No. 198/1941, the first and second paragraphs of the *Collection* give a broader definition of a Jew and Jewish cross-breed than the German law. (Cf. *Reichgesetz Blatt* No. 125, 14 November 1935. *Erste Verordnung zum Reichsbuergergesetz*, paragraphs 22-5.)

51. Oddo, *Slovakia and Its People*, pp. 289-290; Sidor, *Šest' rokov*, pp. 135-136.

52. T-66, R-580, *Berliner Dokumente, Slowakische Politik*, 28 October 1941: "It has to be stated that President Tiso did not by and large (*im grossen und ganzen*) put any obstacles in the way of the enactment of the Law." Cf. *Pravda* (Bratislava), 13 February 1947, p. 2, testimony of Sokol at Tiso's trial. All Ludak emigrant writers today claim that the president had misgivings about the law. Caustic comments about Tiso's role found in SD documents may support the emigrants' claims (T-175, R-518, 9385991, note to file, 4 March 1943).

53. T-120, R-4744, K403503, telegram, Ludin to the German Foreign Office, 20 February 1942.

54. T-120, R-4744, K4035504, telegram, Ludin to the German Foreign Office, 20 February 1942.

55. After the war, opinions split on this matter. Slovaks such as Tiso, Tuka, and Mach claimed heavy pressure; the Germans (Weizsaecker and Woermann) denied it. Among the Germans, only Ludin confirmed its existence, yet SS *Hauptsturmfuehrer* Dieter Wisliceny, the "adviser" for the Jewish question, was firm and said several times at Nuremberg and in Bratislava that the Slovaks presented their Jews voluntarily. A telegram of Ludin to the German Foreign Office of 6 April 1942 (T-120, R-4744, K4035512), dealing with the deportation of *all* 89,000 Slovak Jews, clearly stated that "The Slovak government agreed to the deportation of all Jews from Slovakia without any German pressure . . ." (*Die Slowakische Regierung hat sich mit Abtransport aller Juden aus der Slowakei ohne jeden Druck einverstanden erklaert*). One has to accept Wisliceny's testimony, who appeared very

cooperative during all his interrogations (Office of U.S. Chief of Counsel for Prosecution of Axis Criminality, Interrogation Division Summary, Interrogations of Dieter Wisliceny, Nuremberg, 15 and 17 November 1945). The payment of RM 500 to the Nazi authorities for every Jew they agreed "to care for" is evidence of Slovak eagerness to have the local Jewry deported. (Moreshet Archives, Israel, the Slovak Collection, duplicates from the State Slovak Archives, hereafter cited as *Moreshet Archives—ŠSÚA*, SSR 370-43, verbal note of the German Embassy to the Slovak Ministry for Foreign Affairs, 29 April 1942; verbal note of the Slovak Ministry for Foreign Affairs to the German Embassy, 23 May 1942.)

56. Head of Department No. 14, Slovak Ministry of the Interior, in which responsibility for the "Jewish question" was centered.

57. *Čas* (Bratislava), 4 July 1946, p. 2; *Pravda* (Bratislava), 4 July 1946, p. 2, the trial of Dr. Vašek.

58. *Čas* (Bratislava), 21 December 1946, p. 2, trial of T-M-D.

59. *Supra* pp. 53-54.

60. *Čas* (Bratislava), 5 March 1947, p. 2; *Pravda* (Bratislava), 4 March 1947, p. 2.

61. T-120, R-1279, 484832, *Europapress-Informationen* 31 March 1942.

62. There were more reasons for this decision, not connected directly to the Party's struggle, such as greed for Jewish property, religious and social hatred, the wish to appear as pioneers in solution of the "Jewish problem" and others.

63. T-120, R-341, 249540, note to files, Martin Luther, head of the "Germany" section in Berlin's Foreign Office, 29 March 1942.

64. T-120. R-4744, K403534-38, dispatch, the German Embassy in Bratislava to the German Foreign Office, 24 April 1942.

65. T-120, R-4744, K403510, dispatch, Ludin to the German Foreign Office, 1 April 1942.

66. T-120, R-4744, K403512, telegram, Ludin to the German Foreign Office, 6 April 1942; T-175, R-514, 9380794, report, SS *Untersturmfuehrer* Urbartke to SD branch Vienna, 25 March 1942.

67. Between March and October 1942, some 57,000 Jews were expelled from Slovakia.

When the transports departed in the spring of 1942, gas chambers were not yet operative. The deportees from Slovakia built the first gas chamber in Auschwitz. However, inhuman persecutions were occurring and the *Einsatzgruppen* was at work, and the president knew it, from three sources: the Slovak soldiers in the east, the Church, and miscellaneous sources. As early as January 1942, General Turanec told him about the extermination by the SS of Jewish women and their children who were working in the field kitchen of the Slovak officers on the eastern front. The Slovak officers witnessed the "work" of an *Einsatzgruppe* and informed the president. [*Čas* (Bratislava) 21 February 1947, p. 3; *Pravda* (Bratislava) 20 February 1947.pp. 1, 2; General Turanec]. Cf. Čatloš' testimony, *Pravda* (Bratislava), 15 January 1947, p. 2; *Čas* (Bratislava), 16 January 1947, p. 2; and Sokol's testimony, *Čas*(Bratislava), 15 February 1947, p. 4. The brother of Tiso's secretary, Dr. Ivan Murin, told a German officer on 2 February 1945, that the Slovak soldiers deserted in the east because they could not stand German cruelties toward Russians and Jews (T-175, R-514, 9380903-905, a report signed by Amtkov; cf. T-77, R-881, 5629599, memorandum, Čatloš to OKW, 8 January 1944).

The Vatican informed Tiso in July 1942 about the fate of the deportees in the Lublin region (Ďurica, *Dr. Joseph Tiso*, p. 12). However, the last transport left Slovakia in October 1942 [Michael Dow Weismandel, *Min Ha-metsar* (New York: Emunah, 1960), p. 61].

156

NOTES

Slovakia's Jews had already gotten some understanding of the Nazi conduct in 1941 from Jewish refugees from Poland (Oral History Division, Catalogue No. 2, No. 121, symposium with leaders of Slovak Zionist youth movements, transcript, p. 19). Therefore, the Jewish leadership expected the worst (Oral History Division, Catalogue No. 2, No. 122, sumposium with some of the leaders of Slovak Jewry, transcript, p. 14; cf. Weismandel, *Min Ha-metsar*, p. 24). On 6 March 1942, the rabbis of Slovakia sent a collective letter to Tiso and the bishops. It included the following: "The law can describe the deportation by any name and may give any reason; the fact remains that it means physical extermination of Slovak Jewry" [Livia Rothkirchen, *Hurban Jahadut Slovakia* (Jerusalem: Yad Washem, 1960), p. 130]. In his trial, Tiso denied knowledge of this appeal. The counsel then submitted to the court the letter. It bore a remark *ad acta*. Only when presented with the documents did Tiso admit seeing them [*Pravda* (Bratislava), 12 February 1947, p. 2]. Also, in July 1942, 632 so-called "asocial elements" of the ethnic Germans were shipped to Germany in accordance with euthanasia [L'ubomir Lipták, "Role of the German Minority in Slovakia in the Years of the Second World War," *Studia Historica Slovaca* 1 (1963): 167). Slovak bishops tried to stop this deportation, while contributing, according to Karmasin, to the wave of rumors that the victims "are to be cooked to soap" [Václav Král, ed., *Die Deutschen in der Tschechoslowakei, 1933-1947* (Prague: Nakladateľstvo Československé Akademie Věd, 1964), p. 480, document no. 388, Karmasin to Himmler, 28 July 1942]. (There is much more evidence about the supplying of information to Tiso and his circle during the spring and summer of 1942, which can be omitted here.)

For circumstances which led to the termination of the deportation, see Neumann, *Im Schatten*; Weismandel, *Min ha-metsar*; Rothkirchen, *Hurban*; Livia Rothkirchen, "The Policy of the Vatican and the Holocaust in 'Independent' Slovakia," *Yad Washem Studies* 6 (1966): 23-45, etc.

68. T-175, R-523, 9392343, report on a discussion between Mach and Vavra, 31 March 1942. This report reflects the connection between the Jewish question and the conflict.

69. T-77, R-778, 5504498-502, report, German military attaché to OKW, 8 April 1942.

70. T-120, R-336, 249553-55, telegram, von Ribbentrop to Ludin, 8 April 1942.

71. T-77, R-778, 5504382, dispatch, German military attaché to OKW, 30 March 1942; cf. T-120. R-341, 249548, telegram, Ludin to the German Foreign Office, 2 April 1942.

72. T-120, R-2198, E085863-E085872, dispatch, Ludin to the German Foreign Office, 19 April 1942. Cf. E085873-E085875, Ludin's letter to Tiso, 8 April 1942.

73. T-120, R-341, 249562, telegram, Ludin to the German Foreign Office, 10 April 1942.

74. T-120, R-2188, E0858663-E085872, dispatch, Ludin to the German Foreign Office, 19 April 1942.

75. *Supra*, p. 70.

76. Jozef Tiso, "Zimná pomoc je zimná práca" [The winter relief is winter work]. *Organizačné Zvesti* (Bratislava, 11 October 1941), p. 1. Cf. Franz Neumann, *Behemoth* (New York: Oxford University Press, 1942), p. 82.

77. "Na okraj dňa: Treba usmerniť spolkovú činnosť na vidieku" [It is necessary to guide the social activities of the countryside], *Slovák* (Bratislava), 27 February 1941, p. 4.

NOTES TO CHAPTER V

78. *Organizačné Zvesti* (Bratislava) 3 (March 1942): 2. Cf. with actual cases: T-175, R-531, 9403227, report, SD agent to SD branch Vienna, 7 July 1944.

79. *Organizačné Zvesti* (Bratislava) 2 (December 1940): 6; 2 (February 1941): 2 (October 1941): 9.

80. *Slovák* (Bratislava) 15 August 1939, p. 6.

81 Men who aryanized Jewish property (aryanizers).

82. *Organizačné Zvesti* (Bratislava) 2 (January 1941): 6; 3 (January 1942): 3; 4 (January 1943): 2.

83. T-580, R-66, *Berliner Dokumente, Slowakische politik.* Cf. *Slovák* (Bratislava) 18 January 1941. editorial: "L'udove hnutie."

84. *Slovák* (Bratislava) 14 March 1941.

85. *Ibid.*, 1 (November 1940): 11; 1 (December 1940): 6; 2 (March 1941): 11.

86. T-175, R-531, 9403141, report of Hans Pehm, 31 January 1941.

87. T-175, R-531, 9403141, report of Hans Pehm, 31 January 1941.

CHAPTER VI

1. Štefan Polakovič, "Ideová stránka slovenského nacionalného socialismu" [The ideological structure of the Slovak national socialism], *Slovák* (Bratislava), 2 February 1941, p. 1, editorial.

2. Štefan Polakovič, *Tisová nauka* (Bratislava, Štátne nakladateľstvo, 1944), pp. 217-219; see also p. 278.

3. *Ibid.*, p. 276.

4. *Ibid.*, p. 118.

5. *Slovák* (Bratislava), 19 September 1939, p. 2, Tiso in the city of Nitra.

6. Polakovič, *Tisová nauka*, pp. 33, 37, 284.

7. *Ibid.*, pp. 33, 262, 266.

8. *Ibid.*, pp. 27, 28.

9. Štefan Polakovič, *Náš duch* (Bratislava, Hlavné veliteľstvo HM, 1943), p. 10.

10. Compare the similar attitude of the leaders of the *Juntas de Ofensiva Nacional-Sindicalista* in Spain. "Unlike Hitler, Ledesma and Onesimo Redondo gave a place to the Catholic religion, which they named as embodying the 'racial' tradition of the Spaniards. Catholicism meant indeed the same to Redondo as Aryan blood did to Hitler." Hugh Thomas, *The Spanish Civil War* (Harmondsworth, England: Penguin Books, 1965), p. 98.

11. Karol Koerper, "Na deň smrti Sv. Metoda" [On the anniversary of the death of St. Methodius], *Slovák* (Bratislava), 6 April 1940, p. 3.

12. Svätopluk (870-894) ruled the Empire of Great Moravia.

13. František Hrušovský, "Naväzujeme na slovenskú historiu," *Slovák* (Bratislava) 26 October 1939, p. 3.

14. "Myšlienka koruny svätoplukovskej"[The idea of Svätopluk's crown], *Slovák* (Bratislava), 31 March 1940, editorial. Cf. Polakovič, *Tisová nauka*, p. 85.

15. "Vzrast silou tradicie" [They grow with the help of tradition], *Slovák* (Bratislava), 7 April 1940, p. 1, editorial.

16. T-81, R-527, 5294179, Jozef Paučo, "Svätopluk a našá dnešná politická orientacia" [Svätopluk and our contemporary political orientation], *Nástup* (Bratislava), 15 May 1940.

17. *Slovák* (Bratislava) 16 October 1939, p. 3. Maroš Madačov, "O smysle slovenských dejin" [On the essence of the Slovak history], 1 May 1940, p. 8; *Gardista*

158

NOTES

(Žilina), 17 October 1940, p. 2; cf. Plakovič, *Tisová nauka*, p. 18.
  18. *Slovák* (Bratislava). 5 December 1939, p. 1.
  19. *Ibid.*, 2 December 1939, p. 4.
  20. Polakovič, *Tisová nauka*, p. 180.
  21. *Slovák* (Bratislava), 1 May 1940, p. 8.
  22. T-175, R-517, 9384326, report of an SD agent, 7 November 1941; Professor of Theology Dr. Ladislav Hanuš, addressing a meeting of HG appointees for culture. According to the informer, the lecture was prepared in understanding with Tiso, the Papal Nuncio, bishops, and others.
  23. *Slovák* (Bratislava) 5 February 1944, p. 1, editorial: "The Sources of National Pride"; Polakovič, *Tisová nauka*, p. 38; cf. Paučo, *Jozef Tiso*, p. 324.
  24. Compare with Croatia, another German satellite. The Catholic faith was in the very soul of *Ustasha* nationalism. The *Ustashi* never forgot to repeat Croatia's mission to serve as a bulwark of Christianity, *ante murale Christianitatis*.
  25. Polakovič, *Náš duch*, p. 188. Cf. *idem.*, *Tisová nauka*, p. 211.
  26. František Hrušovský, *Slovenské dejiny* (Turčiansky Sv. Martin: Matica Slovenská, 1939). This work by the Slovak court historian represented the synthesis of the Ludak image of Slovak history. When published for the first time, the book was greeted by a journalist as "the national catechism." *Slovák* (Bratislava) 10 October 1939, editorial.
  27. Polakovič, *Tisová nauka*, p. 340.
  28. *Collection of Slovak Laws*, No. 185/1939, Section 79 (2), Cf. Polakovič, *Tisová nauka*, pp. 321, 331, 332.
  29. Polakovič, *Tisová nauka*, p. 118.
  30. *Ibid.*, p. 118.
  31. *Ibid.*, p. 119.
  32. *Ibid.*, p. 340.
  33. *Ibid.*, pp. 372, 373, 382.
  34. *Ibid.*, p. 115.
  35. "Arizovať je národnou povinosťou" [Aryanization is a patriotic obligation]. *Slovák* (Bratislava), 7 February 1941, p. 6.
  36. Štefan Polakovič, *Slovenský národný socializmus* (Bratislava: Nakladateľstvo HSLS, 1941), p. 264.
  37. *Idem.*, *Náš duch*, p. 122.
  38. Joseph N. Moody, ed., *Church and Society, Catholic Social and Political Thought and Movements, 1789-1950* (New York: Arts, Inc., 1953), pp. 366-434.
  39. *Ibid.*, pp. 501-508.
  40. *Ibid.*, pp. 506-507.
  41. Ignác Gašparec, "Hospodárstvo v stavovskom štáte," *Slovák* (Bratislava), 11 August 1939, p. 8; cf. *Slovák* (Bratislava) 20 August 1939, p. 3; T-120, R-1307, 489862-863, dispatch, the German Legation in Bratislava to the German Foreign Office, 3 June 1940.
  42. Polakovič, *Tisová nauka*, p. 124. Cf. Diamant, *Austrian Catholics*, p. 253. Diamant quotes Austrian Monsignor Ignatius Seipel, who raised the slogan "democracy of true responsibility, in place of democracy of mere voting."
  43. Polakovič, *Tisová nauka*, p. 124.
  44. Ján Rekem, "O principe autority" [On the principle of authority], *Slovak* (Bratislava), 28 October 1939, p. 7. Cf. *Slovák* (Bratislava) 23 April 1942, editorial.
  45. *Slovák* (Bratislava), 15 August 1939, p. 5. Cf. Polakovič, *Tisová nauka*, pp. 161, 164.

46. Compare with Fascist Italy where "The dictatorship is the necessary rack and screw of the corporate system; all the rest is subordinate machinery." Hermann Finer, *Mussolini's Italy* (New York: The Universal Library, 1965), p. 499.

47. T-81. R-550, 5324374, Tiso's speech in the city of Považská Bystrica, on 9 September 1941.

48. Rommen, *The State*, p. 500.

49. Diamant, *Austrian Catholics*, p. 193.

50. Polakovič, *Tisová nauka*, p. 23.

51. *Ibid.*, p. 378.

52. *Ibid.*, p. 22.

53. *Ibid.*, p. 16.

54. *Ibid.*, p. 23.

55. *Ibid.*, pp.286, 287.

56. *Ibid.*, p. 142.

57. *Slovák* (Bratislava), 26 November 1942, p. 1.

58. Polakovič, *Náš duch*, p. 182.

59. *Idem.*, *Tisová nauka*, pp. 157, 158; see also p. 81, where Tiso requested totalitarian administration (*totalitné zariadenie*) of a state, in opposition to a totalitarian state (*totalita statu*).

60. Gejza Medrický, "Poslanie HSL'S v slovenskom národe" [The mission of HSL'S in the Slovak nation], *Slovák* (Bratislava), 14 March 1941, p. 17.

61. *Slovák* (Bratislava), 8 September 1942, p. 6.

62. *Čas* (Bratislava), 12 March 1947, p. 3. Trial T-M-D.

63. *Slovák* (Bratislava), 30 September 1942, p. 2.

64. Polakovič, *Tisová nauka*, p. 38.

65. *Ibid.*, p. 54.

66. Anton Jurovský, *Slovenská národná povaha*, Vol. II of *Slovenská vlastiveda* (5 vols.; Bratislava, Slovenská akademia vied a umeni, 1943-1948), pp. 11, 394.

67. Paul, *Grundzuege*, p. 20.

68. *Ibid.*

69. T-81, R-668, 5476384, note to file on a discussion of an unidentified employe of the Institute for Germans Living Abroad (*Deutsches Ausland-Institut*, DAI) in Stuttgart, with the SD agent, journalist Kuno Goldbach, 15 November 1938. Cf. T-175, R-518, 9383228, note to files of an unidentified SD agent, 22 January 1941.

70. U.S. Legation, Prague, 811.11, Vol. III, dispatch, George F. Kennan to the secretary of state, 12 March 1939; *Slovák* (Bratislava), 15 March 1939, p. 5.

71. "Najvyšši zákon doby" [The supreme law of the time] *Slovák* (Bratislava), 23 March 1941, p. 1, editorial. There are good reasons to believe that this article was published, if not with Tiso's approval, at least with his knowledge. Dr. Jozef Paučo, the editor of *Slovák* wrote: "Usually Dr. Tiso gave no directions how any article was to be written. On the other hand, however, he willingly read the more delicate articles before they went to print." Joseph Paučo, "I was Editor of President Tiso's Newspaper," *Slovakia* 7 (March 1957): 11.

72. An American visitor in Slovakia during World War II recorded a most extreme attempt to cut relations with the Slavs. He was told that the Slovaks originally were not Slavs but Celts. [Edward L. Delaney, "I was in Slovakia," *Slovakia* 2, (March 1952): 29.] Similar notions occurred in Croatia also. The Croats were proclaimed to be descendants of Goths. [Richard Patee, *The Case of Cardinal Aloysius Stepinac* (Milwaukee, Wis.: The Bruce Publishing Company, 1953), p. 129.]

160

NOTES

73. T-77, R-880, 5628889, *Grenzbote* (Bratislava), 5 May 1943, Tiso's address to new army officers.

74. Polakovič, *Náš duch*, p. 129; Johann O. Petreas, *Nová Europa a Slovensko* (Bratislava: Tatra, 1942), p. 64. Cf. Jozef Paučo, "Svätopluk a naša dnešná politická orientacia," *Nástup* (Bratislava) 15 May 1940, p. 1l.

75. Polakovič, *Tisovd nauka*, p. 187.

76. *Ibid*, p. 127; cf. Jan Buban, *Najhlbší koreň vlastnenia* (Trnava: Spolok sv. Vojtecha, 1942), p. 172.

77. Valentin Beniak, *Sebe i Vám* (Ružomberok: Obroda, 1943), p. 128; Ladislav Hanuš, *Rozprava o kulturnosti* (Ružomberok: Obroda, 1943), p. 18 (hereafter cited as *Rozprava*).

78. Polakovič, *Tisovd nauka*, pp. 58, 346. Cf. *Slovák* (Bratislava), 11 November 1942, p. 1, editorial.

79. *Collection of Slovak Laws*, No. 46/1940.

80. *Slovák* (Bratislava), 23 February 1940, pp. 1. 2. Cf. Polakovič, *Tisová nauka*, p. 346.

81. *Slovák* (Bratislava), 2 April 1940, p. 3. Cf. Neumann, *Behemoth*, p. 384.

82. Anton Viršík, "Zo študia narodnosocialistickej hospodárskej politiky," *Sborník spolku záhorských akademikov, 1932-1942*, ed. Julius V. Trebišovský (Trnava: G.A. Bezo, 1942), p. 278. Cf. Polakovič, *Tisová nauka*, p. 385.

83. Polakovič, *Tisová nauka*, p. 385.

84. *Slovák* (Bratislava), 30 January 1941, p. 7; T-175, R-531, 9403141, report of Hans Pehm, 31 January 1941. The author of this report wrote with anger that the Slovak Robin Hood, Juraj Jánošik, was declared the first local Nazi. "*Jánošik, der Raeuberhauptmann*," wrote Pehm,"*das ist eine Frechheit.*"

85. In an article of 550 words, headlined "The Ludak Spirit is Moving upon the Face of Slovakia" [*Organizačné Zvesti* (Bratislava), 3 (November 1942): 1, editorial] , Tiso utilized variations of the word "spirit" twenty-three times, or every twenty-seven words. Cf. Hanuš, *Rozprava*, p. 8. The author here used the expression "spirituality" eight times in 210 words. The average in the whole book is three to four times a page.

86. Štefánek, *Základy sociografie*, p. 9.

CHAPTER VII

1. Husák, *Svedectvo*, p. 42. Cf. *Slovenské Národné Povstanie roku 1944* (Bratislava: Slovenká akademia vied, 1965), pp. 69-70, Michael Zibrin to Juraj Slávik, August 1942.

2. The passage on the ordeal of Slovak Jewry is based on oral testimony collected by me, as well as on printed material. It should be noted that even some of the anti-government elements had seen little wrong in the aryanization. Prečan, *Dokumenty*, Document No. 5, dispatch of Dr. J. Kopecký to the government in exile, 4 March 1943, p. 67; No. 93, dispatch of Dr. J. Kopecký to the government in exile, 12 and 14 July 1944, p. 229.

3. T-77, R-880, 5628377, dispatch, the German military attaché in Slovakia to OKW, 30 May 1942; T-77, R-880, 5628192, protocol of a meeting of a German military mission with Tiso, 16 October 1942.

4. T-175, R 524, 9394614, 16 April 1942; T-175, R-515, 9382680, 23 October 1942, etc.

NOTES TO CHAPTER VII

5. *Gardista* (Žilina), 17 November 1942, p. l.

6. T-175, R-517, 9384303, report, SD branch Bratislava, 15 May 1942.

7. *Slovák* (Bratislava), 30 May 1942, p. 2.

8. T-175, R-518, 9385877, report, SD branch Bratislava, 27 May 1942. (*Gardista* was the official organ of the HG.)

9. *Supra*, p. 35.

10. T-120, R-341, 249594, memo, Woermann to von Ribbentrop, 23 May 1942. Cf. telegram of the German charge d'affaires in Bratislava, Ringelmann, to the German Foreign Office, 5 June 1942, the same frame.

11. T-120, R-341, 249418, memo to files, Weizsaecker, 16 May 1942. Cf. T-175, R-516, 9386011, report, SD branch Bratislava on the visit of Slovakia's leaders by Hitler on 28 May 1943.

12. *Infra*, pp. 94.

13. T-175, R-518, 9385917, report, SD branch Bratislava, 1 January 1943; cf. 9385919, report, SD branch Bratislava, 4 January 1943.

14. T-175, R-75, 2593670, report, Berger to Himmler, 16 January 1943.

15. *Organizačné Zvesti* (Bratislava) 3 (April 1942): 6. I was not able to obtain any reliable data on Party membership. Dr. Hoensch doubts Dr. K.O. Rabl's number of 80,000 Party members in 1939-1940 (*Die Slowakei*, p. 139). Another source gave the membership as 280,000 in April 1943 (Záděra, *Děset let*, p. 90.)

16. *Organizačné Zvesti* (Bratislava) 3 (June 1942): 3.

17. *Ibid.*, 3 (November 1942): 6.

18. *Ibid.*, 3 (September 1942): 7.

19. *Collection of Slovak Laws, Slovenska pracujuca pospolitosť* No. 70/1942.

20. *Ibid., Sdruženie vysokoškolského študenstva*, No. 78/1942.

21. *Ibid., Socialný ústav HSĽS*, No. 80/1942.

22. *Ibid., Zákon o Hlinkovej Slovenskej Ľudovej Strane*, No. 215/1942.

22a. *Supra*, pp. 54, 55.

23. T-77, R-880, 5628894, transcript of the speech, 5 March 1945.

24. T-175, R-524, 9393578, dispatch, SD branch Prague to RSHA, 13 December 1943. Cf. T-175, R-524, 9392887, situation report, SD branch Bratislava, 15 1943.

25. T-175, R-518, 938514, report of an SD agent, May 1942.

26. T-175, R-534, 9407048, note to files, SD branch Vienna, 15 January 1944.

27. T-175, R-516, 9383462, report, SD branch Vienna to RSHA, 25 August 1943.

28. T-175, R-517, 9384495, report, SD branch Bratislava, 27 October 1943.

29. T-175, R-75, 2593670, report, Berger to Himmler, 16 January 1943. Cf. T-175, R-534, 9407057, telegram, SD branch Vienna to RSHA, 13 March 1944.

30. T-175, R-597, 9384495, report, SD branch Bratislava, 27 October 1943.

31. T-175, R-516, 9386011-016, report, SD branch Bratislava, 28 May 1943.

32. T 77, R-879, 5627944, report, the German military attaché to OKW, 15 January 1942.

33. T-77, R-880, 5628844, note for an oral report in OKW, 3 June 1943.

34. T-175, R-563, 94392233, dispatch SS *Standartenfuehrer* Dr. Ehlich to SS *Brigadenfuehrer* Ohlendorf, 19 January 1944. Cf. T-77, R-881, 5629663, dispatch, Ludin to the German Foreign Office, 21 December 1943. This episode denies the claim of a Ludak-emigrant writer that the only reason for Slovakia's joining the war was the desire to fight Communism. [Jozef Paučo, *Slováci a komunismus* (Middletown, Pa.: Y.Y. Lach, 1957), p. 106.] Hitler's own plans prevented Slovak troops from being sent to fight the Western Allies.

35. T-77, R-881, 5629932, dispatch, the German general attached to the Slovak Ministry of National Defense to OKW, 4 September 1943.

36. Čas (Bratislava), 8 January 1947, p. 2, trial T-M-D. For details, see *Supra*, pp. 52, 53, 108, 109, 111, 112.

37. T-175, R-514, 9380837, memo to the files, 31 March 1943; 9380841, memo to the files, 7 April 1943.

38. T-175, R-524, 9392845, press clippings.

39. T-175, R-524, 9393805, report, Gestapo Vienna to RSHA, 23 August 1943; T-175, R-523, 9392812, dispatch, SD branch Vienna to RSHA, sent on 27 August 1943; T-175, R-524, 9393581, memo on Dr. Milán Hanko, SD branch Vienna, 24 September 1943.

40. T-120, R-779, 372502, telegram, Ludin to the German Foreign Office, 30 March 1944.

41. *Ibid*.

42. *Gardista* (Žilina), 10 June 1943, p. 3. Cf. T-175, R-516, 9386010, report of an SD agent, 11 June 1943.

43. T-175, R-516, 9386075, report of an SD agent, 2 August 1943.

44. *Collection of Slovak Laws*, No. 225/1941.

45. *Gardista* (Žilina), 19 December 1943, p. 3.

46. T-175, R-524, 9394103, report of an SD agent, 11 July 1944. Cf. *Pravda* (Bratislava), 13 February 1947, p. 1, trial T-M-D. The testimony of Dr. Martin Sokol.

47. Jozef Tiso, "Politická skuška" [The political test], *Organizačné Zvesti* (Bratislava) 5 (April 1944): 1.

48 *Ibid*.

49. T-175, R-518, 9386765, report on a meeting of eight leading Guardists with Tiso, 12 August 1944.

50. T-175, R-524, 9392887-88, press clippings.

51. T-175, R-517, 9385011, report of an SD agent, 18 May 1944. Cf. Moreshet Archives, Israel, ŠA Radvan, ŽU 757/44 prez, protocol of meetings of the Banská Bystrica district officials with Minister Mach, 24 February 1944.

52. Arnold H. Schwengeler, *Slowakische Reise, 1944* (Bern: Buchdruckerei F. Ponchon Jent, 1944), p. 16. Cf. Prečan, *Dokumenty*, Document No. 55, report on the internal affairs of Slovakia, March 1944, pp. 182, 183.

CHAPTER VIII

1. T-120, R-336, 248516, Tiso's speech of 20 January 1941.

2. Ministerstvo školstva a národnej osvety, *Päť rokov slovenského školstva 1939-1943* (Bratislava: Štátne nakladateľstvo, 1944), p. 42 (hereafter cited as *Pat' rokov*).

3. *Collection of Slovak Laws*, Nos. 308/1940, 168/1939.

4. *Slovák* (Bratislava), 5 March 1944, p. 3, decree of Ministry of Education No. 560/44 prez., 1 March 1944.

5. T-175, R-520, 9388493, collective declamation in the city of Piešťany, 5 May 1942.

6. T-175, R-515, 9382292, order of the Ministry of Justice, No. 17346/1939-2, of 7 September 1939.

7. For an example, see T-175, R-530, 9401219, circular letter of the chairman of the Institute for Worker's Social Security, of 14 February 1941. The chairman warned the employes of his office to change alien names, or otherwise be prepared for trouble, when applying for a salary raise.

NOTES TO CHAPTER VIII

8. *Collection of Slovak Laws*, No. 31/1942.

9. *Ibid.*, No. 255/1939.

10. "Kdo je, a kdo nie je štátnym ob čanom?" [Who is, and who is not a citizen?] *Slovák* (Bratislava), 28 October 1939, p. 4.

11. T-81, R-527, 9294654, draft of the law.

12. *Collection of Slovak Laws*, Nos. 185/1939 and 121/1940.

13. Štefánek, *Základy sociografie*, pp. 179, 180. In addition to the political laxities in census procedures (described elsewhere in the text), Štefánek's numbers leave much to be desired. Missing are a clear number of ethnic Slovaks in Slovakia, since his statistics include Slovaks, Czechs, Jews, and Gypsies in the same category. Various sources set the numbers of the Czechs between 24,000 and 40,000 [*DGFP*, Ser. D, Vol. XI, p. 683, document 393, 26 November 1940; *Slovák* (Bratislava), 19 February 1944]. One may assume that the numbers were even higher, as many Czechs tried to hid their real identity. Štefánek's statistics do not provide any information on the division between refugees from the Soviet Union and native "Russians and Ukraines," and they neglected Gypsies entirely. One wonders also about such factors as ambiguites in the numbers of Jews. The major problem is the source of Štefánek's numbers, as he did not document them.

14. Pavol Čarnogurský, "Národný štát" [A national state], *Slovák* (Bratislava), 5 April 1939, p. 1, editorial. The Sidorite Čarnogurský served at this time as the secretary-general of the Slovak League. The League was officially an organization for the preservation and development of Slovakhood; it was in fact, however, deployed as a tool for nationalization.

15. *Ibid.* Čarnogurský refers to the traditional Slovak national emblem.

16. T-77, R-878, 5626203, dispatch, the German military attaché to OKW, 9 January 1940. Cf. T-175, R-524, report of an SD agent, 11 September 1940.

17. T-120, R-1301, 479830, memorandum for von Ribbentrop about a discussion between Karmasin and Ambassador Rudolf Likus, 18 November 1939. Not all ethnic Germans willingly supported the Nazis. The leaders of the minority, several of them not natives of Slovakia, terrorized the opposition.

18. T-81, R-524, 5294846, letter of Carl Hauskrecht, head of the Office for Press and Propaganda in the German Party to DAI (Stuttgart), 17 May 1940.

19. *Supra*, pp. 98, 103.

20. A survey in my possession prepared on my behalf by the Research Institute for Minority Studies on Hungarians Attached to Czechoslovakia and Carpathoruthenia, Inc., New York, 1964, 5 p.

21. Count Janos Eszterházy, Magyar representative in the parliament, cast the single vote against the Law of Deportation of Jews. *Ibid.*

22. T-175, R-522, 9391612, report of an SD agent, 23 April 1941. Cf. *Slovák* (Bratislava), 16 February 1940, p. 3, a meeting of the Slovak League.

23. Here I follow the terminology used in Slovakia today. This group, which should linguistically be classified with Eastern Slavs, was variously described as Ruthene, Russin, Rusniak, Russian, and Ukrainian; it is not my intention to select the proper name.

24. *Ibid.*, p. 180.

25. *Slovák* (Bratislava), 22 March 1941, p. 7, on the first Greek-Catholic prayerbook.

26. During the census of 1940, the people were made to read Russian texts. When, naturally, they were not able to do so, the officers proclaimed them Slovaks

NOTES

(T-175, R-522, 9391570, official documents; decision of a census officer, and verdict of an administrative court).

27. T-175, R-522, 9391583, letter from the meeting of Ukrainian leaders, 17 November 1940. The dispute as to whether they were Ukrainian, Russian, or Russin (Ruthene, Rusniak) divided these people.

28. See, for example, the Guardist pressure on Bishop Gojdič to change the language in the cathedral of Presov, his seat. (T-81, R-528, 5295653, newspaper clipping of *Gardista* (Žilina), 1 December 1940).

29. T-175, R–522, 9391550, report of an SD agent, 11 February 1941.

30. Citizens of several districts on the borders between Slovakia and Poland, known as Gorals, were of undetermined nationality. Both Slovaks and Poles claimed that the Gorals' national consciousness was latent and had to be awakened. [Andrej Bielovodský, *Severné hranice Slovenská* (Bratislava: Slovenska liga, S.A.), p. 83 (hereafter cited as *Severné hranice*; Wladislaw Semkowicz, ed., *Słowacja i Słowacy* (Cracow: Nakladem Sekciji Słowackiej Towarystwa Słowianskiego, 1937), Vol. II, p. 242.] In 1920 the disputed territory was divided between Czechoslovakia and Poland. After Munich, Warsaw occupied the districts awarded to Czechoslovakia, as well. The Poles were busy "awakening" the national consciousness of the Gorals. When the Germans transferred the whole region to the government of Bratislava, it worked hard to "reawaken" Slovakhood.

31. *Proces proti vlastizradným biskupom Vojtaššákovi, Buzalkovi, Gojdičovi* (Bratislava: Ministerstvo spravodlivosti, Tatran, 1951), pp. 26, 57, 58 (hereafter cited as *Proces*).

32. Bielovodský, *Severné hranice*, pp. 13-15.

33. *Slovák* (Bratislava), 2 December 1939, p. 3, Tuka presents the program of the new cabinet.

34. Žela Inovecká, "O národnostne miešaných manželstvách" [On the nationally mixed marriages], *ibid.*, 10 December 1939, p. 8.

35. *Slovák* (Bratislava) 17 December 1939, p. 10, letters to the editor.

36. T-81, R-550, 532383, report of an SD agent, 29 April 1941.

37. T-175, R-520, 9389298, letter of a German specialist for the "Gypsy problem," to the police attache in the German Embassy in Bratislava of November 1942 (the exact day is unclear). Cf. *ibid.*, 9389296, report of an SD agent, 23 October 1943.

38. T-77, R-778, 5504525, report sent by an unknown high-ranking German personality to Commodore Buerkner, German Army Intelligence, 10 April 1942. Cf. "Po Židoch, Cigáňov" [After the Jews, the Gypsies], *Slowakische Rundschau* (Bratislava) 15 May 1942, p. 15.

39. T-175, R-514, 9380582, Tiso in an interview with a Dutch Catholic journalist, 21 May 1939.

40. The documentation available reveals much less than should be said on this topic. My repeated efforts to acquire more sources in the Vatican met with negative answers.

41. T 175, R-530, 9401415, *Grenzbote* (Bratislava), 24 June 1941, newspaper clipping.

42. T-175, R-530, 9401398, *Grenzbote* (Bratislava), 1 April 1941, newspaper clipping.

43. The leading Slovak national institution for promotion of culture.

44. Štefan Pasiar and Pavel Paška, *Osveta na Slovensku, jej vznik, počiatky a vývoj* [Cultural enlightenment in Slovakia, its origin, beginning, and development] (Bratislava: Osveta, 1964), p. 293.

45 *Slovák* (Bratislava), 5 January 1940, p. 4, announcement for the ministers and the members of parliament.

46. T-175, R-528, 9398504, order of the minister of the interior, No. 3690/1940, 12 September 1940.

47. Compare with the outlawing of the Old Catholic Church in Croatia under the *Ustashi* government during World War II. [Viktor Novak, *Velika optužba* (Sarajevo, 1960), p. 102].

48. T-175, R-514, 9581100-9581109, report, SD branch Vienna to RSHA, 24 September 1942.

49. *Katolické Noviny* (Bratislava), 9 February 1941, editorial.

50. *Ibid.*, The attack on Nazism is clear. The editorial was part of a dispute between the clerical camp of Tiso and the Hlinka Guard.

51. Alexej Izakovič, "Ucelená národná výchova mládeže" [The strong national education of the youth], *Slovák* (Bratislava), 28 February 1940, p. 1. editorial.

52. *Collection of Slovak Laws*, No. 308/1940, Section 10.

53; *Slovák* (Bratislava), 29 May 1940, p. 4, Sivák in the Committee for Culture of the Parliament.

54. *Ibid.*, 12 January 1939, p. 8, Ministry of Education order no. 86.600-39-1.

55. T-175, R-519, 9386894, SD branch Bratislava reporting to SD branch Vienna on publication of order no. 1266 of the Ministry of Education, 22 March 1941.

56. *Collection of Slovak Laws*, No. 244/1941.

57. *Ibid.*, No. 308/1940.

58. Ministerstvo školstva, *Pät' rokov*, p. 196.

59. *Slovák* (Bratislava) 22 May 1939.

60. O. Formánek, "O význame matky" [On the value of a mother], *Slovák* (Bratislava), 30 January 1940, p. 7.

61. Ministerstvo školstva, *Pät' rokov*, p. 217.

62. *Ibid.*, p. 219.

63. *Ibid.*, pp. 153-155.

64. T-120, R-1450, D588278, report of Eduard Frauenfeld to the German Foreign Office, 18 May 1940.

65. Vlado Clementis, *Usmerňované Slovensko* (London: Williams, Lea & Co., 1942), p; 46. On the Index were also works by Sigmund Freud, Erich Kaestner, Erika Mann, Upton Sinclair, R. W. Seton-Watson, Romain Rolland, Maxim Gorki, Otto Strasser, Th. H. Van Velde (the Dutch writer on sex and family life), and others (Moreshet Archives, Slovak Collection, ŠA Bratislava, ŽU 234/43 prez., decree of the Office of the Minister of Interior, 28 June 1943.

66. *Proces*, p. 53, decree of the Central Office for Economy, 28 March 1942.

67. Ministerstvo školstva, *Pät' rokov*, p. 435. The State Land Office was responsible for aryanization of real estate in agriculture, and for land reform.

68. *Ibid.*, p. 436. Cf. T-175, R-514, 9380942, report of Nageler to RSHA, 29 December 1943.

69. Cf. Neumann, *Behemoth*, p. 81.

70. *Organizačné Zvesti (Bratislava)* 2 *(November* 1941): 13, statutes of the corporations. The corporate structure became law in the summer of 1942, p. 94.

71. T-175, R-518, 9385778, report of an SD agent, summer 1939.

72. *Gardista* (Žilina), 12 July 1942, p. 1, editorial.

73. *Slovák* (Bratislava), 18 December 1941, p. 1, Tiso in the city of Bánovce: "One gets desperate watching the public life (of the state) and observing this enormous egotism."

166

NOTES

74. T-175, R-514, 9381110, dispatch, Ludin to the German Foreign Office, 13 April 1942. Cf. Political Archives of the FGR Foreign Office, Bonn, File Inland I-D, Slowakei, Kirche, 3. *Der Reichsminister für die Kirchen Angelegenheiten* to the German Foreign Office, No. 1685/41, 25 November 1941.

75. Polakovič, *Tisová nauka*, p. 220.

76. Collection of Slovak Laws, "The Law About Offenses Against the State," No. 320/1940.

77. *Supra*, p. 48.

78. The American consulate general in Prague, 860F.00/933; dispatch, Irving N. Linnel to the secretary of state, 1 February 1940; cf. letter of Prof. F. Ďurčanský to me on 3 December 1965.

79. *Slovenská Republika*, Konštantín Čulen: "Snem a vláda Slovenskej Republiky," p. 120.

80. T-120, R-779, 372498-372500, telegram, Ludin to the German Foreign Office, 7 June 1944.

81. *Slovák* (Bratislava), 31 May 1939, p. 5.

82. T-175, R-518, 939591, 9385796, reports of the SD branch Bratislava from the period between 1 May and 31 May 1939.

83. *Pravda* (Bratislava), 7 November 1947, trial of the members of the Slovak government; T-175, R-518, 9385914, report of an SD agent, May 1942.

84. Eduard Táborský, "Local Government in Czechoslovakia, 1918-48," *The American and East European Review* 10 (October 1951): 212.

85. The examples used here were the obvious ones. Similar cases can also be found in other fields of Slovak legislation.

86. For an example, the "Order with Force of Law on the Legal Position of Jews" (the so-called Jewish Codex), No. 194/1941 of the *Collection of Slovak Laws*, suspended all previous laws and orders dealing with Jewish matters.

87. *Ibid.*, "The Constitutional Law on Deportation of the Jews," No. 68/1942, 16 June 1942.

88. Vietor, *Príspevok*, p. 502.

89. *Collection of Slovak Laws*, No. 44/1944.

90. *Ibid.*, *Vyhláška predsedu Snemu* [Announcement of the speaker], No. 162/1941.

91. *Slovák* (Bratislava), 18 January 1940, editorial; *Slovensky Robotnik* (Bratislava), 2 January 1941, interview with Speaker Dr. Sokol.

92. Cf. Neumann, *Behemoth*, p. 84.

93. T-175, R-534, 9405278, Tiso's letter concerning the formulation of the law about the Office of Propaganda, No. 11.35/1940, 17 September 1941. T-175, R-523, 9392201, a concluding report on the anti-Jewish measures in Slovakia, SS *Hauptsturmfuehrer* Eduard Hermann, September 1943. According to this report, when the law about the deportation of Jews was formulated, Tuka proposed to deport only those Christianized Jews baptized before 30 January 1942. A counter-proposal of Tiso, putting the date on 14 March 1939, exposed additional hundreds to deportation.

94. The president and the government are due the respectable credit of not having executed anyone in the country until September 1944. On the other hand, murders of a few political prisoners and of Jews by the state's forces and private citizens went unpunished.

95. For an example, see Moreshet Archives, ŠA Bojnice, ŽU 1456/43 prez, letter, District Lieutenant Haššik to Mach, 1 December 1943.

96. T-175, R-515, 9383699-9382702, protocol of a meeting of German propaganda workers, 27 and 28 November 1942; 9381660, memo to files, SD branch Vienna, 30 September 1943.

97. Štefánek, ¡Sociografia Slovenska, p. 305. According to Štefánek, some 7,000 volumes were removed between 1939 and 1944.

98. Ministerstvo školstva, Pät rokov, p. 514.

99. Slovák (Bratislava), 26 October 1939, p. 8, Ďurčanský in opening of the national exhibition of art. Cf. ibid., 11 February 1940, p. 3, interview with the Minister of Education.

100. Ibid., 12 November 1942, p. 8, editorial. The silence of many was rather self-imposed. The outstanding novelist Janko Jesenský may serve as an example. The so-called "writing for drawers" (priečinková literatura) was another sign of the time; the writer would wait with his products for better days.

101. "Čo čakame od slovenskej vedy?" [What are we expecting from the Slovak science?] , Ibid., 24 December 1939, p. 7.

102. Ibid., 7 May 1939, p. 9; 19 July 1939, p. 1; 27 July 1939, p. 1; 3 January 1940, p. 2; 9 November 1941, p. 7; Gardista (Žilina), 13 August 1943, p. 2.

103. Clementis, Usmerňované Slovensko, pp. 44, 45.

104. Vojtech Krajčovič, Die Struktur der slowakischen Wirtschaft (Bratislava: Čas-Verlag, 1941), p. 11 (hereafter cited as Die Struktur).

105. Anton Virsik, "Zo študia narodnesocialistickej hospodárskej politiky," Sbornik, p. 276.

106. Slovák (Bratislava), 31 May 1939, p. 1, editorial; ibid., 21 June 1939, p. 1, editorial.

107. Collection of the Slovak Laws, No. 297/1940.

108. Supra, p. 94.

109. Collection of Slovak Laws, No. 142/1939.

110. Štefan Horváth, "Po dvoch rokoch" [After two years] , Slovák (Bratislava), 14 March 1941, p. 11.

111. Collection of Slovak Laws, Nos. 129/1940 and 248/1940.

112. Supra, p. 94.

113. Tiso's relatives and their close families and friends were extremely involved both in political and economic activities. The families of Tiso, Turček, Fundárek, and Dobiaš held dozens of public and economic positions, with their income and property reaching millions of Slovak crowns. The same thing may be said of the Danihels, Klinovskýs, and others. A sociometrical study would prove that nepotism played an extremely important role in the political, social, and economic life of the Slovak state. Such a study would also show that a relatively small number of men, a kind of oligarchy, held most of the key positions of the state, and had a close relationship with each other.

To a certain degree, the Ludak regime was a revolution of Catholic Homines Novi against the traditional Protestant establishment, which had led the nation since the early years of the nineteenth century. The Protestant supremacy, so enhanced in the Czechoslovak Republic, thus came to an end. The Homines Novi could be seen in the political life, while other members of the same family were busy in the economy, army, and other fields. Often the father was still a peasant, and his children already held political, economic, or social positions in the capital or district towns. It frequently happened that the so-called "political struggle" among groups was

168

NOTES

simultaneously a nepotistic fight over jobs. The social mobility was enormous. The social and sociological implications of the Ludak regime deserve a deeper research and analysis.

114. "Časové otázky roľníctva" [Contemporary problems of the peasantry], *Slovák* (Bratislava), 19 July 1939, p. 11.

115. T-580 R-458, press service of the German Party in Slovakia, 16 December 1943.

116. The man, a Nástupist, Dr. Dominik Filipp, eventually appeared on quite a few boards of trustees as well, probably to represent the Party there.

117. To guide (*usmerňovat'*) was an expression very popular with the Ludaks.

118. *Slovák* (Bratislava), 3 October 1939, p. 5, interview with Dr. Dominik Filipp.

119. *Collection of Slovak Laws*, No. 137/1939.

120. *Ibid.*, No. 42/1940.

121. Ľudovit Kováčik, *Slovensko v sieti nemeckého finančného kapitálu* (Bratislava: SVOL, 1955), p. 121.

122. Reconciliation with the Sidorites after Salzburg may be observed in the important posts they held in the financial and business life of the country. Sidorites held chairs on the board of directors of the Peasant Bank, too.

123. T-175, R-529, 9399481, 9399520, lists of the members of the Board.

124. T-81, R-550, 5324335, press clippings, *National Zeitung* (Essen), 16 October 1941.

125. Typical of the kind of people so endorsed by the Party were the instructions for the would-be aryanizers, published in *Organizačné Zvesti* under the title "How to Aryanize?"[*Organizačné Zvesti* (Bratislava) 2 (May 1941): 12]. The author described people coming to the Party's secretariat for consultation. They decided to aryanize, but did not know how. The paper came to aid these helpless individuals: the application for aryanization is so simple, remarked the author, that anybody can fill it out for himself.

126. See such authors as Stanek, Kováčik, Rafas, and Olšovsky.

127. Vratislay Bauch, *Poľnohospodárstvo za Slovenského štátu* (Bratislava: SNPL, 1958), pp. 44-49. Accordingly, only 2.7 percent of the fields predestined for reform were actually divided; of this contingent, 45 percent were assigned to forty-four individuals.

128. *Organizačné Zvesti* (Bratislava) 3 (September 1942): 5. T-81, R-550, *Grenzbote* (Bratislava), 22 October 1941, newspaper clippings. Dr. Karol Klinovský to a reporter of *Slovák*.

129. Dr. Michal Sahulčik, "Pôda sa nebude pridelovat' zadarmo" [The land will not be allocated free of payment]. *Slovák* (Bratislava), 6 March 1940, p. 5.

130. *Organizačné Zvesti* (Bratislava) 3 (March 1942): 9; (August 1942), p. 9.

131. *Ibid.* 2 (April 1941): 6.

132.*Slovenská Politika* as quoted in *Slovák* (Bratislava), 29 February 1940, p. 6. "Pozemková reforma, aká ma byt'" [A genuine land reform].

133. *Organizačné Zvesti* (Bratislava) 3 (September 1942): 4.

134. Krajčovič, *Die Struktur*, p. 20. Of all peasants, 98.5 percent held 44.4 percent of the arable land.

NOTES TO CHAPTER IX

1. *Slovák* (Bratislava), 20 August 1944, p. 3.
2. Tiso's problems with the armed forces intensified in 1944. Several times he

was compelled to take the initiative. Lack of a more suitable personality than Čatloš kept the general in this position. (T-77, R-881, 5629669, personal letter, Ludin to Ritter, 27 January 1944; 5629561, memo to the files, Vice Admiral Buerkner, 7 March 1944).

3. T-175, R-518, 9386296, report of an SD agent, 10 August 1944.

4. T-175, R-518, 9386765-774, report, SD branch Vienna to RSHA, 12 August 1944.

5. T-175, R-518, 9386775-780, report, SD branch Vienna to RSHA, sent on 21 Auust 1944.

6. T-120, R-779, 372491, telegram, Ludin to the German Foreign Office, 21 August, 1944.

7. T-120, R-770, 372488, telegram, Ludin to the German Foreign Office, 27 August 1944. Prof. Ďurčanský repeated this stand in a letter to me on 3 December 1965. He wrote "I realized fully the disaster which the entrance of the Red Army would mean for Slovakia. Therefore I saw it as my human duty to do everything in order to prevent its entrance, or at least to delay it. In hope that perhaps through a miracle some change would occur in the great policy, I proceeded without paying attention to the German satisfaction because I followed not theirs but Slovak intentions. I could not speak for the Americans because they took a stand unacceptable for us: their attitude meant enslavement of Slovakia." Analyzing these words, one would conclude that, according to Prof. Ďurčanský, not the German but the Allies' atttitude meant enslavement. Yet, it is clear that any obstacles in the way of the Red Army at this time cost lives not only of Russian soldiers, but of American and British soldiers as well. Prof. Ďurčanský admits helping the German war efforts whatever his reasons might have been. His expectations for a miracle, like those of Hitler and Himmler, only reveal the lack of political realism and the daydreams of the Slovak leadership.

8. T-120, R-779, 372485, personal telegram, von Ribbentrop to Ludin, 29 August 1944.

9. The diary of Joseph Tiso's closest collaborator and last prime minister of Slovakia, Dr. Štefan Tiso, reflected the deep shock. The pages of the diary are full of lament, anger, and disappointment over the action of the Slovak people and the failure of the Slovak state. See Diary of Dr. Štefan Tiso (manuscript, in Slovakia T-614, Vault Annex I, The Hoover Institute, Stanford, Calif. (hereafter cited as Diary).

10. Tido J. Gašpar, "Z pamäti," Slovenské Pohľady 12 (December 1968): 79 (hereafter cited as Z pämati).

11. Culen, Po Svätoplukovi, p. 289; cf. Tiso, Diary.

12. Gašpar, Z pamäti, pp. 79, 80; Ferdinand Ďurčanský, "Es war nur eine sowjetische Partisanenaktion," Politische Studien, 157, (1963): 567-575; František Vnuk, Neuveritelné sprísahanie (Middletown, Pa., 1964).

13. Paučo, Sa poznali, pp. 48-50, 53, 54, 144, 145, 150, 154, 165. Cf. various reports of the SD agents: T-175, R-517, 9384593 of 18 September 1944; R-531, 9403246 of 19 September 1944; R-531, 9403243 of 20 September 1944; and R-527, 9397221 of 20 September 1944, etc.

14. Tiso, Diary.

15. T-120, R-779, 372482-484, dispatch, Ludin to the German Foreign Office, 30 August 1944.

NOTES

16. Library of Congress, Himmler Files, report, Berger to Himmler, 2 September 1944. Cf. T-120, R-779, 372470, telegram, Ludin to the German Foreign Office, 5 September 1944. At Nuremberg, Berger denied the initiation of change (SS Lt. General Gottlob Berger, interrogated by Dr. Gero, president of the National Court at Bratislava, and Mr. De Vries on 23 January 1947: Interrogation Summary No. 1086, Office of U.S. Chief of Counsel for War Crimes, APO 686-A, Evidence Division, Interrogation Branch).

17, Library of Congress, Himmler Files, report, Berger to Hitler, 2 September 1944.

18. *Pravda* (Bratislava), 19 December 1946, p. 1, trial T-M-D.

19. *Čas* (Bratislava), 26 October 1947, p. 2, trial of the members of the Slovak government. Cf. Library of Congress, Himmler Files, Ludin: *Vorschlaege*.

20. T-580, R-458, *Grenzbote*, 3 November 1944.

21. T-175, R-517, 938472, report, SS *Obersturmbannfuehrer* Viktor Nageler to RSHA, 3 November 1944. Cf. Library of Congress, Himmler Files, Ludin: *Vorschlaege*.

22. T-175, R-518, 9385752-759, report, Witiska to General Hoeffle, 26 September 1944. Cf. Library of Congress, Himmler Files, Ludin: *Vorschlaege*.

23. T-175, R-517, 9384593, report of an SD agent on conversation with Dr. Viliam Ries, 18 September 1944. Cf. 9384596, memorandum of Kubala, 21 February 1945.

24. T-175, R-527, 9397221, report of an SD agent, 20 September 1944.

25. *Pravda* (Bratislava), 5 March 1947, p. 1, trial T-M-D. Cf. Prečan, *Dokumenty*, Document No. 320, memorandum of the "Young Ludaks," 20 September 1944, pp. 541, 542.

26. *Pučisti* is the terminology used since in Ludak writing to avoid the semantic recognition of the fact that the uprising was staged against them.

27. *Čas* (Bratislava), 15 February 1947, p. 4, trial T-M-D. Sokol's witnesses.

28. T-175, R-536, 9409054, report of an SD agent, 16 January 1945; 9409027, report of an SD agent, 7 February 1945.

29. T-175, R-517, 9384596, Kubala's letter of 21 February 1945.

30. T-175, R-517, 9385236, the circular letter, 24 November 1944.

31. *IMT*, Nuremberg, NG 3490, letter, SS *Standartenfuehrer* R. Brand to SS *Standartenfuehrer Geheimrat* Wagner, 21 December 1944.

32. The emphasis is mine. Library of Congress, Himmler Files: letter, Himmler to Ludin, 31 January 1945.

33. Dr. Bohdan Galvánek, the new Slovak minister to Berlin, while paying his initial visit to the German Foreign Office, informed his host, von Thaden, that both President Tiso and he wished to support the Germans in every respect in dealing with the Jews, who must be deported without humanitarian consideration (T-120, R-1175, 477147, memo to the files, von Thaden, 5 October 1944). It is possible, however, that Galvánek used Tiso's name without being authorized to do so.

NOTES TO CHAPTER X

1. A traditional conservative "is disposed to maintain existing institutions" (OED), while the modern rightist party strives to change the reality in the spirit of its own ideology.

2. Josef Chmelar, *Political Parties in Czechoslovakia* (Prague: Orbis, 1926), p. 59.

3. Polakovič, *Náš duch*, p. 14.

4. The writer is following Timasheff's definition, *Supra*, p. 54.

APPENDIX

Localities in Slovakia

Slovak Name	German Name	Hungarian Name
Bánovce nad Bebravou	Banovitz	Trencsenbán
Banská Bystrica	Neusohl	Besztercebánya
Bratislava	Pressburg	Pozsony
Handlová	Krickerhäu	Nyitrabánya
Košice	Kaschau	Kassa
Liptovský Sv. Mikuláš	Liptau-Sankt-Niklaus	Liptószentmiklós
Nitra	Neutra	Nyitra
Piešťany	Pistyan	Pöstyén
Považská Bystrica	Waagbistritz	Vágbeszterce
Prešov	Preschau	Eperies
Ružomberok	Rosenberg	Rózsahegy
Trenčianske Teplice	Trentschinteplitz	Trencsénteplic
Trenčín	Trentschin	Trencsén
Trnava	Tyrnau	Nagyszombat
Turčiansky Sv. Martin	Sankt Martin	Turócszentmárton
Žilina	Sillein	Zsolna
Zvolen	Altsohl	Zólyom

BIBLIOGRAPHY

Documents, Unpublished and Published

The Hebrew University of Jerusalem, The Institute of Contemporary Jewry. Oral History Division Catalogue No. 2 (English), Jerusalem 1965, No. 1 (Hebrew) Jerusalem 1965. *Jewish Resistance Activity in Slovakia during World War II*. The Interviewer: Yeshayahu Jelinek. Copies of 44 testimonies, and transcripts of two symposia listed in the catalogue no. 2 are in the possession of the writer.

Moreshet Archives, Givaat Havivah, Israel. The Slovak Jewry section.

Political Archives of the Foreign Office, Bonn, FGR. Inspected files dealing with Slovakia, and not microfilmed previously

U.S. Department of State, Historical Office. Washington, D. C., American Legation, Prague, 1938, Vo. IX. Correspondence. American Legation, Prague, 1939, Vol. III. Correspondence. American Consulate General, Prague, 1940, Part 25, 26, 27. American Embassy, Prague (sic!), 1941, Vol. I. Correspondence. Scattered documents marked 740.0011, 860F.00

U.S. Library of Congress, Manuscript Division, Washington, D. C. Captured German Documents. Himmler Files. Containers No. 390, 393. The Institute for Germans Living Abroad (Deutsches Ausland-Institut, DAI) Files. Containers 277 (A), 158 (A, B, C); Folders 91, 92, 93.

U.S. National Archives. Washington, D. C. German Records Microfilmed at Alexandria, Va. World War II Records Division. The documents in the National Archives are identified by the film serial (S) number, by the roll (R) number and by the frame numbers. Each collection has its own National Archives Microcopy number (T). The following tables identify the German files, giving their roll (R) and serial (S) numbers. The serial numbers have been omitted in the footnotes.

T-77 Headquarters, Armed Forces High Command. (*Oberkommando der Wehrmacht*, OKW).

RS 296 Diary of the German Military Mission in Slovakia

RS 297 Diary of the German Military Mission in Slovakia

RS881 German Military Attaché, Bratislava

RS896 *Amstgruppe Ausland*

RS721 *Gruppe Wehrwirtschaft*

RS734 OKW—Miscellaneous

RS778 OKW—Miscellaneous

RS877-RS880 Og *Ausland* Files

BIBLIOGRAPHY

T-81, The Institute for Germans Living Abroad (*Deutsches Ausland-Institut*, DAI). Documents on Slovakia in the files of DAI are mixed with miscellaneous material from other countries. Hereafter given the R and S numbers of used microfilms. R337–S555, R374-S592, R397-S597, R413-S631, R416-S634, R418-S634, R420-S638, R527-S745, 528-S746, R536-S754, R550-S768, R555-S773, R564-S782, R565-S785, R577-S795, R597-S815, R601-S819, R668-S886.

T-120, German Foreign Ministry and Chancellery Records.

R-12, 13-S28	German Legation in Czechoslovakia
R17-S33	Director Political Department
R59-S67	Secret Files of Paul Otto Schmidt
R65, 66-S73	State Secretary
R154-S140	State Secretary
R197-S230	State Secretary
R239-S269	Head of the *Auslandsorganisation*
R257-S331	Under State Secretary
R259-S334	Under State Secretary
R277-S350	Under State Secretary
R280-S371	Under State Secretary
R310-S506	State Secretary
R336-S610,611	State Secretary
R341-S613	Pol. *geheim*
R362-S737	Political Department
R715-S1164	*Handakten* Luther
R748-S1243	*Handakten* Luther
R757-S1271	*Handakten* Keppler
R777-S1532	Reich Chancellery
R779-S1515	Reich Chancellery
R783-S1551	State Secretary
R916-S1613	Pol. *geheim*
R1030-S1797	Political Department
R1074-S1918	Pol. IV
R1094-S2050	State Secretary
R1094-S2080	State Secretary
R1139-S2006	Pol. IV
R1141-S2002, S2003	Pol. IV
R1159-S2139	Economic Policy Department
R1175-S2244-2248	Reich Chancellery
R1279-S2313	State Secretary
R1301-S2276	Pol. *geheim*
R1307-S2367	Pol. IV

R1308-S2369   Pol. IV
R1318-S2380, S2381 Pol. IV
R1320-S2383   *Handakten* Keppler
R1321-S2409-2419   Pol. IV
R1327-S2491   Legal Department
R1419-S2871   Political Department
R1420-S2871   Political Department
R1421-S2904, S2405 Pol. IV
R1422-S2919   Pol. II
R1449-S3013   Pol. IV
R1450-S3011   Under State Secretary
R1817-S3998, 3989 German Embassy in Poland
R2200-2206-S4436-4440 Pol. IV
R2433-S4738   German Legation in Slovakia
R2677-S5611   *Inland* A/B
R2682-S5572   *Handakten* Ritter
R3284-S7815   Economic Policy Department
R3307-S8294   Legal Department
R3307-S8296   Legal Department
R3622-S9900   *Inland Geheim*
R4354-SK819   *Inland Geheim*
R4637-4641-SK1500 *Inland* A/B
R4659-4668-SK1509 *Inland* A/B
R4744-SK1643, SK1644 German Legation in Slovakia

T-175, Reichsfuehrer SS and Chief of the German Police, Heinrich Himmler. Fifty-six rolls of microfilms (RS514-RS570) contain some 67,000 documents. These documents cover all fields of Slovak political, social, cultural, intellectual, religious as well as economic life from October, 1938, to April, 1945. Additional material may be found in RS29, RS32, RS48, RS49, RS59, RS60, RS66, RS74, RS75, RS80, RS120, RS123, RS125,

T-580, Captured German Documents, filmed at Berlin for the American Historical Association. Miscellaneous documents in R66, R355, R432, R458, R459, R877. These microfilms do not have serial numbers.

U.S. National Archives. Washington, D. C. The records of the Office of the U.S. Chief of Counsel for War Crimes. Nuremberg, Germany. Official Record U.S. Military Tribunals. Nuremberg. Case No. 11, Tribunal IV (IVA), U.S. vs. Ernst von Weizsaecker, *et. al.*
Interrogations and Witnesses, mimeographed (in English)

BIBLIOGRAPHY

Gottlob Berger: 20, 21, 24-28 May; 1, 2 June; 27 October 1948
William Keppler: 16, 19-21 July; 1-3 September 1948
Hans Lammers: 3, 7-10, 13-17, 20-23 September 1948
Karl Ritter: 12-16 July 1948
Adolf Steengracht von Moyland: 23-25, 28-30 June, 1 July 1948
Edmund Veesenmayer: 21-23 July 1948
Ernst von Weizsaecker: 7-11, 14-18, 21 June 1948
Ernst Woermann: 2, 6-9 July; 28 October 1948
Collection of documents. Inspected thoroughly: NG (Nuremberg, Government); NI (Nuremberg, Industrialists). Inspected partially: L (London); PS (Paris—Storey); R (Rothschild); BBT (Berlin Branch—Thayer); D (German Industry and Slave Labor Camps).
Interrogations:
    Gottlob Berger by Dr. Gerö and Mr. DeVries on 23 January 1943, Nuremberg, Germany
    Hans Elard Ludin by Dr. Arthur Fanta on 6 October 1947, Bratislava, Czechoslovakia
    Wilhelm Keppler by Col. Curtis L. Williams on 24 November 1945, Nuremberg, Germany
    Adolf Steengracht von Moyland by Dr. R. M. W. Kempner on 31 July 1947, Nuremberg, Germany
    Dieter Wisliczeny by Lt. Col. Smith W. Broockhart, Jr., on 15, 17, 24 November 1945, Nuremberg, Germany; by Dr. Arthur Fanta on 7 October 1947, Bratislava, Czechoslovakia
    Ernst Woermann by Dr. R. M. W. Kempner on 22 May 1947; by Mr. Beauvais on 9 July 1947, Nuremberg, Germany.

Yad Vashem, Martyrs and Heroes Memorial Authority, Archives, Jerusalem, Israel. The Slovak Jewry (Steiner) Collection. Inspected partially.

Aperçu Statistique de la République Tchécoslovaque. Prague, 1930.

Five Great Encyclicals. New York: The Paulist Press, 1939.

International Military Tribunal, Nuerenberg. Trial of the Major War Criminals Before the International Military Tribunal, Nuerenberg, November 14, 1945-October 1, 1946. Vols. I-XLII, Nuremberg, Germany, 1949.

Kennan, George F., *From Prague After Munich. Diplomatic Papers 1938-1947.* Princeton, N.J.: Princeton University Press, 1968.

Král, Václav, cop. *Die Deutschen in der Tschechoslowakei 1933-1947.* (Acta occupationis Bohemiae et Moraviae), Prague: Academia, 1964.

BIBLIOGRAPHY

Prečan, Vilém, ed. *Slovenské národné povstanie. Dokumenty.* Bratislava: Vydavateľstvo politickej literatury, 1965.

—————. *Slovenské národné povstanie. Nemci a Slovensko.Dokumenty.* Bratislava: Epocha, 1970.

Rasla, Anton. *Tiso a povstanie. Dokumenty.* Bratislava: Pravda, 1947.

Rothkirchen, Livia. *Hurban yahadut slovakia:T'eur history b'teudot.* (The destruction of Slovakian Jewry: a documentary history). Jerusalem: Yad Vashem, 1961.

Slovakia. Slovenský štatistický ústav. *Uzemie a obyvateľstvo Slovenskej republiky a prehľad obci obstupených Nemecku, Maďarsku, a Polsku.* Bratislava: Štátny štatistický ústav, 1939.

Slovenský zákonnik. 7 vols. Bratislava: Štátne nakladatelstvo, 1939-1945.

Stattisches Jahrbuch der Cechoslowakischen Republik. Prague, 1936.

Steiner, Bedrich, ed. *Shoat yehudei slovakia. The Tragedy of Slovak Jewry.* Bratislava: Documentation Centre of CUJCR, 1949.

Secrétaire d'état de sa Sainteté. *Actes et Documentes du Saint Siège relatifs à la Seconde Guerre Mondiale.* Edités par Pierre Blet, Angelo Martini, Robert A. Graham, Burkhart Schneider. Città del Vaticano: Libraria Editrice Vaticana. Used volumes:
1. Le Saint Siège et la Guerre en Europe, Mars 1939-Août 1940.(1966).
2. Lettres de Pie XII aux Evêques Allemands, 1939-1944. (1966).
3. Le Saint Siège et la Situation religieuse en Pologne et dans les Pays Baltes, 1942-1945. (1967).
4. Le Saint Siège et la Guerre en Europe, Juin 1940-Juin 1941.(1967).
5. Le Saint Siège et la Guerre Mondiale, Juillet 1941-Octobre 1942. (1969).

Tiso, Štefan. *Diary.* (Manuscript). Stanford, California: The Hoover Institution on War, Revolution, and Peace. No. Tu. Slovakia, T 614, Vault Annex I.

Two Years of German Oppression in Czechoslovakia. London: Czechoslovak Ministry of Foreign Affairs, 1941.

U.S. Department of State. *Documents on German Foreign Policy, 1919-1945.* Series D (1937-1945). Washington, D.C.: U.S. Government Printing Office. Used volumes:
5. Poland, the Balkans, Latin America, the Smaller Powers, 1937-1939. (1953)
6. The Last Months of Peace. March-August, 1939. (1956).
7. The Last Days of Peace. August 9-September 3, 1939. (1956).
8. The War Years, 1939-1940. (1954).
9. The War Years, 1940. (1956).

10. The War Years, June 23-August 1, 1940. (1957).
11. The War Years, September 1, 1940-January 31, 1941. (1960).
12. The War Years, February 1-June 22, 1941. (1961).
13. The War Years, June 23-December 11, 1941. (1964).
U.S. Military Tribunal, Nuernberg. *Trials of War Criminals Before the Nuernberg Military Tribunals. The Ministeries Case. (No. 11, Ernst von Weizsaecker, et. al.)* Vols. XII, XIII, XVI. Washington, D.C.: Government Printing Office, 1952.

Newspapers and Periodicals

Čas (Bratislava), Organ of the Slovak Democratic Party, 1945-1948.
Gardista (Žilina), Published by the Hlinka Guard, 1942-1945.
News Flashes From Czechoslovakia (Chicago), Czechoslovak National Council of America, 1940.
News from Czechoslovakia (New York), American Friends of Czechoslovakia, 1939-1944.
Organizačné Zvesti HSLS (Bratislava), Published by the Secretary General of Hlinka's Slovak People's Party, 1940-1945.
Pravda (Bratislava), Organ of the Slovak Communist Party, 1945-1948.
Rok Matice Slovenskej (Turčiansky Sv. Martin), Published by Matica Slovenská, 1943.
Slovák (Bratislava), Organ of Hlinka's Slovak People's Party, 1939-1945.
Slowakische Rundschau (Pressburg), Published by Tatra-Verlag, 1942.

Memoirs, Biographies, Autobiographies and Speeches

Beneš, Edvard, *Memoirs, from Munich to New War and New Victory.* London, 1954.
Bor, Ján E. (Ernest Zaťko), *Vojtech Tuka, úvod do života a diela.* Turčiansky Sv. Martin, 1940.
——————. *Pomotané vlákno.* Trnava, 1942.
Brezovský, Ján. *Cesta k samostatnosti—na okraj Tukovej tvorby.* Bratislava, 1941.
Čulen, Konštantín. *Po Svätoplukovi druhá naša hlava. Život Dr. Jozefa Tisu.* Middletown, Pa., 1947.
Faguľa, L. G. *Andrej Hlinka.* Bratislava, 1943.
Husák, Gustav. *Svedectvo o Slovenskom Národnom Povstani.* Bratislava, 1964.
Kukliš-Kunovský, Pavel. *Ako je na Slovensku?* Pittsburgh, Pa., 1940.
Neumann, Jirmijahu Oskar. *Im Schatten des Todes.* Tel-Aviv, 1956.

BIBLIOGRAPHY

Paučo, Jozef, ed. *Dr. Jozef Tiso o sebe; obhajobna reč pred tzv. Národným súdom v Bratislava, 17 a 18 marca 1947.* Passaic, N.J., 1952.

—————. *Karol Sidor, Politik, novinár, spisovatel.* Middletown, Pa., 1962.

—————. *Pädesiatnik Dr. Jozef Kirschbaum.* Middletown, Pa., 1963.

—————. *Tak sme sa poznali.* Middletown, Pa., 1967.

Rašla, Anton. *Civilista v armáde. Spomienky na roky 1938-1945.* Bratislava, 1967.

Sidor, Karol, *O vzniku slovenského štátu.* Bratislava, 1945.

Šimončič, Albert, and Jozef Polčin. *Dr. Jozef Tiso, prvý prezident Slovenskej republiky.* Bratislava, 1941.

Široký, Viliam. *Za šťastné Slovensko v socialistickom Československu.* Prague, 1952.

Tiso, Jozef. *Politika a náboženstvo.* Bratislava, 1940.

—————. *Za česť národa a budúcnosť štátu.* Bratislava, 1941.

—————. *Die Warheit ueber die Slovakei.* Munich, 1948.

Tuka, Vojtech. *Usmievavé Slovensko.* Bratislava, 1939.

——————.*Slovenský národný socializmus.* Bratislava, 1940.

—————. *Slovenský národný socializmus a roľnictvo.* Bratislava, 1941.

Weismandel, Michael Dow. *Min ha-metsar.* New York, 1960.

Monographs and Symposia

Anderle, Josef, "The Establishment of Slovak Autonomy in 1938," in Miloslav Rechcigl, Jr., ed. *Czechoslovakia, Past and Present.* The Hague, 1969, Vol. I, pp. 76-97.

Akademia nauk SSR, Institut slavianovedenia. *Istoria Chekhoslovakii.* 3 vols. Moscow, 1956-1960.

Arndt, Karl, ed. *Rechtsverkehr mit der Slowakei.* Berlin, 1944.

Baron, Salo W. *Modern Nationalism and Religion.* New York, 1947.

Bauch, Vratislav. *Poľnohospodárstvo za Slovenského štátu.* Bratislava, 1958.

Bednárik, Rudolf. *Príručka pre narodopisný výskum slovenského ľudu.* Bratislava, 1942.

—————. *Slowakische Volkskultur.* Bratislava, 1943.

Beer, Ferdinand, et. al. *Dejinna križovatka. Slovenské národné povstanie-predpoklady a výsledky.* Bratislava, 1964.

Beer, Ferdinand. *KSČ v čele narodne osvobozeneckého boje českého a slovenského lidu (1938-45).* Prague, 1956.

Benčik, Antonín, et. al. *Partizanské hnutí v Československu během druhé světové války.* Prague, 1961.

BIBLIOGRAPHY

Beniak, Valentin. *Sebe i Vám*. Ružomberok, 1943.

Benovský, Pavol. *Poznámky k narodnostnému principu*. Trnava, 1942.

Bielovodský, Andrej. *Severné hranice Slovenska*. Bratislava, (S.A.).

Bokes, František, *Dejiny Slovenska a Slovákov*. Bratislava, 1946.

——————. *Slovenský životný priestor v minulosti a dnes*. Bratislava, 1943.

Borsody, Stephen. *Magyar-szlovak kiegyzes, a czeh-szlovak-magyar viszony utolso szaz eve*. Budapest, 1945.

Braunias, Karl. *Die Slowaken*. Stuttgart-Berlin, 1942.

Buban, Jan. *Najhlbši koreň vlastnenia*. Trnava, 1942.

Bullock, Alan. *Hitler, A Study in Tyranny*. New York, 1953.

Čavojský, Rudo. *Odborová organizacia slovenských robotnikov*. Bratislava, 1941.

Chmela, Leopold. *The Economic Aspects of the German Occupation of Czechoslovakia*. Prague, 1948.

Chmelar, Josef. *Political Parties in Czechoslovakia*. Prague, 1926.

Čik, P. Xaver Stanislav. *Dejiny Mariantalu*. Marianka, 1942.

Clementis, Vlado, comp. *Hnev svätý, z veršov odbojného Slovenska*. London, 1947.

Clementis, Vlado. *Usmerňovane Slovensko*. London, 1942.

de Colonna, Betram. *Czecho-Slovakia Within*. London, 1938.

Čulen, Konštantín. *Boj Slovákov za slobodu*. Bratislava, 1944.

——————. *Zum slowakisch-ungarischen Verhältnis. Rede in Slowakischen Parlament*. Bratislava, 1940.

——————. *Pohľady na dnešok*. Bratislava, 1944.

Czechoslovakia, Ministerstvo spravedlivosti. *Proces proti vlasti-zradným biskupom*. Bratislava, 1951.

Današ, Jozef. *O účasti HSLS na rozbití Československa hitlerovským Nemeckom, študijný material*. Bratislava, 1958.

——————. *Ľudácky separatizmus a hitlerovské Nemecko*. Bratislava, 1963.

Daxner, Igor. *Ľudáctvo pred narodným súdom,* Bratislava, 1961.

Derer, Ivan. *Slovenský vývoj a ľudácka zrada*, Prague, 1946.

Diamont, Alfred. *Austrian Catholics and the First Republic; Capitalism and the Social Order, 1918-1934*. Princeton, N.J., 1960.

Doležal, Jiři. *Slovenské narodni povstaní. Prispevok k jeho vzniku a průběhu*. Prague, 1954.

Doležal, J. Ivan. *Fašistický režim na Slovensku a jeho protinarodný charakter*. Martin, 1954.

Dress, Hans. *Slowakei und faschistische Neuordnung Europas 1939-1941*. Berlin, 1971.

BIBLIOGRAPHY

Ďurčanský, Ferdinand. *Die Weg zur slowakischen Freiheit.* Pressburg, 1945.

Durica, Milan S. "L'autonomia della regione Slovaca nella 'Seconda repubblica' di Cecco-Slovacchia", *Studii in onore di Arturo Cronia.* Padua, 1967, pp. 131-183.

—————. *Die slowakische Politik 1938-1939 in Lichte der Staatslehre Tisos.* Bonn, 1967.

—————. *La Slovacchia e le sue relazioni politiche con la Germania, 1938-45.* Vol. I. Padua, 1964.

Dvorák, Josef. *Slovenská politika včera a dnes.* Prague, 1947.

Elias, Andrew. "The Slovak Uprising of 1944," in Miloslav Rechcigl, ed., *Czechoslovakia, Past and Present.* The Hague, 1969, Vol. I.

Erdely, Eugen V. *Germany's First European Protectorate, The Fate of the Czechs and Slovaks.* London, 1942.

Faith, Štefan. *Činný katolicizmus.* Trnava, 1944.

Falťan, Samo. *Partizanská vojna na Slovensku.* Bratislava, 1959.

—————. *Slovenská otázka v Československu.* Bratislava, 1964.

—————. *O slovenskom národnóm povstani.* Bratislava, 1964.

Feuring, Wilhelm, *et. al. Slowakei, Land und Leute.* Munich, 1944.

Fillo, Mikuláš. *Greko-katolicki Slováci v minulosti a pritomnosti.* Michalovce, 1943.

Finer, Hermann. *Mussolini's Italy.* New York, 1935.

Franek, Ľudovit. "Antropologia," in Ľudovit Novák, ed., *Slovenská Vlastiveda.* Bratislava, 1943, Vol. II.

Friedrich, Carl J., ed. *Totalitarianism.* Cambridge, Mass., 1954.

Friedrich, Carl and Zbigniew K. Brzezinski. *Totalitarian Dictatorship and Autocracy.* New York, 1961.

Gajdoš-Breza, Juraj. *Dni obrody. Články a kurzivky, 1939-1940.* Prešov, 1940.

Ganzer, Richard K. *Das Reich als europaeische Ordnungmacht.* Hamburg, 1941.

Gašpar, Tido J. *Pre dobro celku.* Bratislava, 1942.

—————. *Ziskožravci.* Bratislava, 1941.

—————. *Das slowakische nationale Bewusstein.* Bratislava, 1939.

—————. *Velký rok.* Turčiansky Sv. Martin, 1940.

Gheorghe, Jon. *Rumäniens Weg zum Satellitenstaat.* Heidelberg, 1952.

Gráca, Bohuslav. *14 marec 1939, z dejín Komunistickéj Strany Slovenska.* Bratislava, 1959.

Gross, Hermann. *Die Slowakei in der Grosswirtschaft Europas.* Bratislava, 1943.

BIBLIOGRAPHY

Gryzlov, Gavril. *Gardistické inferno, O zločinoch prislušníkov POHG; Reportáže, proces, dokumenty.* Bratislava, 1958.

Gulick, Charles A. *Austria from Habsburg to Hitler.* Berkeley, 1948.

Gutachten des Instituts fuer Zeitgeschichte. Vol. I, Munich, 1958, Vol. II, Stuttgart, 1966.

Halečka, Tibor, *Ľudáctvo a náboženstvo.* Martin, 1957.

Hanuš, Ladislav. *Rozprava ò kultúrnosti.* Ružomberok, 1943.

✓ *Die Hlinka Partei. Geschichte, Ideologie, Organisation, Kultur, Wirtschaft, Sozialpolitik.* Bratislava, 1943.

Hoensch, Jörg K. *Die Slowakei und Hitlers Ostpolitik: Hlinkas Slowakische Volkspartei zwischen Autonomie und Separation, 1938-1939.* Köln-Graz, 1965.

—————. *Der ungarische Revisionismus und die Zerschlagung der Tschechoslowakei.* Tuebingen, 1967.

✓ Holotík, Ľudovit, ed. *Dejiny Slovenska.* Bratislava, 1961.

Holotík, Ľudovit, et. al. *Nemecká otázka a Československo, 1938-1961.* Bratislava, 1962.

Holotík, Ľudovit , ed. *O vzajomných vztahoch Čechov a Slovákov.* Bratislava, 1965.

—————, *Slovenské národné povstanie roku 1944.* Bratislava, 1965.

—————, *Prispevky k dejinám fašizmu v Československu a Maďarsku.* Bratislava, 1969.

✓ Hronek, Jiři, *Volcano under Hitler; the Underground War in Czecho-Slovakia.* London, 1941.

Hrušovský, František, *Die Geschichte der Slowakei.* Bratislava, 1942.

✓ Hrušovský, Francis. *This is Slovakia, A Country You Do Not Know.* Scranton, Pa., 1953.

Hudak, Adalbert. *Die Kirche unserer Väter. Weg und Ende des deutschen Luthertums in der Slowakei.* Stuttgart, 1953.

Huška, Miroslav A. *Proti ľudu cestou kľamstva.* Banská Bystrica, 1962.

Hysko, Miroslav. *O protinárodnej politike ľudackého fašizmu.* Bratislava, 1954.

—————. *Tlač v Čechách a na Slovensku v rokoch 1939-45.* Bratislava, 1961.

Hysko, Miroslav and Miroslav Kropilák. *Z veľkých dni boja slovenského ludu. Chronologický prehľad významných údalosti.* Bánska Bystrica, 1959.

Ivanka, Milan. *Proti tajnej iredente,* Bratislava, 1928.

Janáček, František. *Dva smery v začiatkoch národného odboja, október 1938, jún 1940.* Bratislava, 1962.

BIBLIOGRAPHY

Jareb, Jere. *Pola stolječa Hrvatske politike*. Buenos Aires, 1960.

Jablonický, Jozef and Ján Pivovarči. *The Slovak National Uprising*. Bratislava, 1969.

Jablonicky, Jozef. *Z ilegality do povstania. (Kapitoly z občianského odboja.)* Bratislava, 1969.

Juraš, Štefan. *Die Slowakei in der Grossraumwirtschaft*. Bratislava, 1941.

Jurovský, Anton. "Slovenská národná povaha," in Ludovit Novák, ed., *Slovenská Vlastiveda*. Bratislava, 1943, Vol. III.

––––––, (Weis-Nagel). *Národné povedomie a charakter*. Turčiansky Sv. Martin, 1940.

––––––. *Vodcovstvo a vodcovská osobnost'. (So zretel'om na naše pomery)*. Bratislava, 1942.

Karmasin, Franz. *War es richtig, Vater Raiffeisen? Das deutsche Genossenschaftswesen in der Slowakei*. Munich, 1956.

Kerner, Robert J., ed. *Czechoslovakia, Twenty Years of Independence*. Berkeley, 1940.

Kirschbaum, Joseph M. *Náš bôj o samostatnost'*. Cleveland, Ohio, 1958.

––––––. *Slovakia: Nation on the Crossroads of Central Europe*. New York, 1960.

Knieža, Emil F. "The Resistance of Slovak Jewry in Slovakia," in Yuri Suhl, ed. *They Fought Back*. New York, 1967, pp. 176-181.

Kociska, Anna. *Robotnici v boji proti fašizmu na Slovensku v rokoch 1938-1941*. Bratislava, 1964.

Kočiš, Aladár. *Cesta k slobode*. Bratislava, 1944.

Kováčik, L'udovit. *Slovensko v sieti nemeckého finančneho kapitálu*. Bratislava, 1955.

Krajčovič, Vojtech. *Die Struktur der slowakischen Wirtschaft*. Bratislava, 1941.

Kral, Václav. *Pravda o okupaci*. Prague, 1962.

Kramer, Juraj. *Iridenta a separatizmus v slovenskéj politike, 1919-1938; Študia o ich vzt'ahu*. Bratislava, 1957.

––––––. *Slovenské autonomisticke hnutie v rokoch 1918-1928*. Bratislava, 1963.

Kubáč, Jaroslav, ed. *O l'udackom fašizme*. Prague, 1956.

Kunoši, Alexander. *The Basis of Czechoslovak Unity*. London, 1944.

Laciak, Ondrej. *Slobodný vyielač Bánská Bystrica*. Bratislava, 1961.

Lettrich, Jozef. *History of Modern Slovakia*. London, 1956.

Lewis, Brackett. *Democracy in Czechoslovakia*. New York, 1941.

Lipscher, Ladislav. *L'udacká autonomia–Ilúzia a skutočnost'*. Bratislava, 1957.

Liptak, L'ubomir. *Franz Karmazin opät' na scéne*. Bratislava, 1962.

BIBLIOGRAPHY

Lipták, Ľubomir. *Ovladnutie Slovenského priemyslu nemeckým kapitálom.* Bratislava, 1960.

——————. *Slovensko v 20. storoči.* Bratislava, 1968.

✓ Macartney, Carlile A. *Hungary and Her Successors, 1919-1937.* London, 1937.

——————. *October Fifteenth.* Edinburgh, 1956.

Maček, Vladko. *In the Struggle for Freedom.* New York, 1957.

Magala, Jozef. *Náš svetonázor.* Bratislava, 1940.

Materna, Jozef. *Minulost' a pritomnost' slovenských autonomistov.* Bratislava, 1923.

Mečiar, Stanislav. *Im Umbruch, Sammlung von Zeitungsaufsatzen.* Bratislava, 1944.

Mederly, Karol. *Ústava slovenskej republiky.* Bratislava, 1939.

Mestrović, Ivan. *Uspomene na politicke ljude i dogadjaje.* Buenos Aires, 1961.

Mikus, Joseph A. *Slovakia, A Political History: 1918-1950.* Milwaukee, Wis., 1963.

Miškovič, Alojz. *Madarské úmysly so Sloviakmi.* Bratislava, 1944.

——————. *Napravená krivda. Vratené kraje vo Spiši, Orave a Čadčianskom okrese.* Turčiansky Sv. Martin, 1940.

✓ Moody, Joseph N., ed. *Church and Society. Catholic Social and Political Thought and Movements, 1798-1950.* New York, 1953.

Mráz, Andrej. *Dejiny slovenskej literatury.* Bratislava, 1948.

Múdry-Šebík, Michal . *Stručné dejiny Slovákov.* Pittsburgh, Pa., 1940.

✓ Muran, J. B. *We Fight On: Slovak Rising in the German Rear.* New York, 1945 (?).

Murgaš, Karol. *Der Pakt der mannhaften Verflichtungen, eine politische Reportage ueber die historischen Tage von 23-26 November 1940,* Turčiansky Sv. Martin, 1941.

——————. *Národ medzi Dunajom a Karpatmi.* Turčiansky Sv. Martin, 1940.

Mussolini, Benito. *Fašistická nauka.* Trans. and Intr. by Dr. Vojtech Košík. Bratislava, 1939.

Muťnanský, Ľudovit. *Slovenská sociálná výstavba, cesta do nového europského socialného poriadku.* Bratislava, 1944.

——————. *Slovenská revolucia na vlnách éteru.* Bratislava, 1942.

——————. *" Tu rišsky vysielač Viedeň . . ."* (*Boj vo svetovom eteri o slovenskú pravdu a budúcnost'*). Vienna, 1939.

Nagy-Talavera, Nicholas M. *The Green Shirts and the Others.* Stanford, California, 1971.

BIBLIOGRAPHY

Neumann, Franz L. *Behemoth: The Structure and Practice of National Socialism.* Toronto, New York (etc.), 1942.

Novák, Jaroslav. *Im Zeichen Zweier Kreuze, Franz Karmazin und Ferdinand Ďurčanský.* *Glanz und Fall.* Prague, 1962.

Novák, Ľudovit. *Jazykovedné glosy k československej otázke.* Turčiansky Sv. Martin, 1935.

Nowak, Robert. *Der kuenstliche Staat: Ostprobleme der Tschechoslowakei.* Oldenburg, O., 1938.

Oddo, Gilbert L. *Slovakia and Its People.* New York, 1960.

Olšovský, Rudolf. *Prehled hospodarského vývoje Československa v letech, 1918-1945.* Prague, 1961.

Pasiar, Štefan and Pavel Paska. *Osveta na Slovensku, jej vznik, počiatky a vývoj.* Bratislava, 1964.

Patee, Richard. *The Case of Cardinal Aloysius Stepinac.* Milwaukee, Wis., 1953.

Pauco, Jozef. *Slováci a komunizmus.* Middletown, Pa., 1957.

—————. *Politicko-narodný program HSLS.* Bratislava, 1944.

—————. *Christian Slovakia under Communism.* Valparaiso, Ind., 1959.

Paul, Gustav. *Grundzuege der Rassen- und Raumgeschichte des deutschen Volkes.* Munich, 1943.

Pavlik, Viktor. *Hospodárska štruktúra Slovenska.* Bratislava-Prešov, 1941.

The Persecution of the Jews in Nazi Slovakia: Report and Documents. London, 1942.

Peroutka, Ferdinand. *Budovani statu.* Prague, 1933-1936.

Pešiak, Jan. *Riešenie slovenskej narodnostnej otázky.* Bratislava, 1962.

Petreas, Johann O. *Nová Europa a Slovensko.* Bratislava, 1942.

—————. *Die Slowakei im Umbruch.* Turčiansky Sv. Martin, 1941.

Pleva, Ján and Miloš Tichý. *Krest'anské odbory na Slovensku.* Bratislava, 1967.

Plevza, Viliam *et al. KSČ a roľnická otázka na Slovensku, 1921-1960.* Bratislava, 1961.

Pokorný, Ctibor. *Židovstvo na Slovensku.* Turčiansky Sv. Martin, 1940.

—————. *Boj za slobodu.* Bratislava, 1941.

Polakovič, Štefan. *Z Tisovho boja.* Bratislava, 1941.

—————. *Tisová nauka.* Bratislava, 1941.

—————. *Náš duch.* Bratislava, 1943.

—————. *Warum eine freie Slowakei.* Bratislava, 1944.

—————. *K základom slovenského štátu.* Bratislava, 1944.

—————. *Slovenský národný socializmus.* Bratislava, 1941.

—————, *Das slowakische Nationalbewusstein.* Vienna, 1943.

186

BIBLIOGRAPHY

Polakovič, Štefan. *Die Entwicklung der Grundideen der slowakischen Politik.* Bratislava, 1945.

Prečan, Vilém. *Slovenský katolicizmus pred februarom 1948.* Bratislava, 1961.

——————. "Die nationalsozialistische Slowakeipolitik 1944," in Ernst Schulin, ed. *Gedenkschrift fuer Martin Goehring.* Wiesbaden, 1968.

Prispevky k dejinám východného Slovenska. Bratislava, 1964.

Proti prežitkom l'udáctva. Sborník prejavov z ideologickéj konferencie Filozofickéj fakulty Slovenskéj univerzity v dnoch 28 a 29 januára 1954. Bratislava, 1954.

Purgat, Juraj. *Od Trianonu po Košice. K mad'arskej otázke v Československu.* Bratislava, 1970.

Radvanyi, Celo. *Ked rinčaly zbrane. Slovenská vojenská tradicia.* Bratislava, 1944.

Rafas, Pavol. *Priemysel Slovenska za kapitalizmu.* Bratislava, 1957.

Revay, Istvan. *Die in Belveder gezogene ungarisch-slowakische Grenze.* Budapest, 1941.

Riedl, Franz. *Das Deutschtum zwischen Pressburg und Bartfeld.* Stuttgart-Berlin, 1940.

Ries-Javor, Viliam. *Kontinent v prerode. Študie o povojnovej Europe, so zretel'om na Slovensko.* Bratislava, 1943.

Roessler, Fritz. *Die Slowakei zwischen Gestern und Heute.* Dresden, 1943.

Rommen, Heinrich A. *The State in Catholic Thought. A Treatise in Political Philosophy.* St. Louis, 1950.

Rudershausen, Julta. *Lebens- und Sozialverhältnisse in der Slowakei.* Bratislava, 1940.

Schwartz, Michael. *Die Slowakei, der juengste Staat Europas.* Leipzig, 1939.

Schwengeler, Arnold H. *Slowakische Reise. 1944.* Bern, 1944.

Schwer, Wilhelm. *Catholic Social Theory.* St. Louis, 1940.

Sedlaková, Maria. *Krycie meno Jozef. O zločinoch prislušníkov POHG. Reportáže, proces, dokumenty.* Bratislava, 1958.

Semkowicz, Władysław, ed. *Słowacja i Słowacy.* Cracow, 1937.

Seton-Watson, Hugh. *Eastern Europe Between the Wars, 1918-1941.* Cambridge, 1946.

Seton-Watson, Robert W. *Slovakia Then and Now.* Prague, 1931.

——————. *The New Slovakia.* Prague, 1924.

——————. *A History of Czechs and Slovaks.* London, 1943.

Sidor, Karol. *Šest' rokov pri Vatikane.* Scranton, Pa., 1947.

BIBLIOGRAPHY

Siracký, Andrej. *Klerofašistická ideologia ľudáctva.* Bratislava, 1955.

Slávik, Juraj. *Zapredané Slovensko.* Chicago, Ill., 1939.

Slimák, Cyprian, ed. *Pod vedenim strany. Sbornik spomienok ilegalných a protifašistických bojovnikov z rokov 1938-1945.* Bratislava, 1959.

Die Slowakei als mitteleuropaisches Problem in Geschichte und Gegenwart. Munich, 1965.

Slovakia, Ministerstvo školstva a národnéj osvety. *Pät' rokov slovenskeho školstva, 1939-1945.* Bratislava, 1944.

Slovakia, Ministerstvo dopravy a verejných prác. *Doprava a verejné práce na Slovensku.* Bratislava, 1941.

Slovakia, Ministerstvo národnéj obrany. *Armáda v obrane a práci. Pät' rokov slovenskéj armády.* Bratislava, 1944.

Slovakia, Kancelaria SNR. *Slovenská národná rada, 1943-1949.*

Der slowakische Judenkodex. Trans. and intr. by Ludwig A. Dosťal. Bratislava, 1941.

Die slowakische Republik. Rueckblick auf den Freiheitskampf und politisches Profil. Bratislava, 1940.

Smida, Josef. *The Tuka Trial.* Bratislava, 1930.

Sochán, Pavel. *Voják v mentalite slovenského ľudu.* Bratislava, 1942.

Soziale Fuersorge und Kulturleben. Bratislava, 1940.

Šprinc, Mikuláš, ed. *Slovenská Republika, 1939-1949.* Scranton, Pa., 1949.

Stanek, Imrich. *Zrada a pád. Hlinkovští separatisté a tak zvaný slovenský stát.* Prague, 1958.

Štefánek, Anton. "Základy sociografie Slovenska," in Ľudovit Novák, ed. *Slovenská Vlastiveda.* Bratislava, 1945, Vol. III.

Street, C. J. C. *Slovakia's Past and Present.* London, 1928.

Strhan, Milan. *Handlovský štrajk 1940.* Bratislava, 1960.

Svetoň, Ján. *Die Europäischen Auslandsslowaken.* Bratislava, 1943.

————. *Obyvateľstvo Slovenska za kapitalizmu.* Bratislava, 1958.

Taborsky, Edward. *Czechoslovak Democracy at Work.* London, 1945.

Thomson, S. Harrison. *Czechoslovakia in European History.* Princeton, N.J., 1953.

Trebišovský, Julius V., ed. *Sborník spolku zahorských akademikov, 1932-42.* Trnava, 1942.

Tropper, Ernst. *Slowakei, Land zwischen Ost und West.* Brno, 1944.

Tuka, Vojtech. *Die Rechtssysteme. Grundriss einer Rechtsphilosophie.* Berlin, 1941.

Uderstädt, E. C. *Das Protektorat Boehmen und Maehren und der Schutzstaat Slowakei.* Berlin, 1939.

Varšík, Branislav. *Narodnosté branice Slovensko-Madarské v ostatných dvoch storočiach.* Bratislava, 1940.

188

BIBLIOGRAPHY

Vašek, Anton. *Die Lösung der Judenfrage in der Slowakei; systematische Uebersicht der antijuedischen Gestzgebung.* Pressburg, 1942.

Venohr, Wolfgang. *Aufstand fuer die Tschechoslowakei. Der slowakische Freiheitskampf von 1944.* Hamburg, 1969.

Vietor, Martin, *Dejiny okupacie južného Slovenska (1938-1945).* Bratislava, 1963.

Vnuk, František. *Dr. Jozef Tiso, President of the Slovak Republic.* Sidney, 1967.

————. *Neuveritelné sprísahanie.* Middletown, Pa., 1964.

Waldeck-Goldschmidt, Rosie. *Athene Palace.* New York, 1942.

Wanklyn, Harriet S. (J.A. Steers). *Czechoslovakia. A Geographical and Historical Study.* New York, 1954.

Weinreich, Max. *Hitler's Professors. The Part of Scholarship in Germany's Crimes Against the Jewish People.* New York, 1946.

Wohland, Ludwig. *Mein Hauerland, Leben und Schicksal einer deutschen Volksinsel im Suedosten.* Stuttgart, 1953.

Wojtko, Mary G. *Slovakia's Road to Statehood.* Whiting, Ind., 1957.

Young, Edgar P. *Czechoslovakia.* London, 1946.

Yurchak, Peter P. *The Slovaks, Their History and Tradition.* Whiting, Ind., 1946.

Zachar, Ludovit. *Katholizismus und slowakischer National-Sozializmus.* Bratislava, 1940.

Zavarský, Jozef. *Chceme žit'.* Trnava, 1941.

Zimmern, Alfred E. *Czechoslovakia Today.* London, 1938.

Zinner, Paul E. *Communist Strategy and Tactics in Czechoslovakia, 1918-1948.* New York, 1963.

Zubec, Theodore J. *The Church of Silence in Slovakia.* Whiting, Ind., 1956.

Essays in Periodical Literature

Batowski, Henryk, "Dziesiec lat dziejow słowackich, 1938-48," *Przegład Zachodni,* V (1949), pp. 481-49.

Bielik, František and Julius Sopko, "Ustredné organy štátnej moci a správy v rokoch 1938-1945," *Sborník archivných prác,* 13 (1963), pp. 96-138.

Bauch, Vratislav and Michal Kontra, "Príspevok k otázke malých rol'-nikov za tzv. slovenskeho štátu," *Ekonomický časopis,* III (1955), pp. 77-96.

BIBLIOGRAPHY

Bodensieck, Heinrich, "Die Politik des Zweiten Tschechoslowakischen Republik (Herbst 1930-Fruejahr 1939)," *Zeitschrift fuer Ostforschung*, IV, 1 (1957), pp. 54-71.

——————. "Das Dritte Reich und die Lage der Juden in der Tschecho-Slowakei nach Muenchen," *Vierteljahrshefte fuer Zeitgeschichte*, IX, 3 (1961), pp. 249-61.

Borsody, Stephen, "The Slovaks in the Carpathian Basin," *Hungarian Quarterly*, VII (1941), pp. 215—27.

Cavalli, Fierelo, "La Santa Sede contro la deportazioni degli ebrei dalla Slovacchia durante seconda guerra mondiale," *La Civilta cattolica*, CXIII, 3 (1961), pp. 3-18.

"Československá otázka v diplomatických spisoch horthyovského Maďarska (1936-1938 do Mníchova)," *Historický časopis*, XV, 1 (1967), pp. 110-34.

Današ, Jozef, "O vsťahoch HSLS s hitlerovský Nemeckom v predvečer vzniku tkzv. slovenského štátu," *Historický časopis*, VIII, 1 (1959), pp. 53-57.

Delaney, Edward L., "I was in Slovakia," *Slovakia*, II (1952), pp. 25-44.

Dress, Hans, "Die Stellung des sogenannten slowakischen Staats im Rahmen der faschistischen Neuordnung Europas (1939-1945), *Zeitschrift fuer Geschichtswissenschaft*, XV, 4 (1967), p. 695.

Ďurčanský, Ferdinand, "Mit Tiso bei Hitler. Die Entstehung der Slowakischen Republik 1939," *Politischen Studien*, VII, 80 (1956), pp. 1-10.

Ďurica, Milan S., "Dr. Joseph Tiso and the Jewish Problem in Slovakia," *Slovakia*, VII, 3-4 (1957), p. 1-22.

——————. "The Slovak Republic," *Slovak Studies*, I, 1 (1961), pp. 105-22.

Falťan, Samo. "Partisan War in Slovakia in the Period 1944—1945," *Studia Historica Slovaca*, V (1967), pp. 57-92.

Gašpar, Tido J., "Z pamäti," *Slovenské pohľady*, LXXXIV, 6 (June 1968), pp. 84-99; 7 (July 1968), pp. 62-79; 8 (August 1968), pp. 76-85; 9 (September 1968), pp. 108-114; 10 (October 1968), pp. 102-10; 11 (November 1968), pp. 104-7; 12 (December 1968), pp. 78-83.

Holotiková, Zdenka, "K činnosti a ideologii ľudáckych odborov na Slovensku v radoch slovenskej robotnickej triedy," *Historický časopis*, IX, 1 (1961), pp. 50-67.

Hoensch, Jörg K., "Das slowakisches Nationalaufstand in der Geschichtesschreibung der CSSR," *Osteuropa*, XVIII, 7 (1965), pp. 509-15.

——————, "Die Grundlage des Programms der Slowakischen Volkspartei vor 1938," *Bohemia*, VII (1966), pp. 320-56.

BIBLIOGRAPHY

Hornová, Adela, "Charakteristika ekonomiky tzv. slovenského štátu," *Ekonomický časopis*, II (1954), 337-48.

——————, "Hlavne crty militarizacie ekonomiky tzv. slovenského štátu," *Ekonomický časopis*, V (1959), pp. 463-83.

——————, "O hmotnom postavení pracujúcich za slovenského štátu," *Ekonomický časopis*, VI (1960), pp. 49-70.

Jelinek, Yeshayahu, "The Role of the Jews in Slovakian Resistance," *Jahrbuecher fuer Geschichte Osteuropas*, Neue Folge, XV, 3 (1967), pp. 415-22.

——————, "Bohemia-Moravia, Slovakia, and the Third Reich During the Second World War," *East European Quarterly*, III, 3 (June pp. 229-39.

——————, "Denník Dr. Štefana Tisu," *Historický časopis*, XVIII, 2 (1970), pp. 270-87.

——————, "Stormtroopers in Slovakia: The Rodobrana and the Hlinka Guard," *Journal of Contemporary History*, VI, 3 (1971),pp. 97-119.

——————, "The 'Final Solution'—the Slovak Version," *East European Quarterly*, IV, 4 (January 1971), pp. 431-41.

"K česko-slovenským vzťahom," *Historický časopis*, XV, 4 (1967), pp. 559-72.

Kamenec, Ivan, "Snem Slovenskej republiky a jeho postoj k problému židovského obyvateľstva rokoch 1939-1945," *Historický časopis*, XVII, 3 (1969), pp. 329-60.

——————, "Židovská otázka a spôsoby jej riešenia v čase autonomie Slovenska," *Nové obzory*, IX, 1960.

Kirschbaum, Joseph M., "Die internationale Anerkennung der Slowakischer Republik," *Die Slowakei*, XI, 2 (1964), pp. 3-12.

——————, "The Politics of Hlinka's Slovak People's Party in the Slovak Republic," *Slovakia*, I, 1 (1951), pp. 43-49.

——————, "Facts and Events behind the Scenes of Slovakia's Declaration of Independence," *Slovakia*, IX, 4 (1959), pp. 1-7.

Krajčovič, Vojtech, "Der Anfang der slowakischen Industrie im Selbstständingen Staate," *Slowakische Rundschau*, VII (1943).

Kramer, Juraj, "Ausländische Einflusse auf die Entwicklung der slowakischen autonomischen Bewegung," *Historica*, III (1961), pp. 179-63.

Lipscher, Ladislav, "Klub slovenských poslancov v rokoch 1918-1920," *Historický časopis*, XVI, 2 (1968), pp. 133-68.

Lipták, Ľubomir, "Podrobenie slovenského priemyslu nemeckým kapitálom," *Historický časopis*, XI, 1 (1955), pp. 3-23.

——————, "Role of the German Minority in Slovakia in the Years of the Second World War," *Studia Historica Slovaca*, I (1963), pp. 150-178.

BIBLIOGRAPHY

Lipták, Ľubomir, "Príprava a priebeh salzburgských rokovani roku 1940 medzi predstaviteľmi Nemecka a slovenského štátu," *Historický časopis*, XIII, 3 (1965) pp. 329-65.

————, "Slovenský štát a protifašistické hnutie v rokoch 1939-1943," *Historický časopis*, XIV, 1 (1966), pp. 161-218.

————, "Maďarsko v politike slovenského štátu v rokoch 1939-1943," *Historický časopis*, XV, 1 (1967), pp. 1-35.

Low, Myron J., "From Autonomous State to Protectorate: German Policy Toward Slovakia," *The Historian*, XXVI, 3 (1964), pp. 405-24.

Mikus, Joseph A., "Slovakia Between Two World Wars," *Slovak Studies*, I, 1 (1961), pp. 95-104.

Paučo, Joseph, "I was Editor of President Tiso's Newspaper," *Slovakia*, VII, 1 (1957), pp. 9-12.

Polakovič, Štefan, "Pocit menejcennosti v národe," *Slovenské pohľady*, LVI, 1 (1940).

Potemra, Ladislav A., "Ruthenians in Slovakia and the Greek Catholic Diocese of Prešov," *Slovak Studies*, 1 (1961), pp. 199-220.

Rothkirchen, Livia, "The Policy of the Vatican and the Holocaust in 'Independent' Slovakia," *Yad Vashem Studies*, VI (1966), pp. 23-45.

Sidor, Karol, "What Led to the Proclamation of the Slovak Republic?" *Slovakia*, II, 3 (1952), p. 1-12.

————, "Ako som sa srazil s Nemcami," *Kalendár Jednoty*, 1947.

Skilling, Gordon H., "The Czechoslovak Struggle for Liberation in World War II," *The Slavonic and East European Review*, XXXIX, 92 (1960), pp. 174-197.

Stanek, Imrich, "Vatikan, spojenec ľudáctva a tzv. slovenského štátu," *Ceskoslovenský časopis historický*, III, 1 (1955), pp. 82-110.

Strhan, Milan. "Živnostenská banka na Slovensku 1918-1938," *Historický časopis*, XV, 1 (1967), pp. 177-218.

Štvrtecká, Anna, "The Communists and the Slovak National Uprising," *Czechoslovak Press Survey*, September 2, 1964, pp. 2-7.

Taborský, Edward, "Local Government in Czechoslovakia, 1918-1948," *American Slavic and East European Review*, X, 3 (1951), pp. 202-15.

Tiso, Joseph, "Die Sendung des Slowakischen Staates," *Slowakische Rundschau*, IV (1943), pp. 65-70.

Toma, Peter A. "Soviet Strategy in the Slovak National Uprising of 1944," *Journal of Central European Affairs*, XIX, 3 (1959), pp. 290-298.

Uršiny, Ján, "Z pamäti," *Matičné čitanie*, October-December 1968.

Vietor, Martin, "Príspevok k objasneniu fašistického charakteru tzv. slovenského štátu," *Historický časopis*, VIII, 4 (1960), pp. 82-508.

BIBLIOGRAPHY

Vnuk, František, "The German Zone of Protection in Slovakia, (A Study in Slovak-German Relations in March-August 1939)," *Slovakia*, IX, 4 (1959), pp. 7-23.

————, "Slovakia's Accession to the Tripartite Pact," *Slovakia* IX, 5 (1959, pp. 6-19.

————, "Die Lebensfähigkeit der unabhängigen Slowakei," *Die Slowakei*, II, 1 (1964), pp. 43-50.

————, "Slovakia's Six Eventful Months (October 1938-March 1939)," Offprint from *Slovak Studies*, Cleveland-Rome, 1964.

————, "Die slowakische Haltung zum Nationalisozializmus," *Die Slowakei*, IV, 1 (1966), pp. 3-9.

————, "Ľudová strana v slovenskej politike," *Literarný almanach Slováka v Amerike*, 1968, pp. 21-45.

INDEX

INDEX

EAST EUROPEAN MONOGRAPHS

The *East European Monographs* comprise scholarly books on the history and civilization of Eastern Europe. They are published by the *East European Quarterly* in the belief that these studies contribute substantially to the knowledge of the area and serve to stimulate scholarship and research.

1. *Political Ideas and the Enlightenment in the Romanian Principalities, 1750-1831.* By Vlad Georgescu. 1971.

2. *America, Italy and the Birth of Yugoslavia, 1917-1919.* By Dragan R. Zivojinovic. 1972.

3. *Jewish Nobles and Geniuses in Modern Hungary.* By William O. McCagg, Jr. 1972.

4. *Mixail Soloxov in Yugoslavia: Reception and Literary Impact.* By Robert F. Price. 1973.

5. *The Historical and Nationalistic Thought of Nicolae Iorga.* By William O. Oldson. 1973.

6. *Guide to Polish Libraries and Archives.* By Richard C. Lewanski. 1974.

7. *Vienna Broadcasts to Slovakia, 1938-1939: A Case Study in Subversion.* By Henry Delfiner. 1974.

8. *The 1917 Revolution in Latvia.* By Andrew Ezergailis. 1974.

9. *The Ukraine in the United Nations Organization: A Study in Soviet Foreign Policy, 1944-1950.* By Konstantin Sawczuk. 1975.

$770057487

10. *The Bosnian Church: A New Interpretation.* By John V. A. Fine, Jr. 1975.

11. *Intellectual and Social Developments in the Hapsburg Empire from Maria Theresa to World War I.* Edited by Stanley B. Winters and Joseph Held. 1975.

12. *Ljudevit Gaj and the Illyrian Movment.* By Elinor Murray Despalatovic. 1975.

13. *Tolerance and Movements of Religious Dissent in Eastern Europe.* Edited by Bela K. Kiraly. 1975.

14. *The Parish Republic: Hlinka's Slovak People's Party, 1939-1945.* By Yeshayahu Jelinek. 1976.